Baile Munna   ⸌⸍ JAN 2020
Ballymun
Tel: 8421890

THE GAYBO REVOLUTION

D0263399

THE GAYBO REVOLUTION

How Gay Byrne Challenged Irish Society

Finola Doyle O'Neill

ORPEN PRESS

Published by
Orpen Press
13 Adelaide Road
Dublin 2
Ireland

email: info@orpenpress.com

www.orpenpress.com

© Finola Doyle O'Neill, 2015

Images © RTÉ Stills Library
Gay Byrne stamp © An Post

1 3 5 7 9 10 8 6 4 2

Paperback ISBN 978-1-909895-90-4
ePub ISBN 978-1-78605-009-0
Kindle ISBN 978-1-78605-010-6
PDF ISBN 978-1-78605-011-3

A catalogue record for this book is available from the British
Library. All rights reserved. No part of this publication may be
reproduced, stored in a retrieval system or transmitted in any
form or by any means, electronic, mechanical, photocopying,
recording or otherwise, without the prior, written permission of
the publisher.

This book is sold subject to the condition that it shall not, by way
of trade or otherwise, be lent, resold, hired out, or otherwise
circulated without the publisher's prior consent in any form
of binding or cover other than that in which it is published
and without a similar condition including this condition being
imposed on the subsequent purchaser.

Printed in Dublin by SPRINTprint Ltd.

For my parents, Kay and Pat Doyle, and my sister, Cliodhna Doyle, whose input was invaluable.

And to my husband, Peter O'Neill, and our children, Ross, Cathy, Rory, Rian and Beth, all of whom suffered not in the least as I toiled!

Finola Doyle O'Neill

Acknowledgements

I would like to acknowledge the assistance of University College Cork's (UCC) College of Arts, Celtic Studies and Social Sciences (CACSSS) publication fund, plus the RTÉ Stills Library, in particular Pearl Quinn. For his mentoring and his willingness to cast a cold eye over this book, I wish to thank Professor Geoff Roberts from the School of History at UCC. I also want to thank Doireann Ní Bhriain for being so forthcoming with information and material at all times. For guiding me in my earlier years as a doctoral student, I wish to express my appreciation to Professor Joe Lee. And for her vigilant proofreading, I wish to thank Jennifer Thompson of Orpen Press.

Finally, I owe thanks to my UCC History students from my second year Media History module; they continue to remain fascinated and inspired by the legacy of Gay Byrne and allow me to teach in the area I am passionate about, Ireland's media history.

Finola Doyle O'Neill

Contents

1

Introduction: The Byrne Identity

If you grow up in Ireland you are never going to be as famous as Gay Byrne.[1]

(Bono, U2)

Shortly before Gay Byrne's retirement from *The Late Late Show* – Europe's longest-running television talk show[2] – in 1998, Lansdowne Market Research conducted a poll to determine the most popular and the most hated public figures in Ireland.[3] Byrne tied with former Taoiseach Charles Haughey as the most hated figure in the country. He was also voted the most popular.

For the past five decades, Byrne has been simultaneously reviled and admired as a broadcaster by both the media and the public, and it is this dichotomy that lies at the core of his appeal. On radio, the characteristics that endeared him to Irish house-wives would prove to be the self-same traits that alienated him from their husbands. He was perceived by many as a 'father

---

[1] Bono, quoted in 'Gay Byrne reveals he doesn't want a celebrity-style bash to mark his big day', *Irish Mirror*, 5 August 2014.

[2] Guinness Book of Records 2015: Ireland's *The Late Late Show* is the second-longest-running talk show in television history, and the longest-running talk show in Europe. NBC's *The Tonight Show* is the longest-running TV talk show in the world, having debuted in 1954.

[3] Cited in the *Irish Examiner*, 16 May 2009.

Leabharlanna Poiblí Chathair Baile Átha Cliath
Dublin City Public Libraries

confessor' to an entire nation, spawning not only talk-show imitators both in Ireland and across the water, but also a plethora of live phone-in radio shows and 'Uncle Gaybo' prototypes.

In 2011, more than a decade after leaving *The Late Late Show*, another poll placed Byrne as the most popular potential candidate to become president of the country.[4] His continuing hold on Irish life and culture is further demonstrated by the many awards and acknowledgements he has received in recent years. These acknowledgements include an honorary doctorate from Trinity College Dublin and the Freedom of the City of Dublin. He is featured on the Irish Leaving Certificate syllabus for History. His face has graced Irish postage stamps, and his likeness stands in the National Wax Museum in Dublin. For fifteen years Byrne was host of the Rose of Tralee,[5] helping to make the pageant a mainstay of popular Irish culture.[6] Throughout the 1980s to the mid-1990s, he also presented the Calor Kosangas Housewife of the Year competition,[7] a role which, along with that of host of *The Gay Byrne Show*, elevated him to the status of quintessential 'mammy's boy', as the housewives of Ireland did battle in the kitchen for national glory.[8]

---

[4] Paddy Power Presidential Poll Report, REDC, 2011. REDC is a Dublin-based research and marketing firm, which uses a telephone-based approach for national political polling.

[5] The Rose of Tralee Festival is an international competition, open to women who were born in Ireland or have Irish roots. It has been held annually each August in Tralee, Co. Kerry since 1959 and is televised live by RTÉ. Gay Byrne was host of the competition from 1974–99, and during his tenure the show received unprecedented television viewer ratings. In his final year as host, viewing figures were 1.5 million.

[6] Ryle Dwyer, *The Rose of Tralee: Fifty Years A-Blooming* (O'Brien Press: Dublin, 2009).

[7] The Calor Kosangas Housewife of the Year competition was hosted by Gay Byrne and ran from 1983–94. The contestants were tested on their ability to produce a meal within a two-hour period, while Byrne interviewed them. A judging panel assessed their personality, appearance and civic spirit. The competition was dropped in the mid-1990s amid complaints that too many women working outside the home were taking part.

[8] '"Rose of Tralee for mammies" that picked out our housewife of the year', *Irish Independent*, 6 October 2012.

In August 2014 Byrne turned 80. Instead of retiring quietly from public view, he, together with his wife of 50 years, Kathleen Watkins, performed his sold-out show, *Gay Byrne: Live on Stage*, in bespoke venues throughout Ireland. At the same time, he was also presenting a jazz programme on RTÉ's Lyric FM and a television show, *The Meaning of Life*, in which he conducted a series of intimate and revealing conversations with well-known people. As Chairman of the Road Safety Authority from September 2006 until June 2014, he took a vocal and crusading stance on the high incidence of road deaths in Ireland. In more recent times he has expressed public outrage at the Government's treatment of two Garda whistle-blowers who disclosed the abuse of the penalty-points system by senior-ranking Gardaí.[9]

However, it was the revelation in October 2014 that Byrne was being sued by the former Anglo Irish Bank over property debts that once again catapulted the veteran broadcaster to centre stage in Irish life.[10] The man who had hosted and harangued the nation as a talk-show host since 1962 had lost €2 million due to a series of property investments, including the purchase of a hotel in Budapest and properties in Dublin's Docklands, brokered by Byrne's friend and tax advisor Derek Quinlan. It was not the first time Byrne had placed his trust in a close friend and accountant only to suffer significant financial losses. In 1986, he discovered that his close friend Russell Murphy, the godfather to his daughter Crona, had defrauded him of more than €200,000.[11] This second loss of money, however, resonated deeply with the Irish public, many of whom had also been victims of an over-heated property market.

The collapse of the housing market, allied to the economic recession that crippled Ireland from 2008 to 2014, affected

---

[9] 'Shatter and Callinan "should apologise" – Gay Byrne', *Irish Times*, 16 March 2014.

[10] 'Gay Byrne's family sued by former Anglo over property debts', *Irish Independent*, 27 October 2014.

[11] *Ibid.*

most Irish householders. Somehow, Byrne's personal experience appeared to mirror that of the nation. There was a bitter poignancy in the fact that he, a notoriously private man, who had certainly done the State some service in his role as host to a nation of talkers, was fated to have his private affairs played out publicly in the Irish courts.

While it is the public persona rather than the private life of this veteran talk-show host that fuels the following chapters of this book – and from conversations with Byrne it is evident that he will brook no intrusion into his family life or, indeed, allow access to his close-knit circle of friends in Co. Donegal, where he has a holiday retreat[12] – it is interesting to explore how certain incidents and events from his personal life have come to inform some of the more controversial moments of his career, affecting the influence and appeal of both the *Late Late Show* television programme and the *Gay Byrne Show* radio programme.

On 6 July 1962 when, at the age of just 26, Byrne first came to public prominence as host of *The Late Late Show*, no one could have anticipated that he would remain at its helm for over 37 years, or that it would herald the beginnings of his mercurial and, at times, fractious relationship with the Irish public. After a stint in the UK on both Granada and BBC Television, Byrne returned to an Ireland which was for him, in the 1960s, a 'tight little, smug little, complacent little place,'[13] a complacency he would later help to shatter and shake as one of Ireland's most prolific broadcasters.

Not content with merely presenting and producing *The Late Late Show*, however, he simultaneously presented the pioneering radio show *The Gay Byrne Hour*, later to become *The Gay Byrne Show*, a position he would ultimately hold for over 26 years.

---

[12] 'Gay Byrne will write his own account of Gay Byrne and under no circumstances are my family or friends in Donegal to be contacted.' Gay Byrne, in conversation with the author, 3 March 2012.

[13] Gay Byrne with Deirdre Purcell, *The Time of My Life: An Autobiography* (Gill & MacMillan: Dublin, 1989) p. 60.

The programme began in 1973,[14] and Byrne soon acquired the appellation 'Uncle Gaybo', as the show itself gradually evolved into a form of public confessional for its almost exclusively female listeners. *The Gay Byrne Show* was initially dubbed a 'housewives' choice' programme as a result of the large numbers of married women who tuned into it on a daily basis.[15] This was due in part to a law in force at the time, known as the 'marriage bar', which decreed that women must give up their jobs upon marriage. Though the law was revoked in 1973, it took almost a decade for married women to return in force to the workplace.

While it may have been unintentional and somewhat reluctant on his part, Byrne's role as a talk-show host was central to the opening-up of uncharted areas of public discourse, highlighting issues which had hitherto remained silent and undisclosed. His gift lay in his ability to shine a spotlight on raw and uncomfortable areas of Irish life that were previously unarticulated in the media. Though Byrne's radio show did not generate the same level of public debates evoked by *The Late Late Show* controversies – such as the Bishop and the Nightie affair or the Playboy Bunnies affair, both of which are discussed in the next chapter – each platform provided a forum of discussion for serious issues such as abortion, contraception and the role of the Catholic Church, while simultaneously showcasing some of the more light-hearted and fun moments in Irish life. It was perhaps this ability to straddle and showcase both sides of Irish life seamlessly that led to much of Byrne's success.

Throughout the course of this book, we take a look at how the wider history and characteristics of the talk-show genre in both television and radio prove central to any discussion on the significance of the talk show in everyday life in Ireland. Moreover, Byrne's mastery of this genre of public confessional still resonates in current radio programmes, such as RTÉ Radio 1's

---

[14] *Ibid.*, p. 30.
[15] 'Housewives' Choice' was also the term used to describe the type of programme presented by popular disc jockey Jimmy Young on BBC Radio 1 from 1967 to 1973.

flagship show *Liveline* and a host of similarly styled shows currently broadcast on the national airwaves.

Yet, Byrne's modest, working-class background gave little indication of the impact he would have on the mindset of Irish audiences. He was born Gabriel Mary Byrne on 5 August 1934, the youngest of six children, and was reared, for the most part, in Dublin's South Circular Road area. He was a pupil of the Christian Brothers School in Synge Street, where he recalls they were beaten 'for failure at lessons and, simply, it seemed, on principle.'[16]

Byrne did not share all the characteristics of a typical Synge-Street-educated Catholic boy, however. His father, Edward, and eight of his father's nine brothers all joined the British Army. Byrne notes that one of his grandfather's proudest days was when he accepted the 'privy purse', an annuity of £10 from his employer, the Earl of Meath, on behalf of the King. It was awarded to him for having sent so many sons to the front.

From an early age Byrne sensed that Catholic, nationalistic fervour was the norm in most Irish households, and one particular incident reminded him of his 'otherness'. A school essay on his father's experiences in the First World War incurred the wrath of a teacher, who ridiculed the young Byrne for its content. Byrne, as indicated in his autobiography, was left troubled by the encounter:

> I still do not truly understand what happened. The only thing I can surmise, based on some of the appalling letters I get on the radio programme from Irish patriots every time there is any reference to the First World War or to Poppy Day, is that John-Joe (the teacher) was a closet nationalist and abhorred the idea of the father of a pupil of his having been in the British Army.[17]

---

[16] Byrne and Purcell, *op. cit.*, p. 30.

[17] *Ibid.*, p. 30.

In later years, during the centenary of the First World War, Byrne revisited the legacy of his father's participation in the war in a documentary aptly titled *My Father's War*.[18] He embarked on a personal odyssey to discover the war secrets his father had never told him. The fact that Byrne's upbringing nurtured a sense of tolerance towards other cultures, in particular towards all things British, offset the nationalist indoctrination he had received from the Christian Brothers. This was to stand him in good stead when dealing with the controversies provoked by his radio and television shows.

Another incident which happened much earlier in his working life was to resonate deeply with Byrne. All of his father's family and all of his siblings had worked for the Guinness Brewery at St James's Gate in Dublin. In the early twentieth century, Guinness was reckoned to be the largest brewery in the world. By the 1940s its provision of medical services, sports and leisure facilities, educational schemes and even housing for employees made it a very attractive place to work. Subsequently, the young Byrne thought that this, too, was to be his career path. However, fate prevailed, and Byrne was turned down for a job at the brewery, perhaps due to a preponderance of Byrnes already in employment there.[19] This, according to Byrne's autobiography, 'was a grave disappointment to us all. In a way it was a source of shame.'[20] Ultimately, it would prove to be one of the biggest factors that cemented his desire to succeed in broadcasting. He briefly entered, and quickly abandoned, the security of an insurance job to later assume the role that would define his life – host of *The Late Late Show*.

Before that, however, and from a very young age, Byrne had hugely admired family friend and broadcaster Eamonn Andrews. In his autobiography, Byrne claims he had a 'huge regard' for Andrews and seemed to admire the fact that Andrews had overcome his working-class background to make

---

[18] Gay Byrne, *My Father's War*, RTÉ 1, 14 April 2015.
[19] Byrne and Purcell, *op. cit.*, p. 33.
[20] *Ibid.*, p. 31.

it big in Britain, first as a quiz-show presenter on BBC radio, then as host of the BBC television show *This Is Your Life*, before ultimately receiving a CBE in 1970 for his services to British broadcasting.[21] Perhaps Byrne admired the ordinariness of Andrews and the fact that he never compromised his Irishness by losing either his accent or his name, retaining both to make him 'the genial Irish Everyman with a broad grin.'[22]

Byrne's involvement in amateur drama was also to prove useful in his career. Indeed, apart from a brief dabble in journalism in the form of a weekly music column for the *RTV Guide* – a precursor to the *RTÉ Guide* in the 1960s[23] – Byrne was an actor at heart, making him an accomplished student of the show-business tradition. He had also worked in Raidió Éireann as host of a pop programme, *Saturday Spin*, and a jazz programme – aptly entitled *Jazz Corner* – broadcast on Monday nights from the old Raidió Éireann studios in Henry Street in Dublin.[24]

By the 1960s, when many television performers were still learning the grammar of the new medium, Byrne sprang into public view with an easy and confident air. This professionalism was the result of a rigorous and difficult apprenticeship at Granada TV, where he was the first person to interview the Beatles. A stint at BBC2 Television was to follow, plus a rather forgettable thirteen-week role as quizmaster for Southampton-based ITV show *That's What You Think*. Described by one critic as 'TV's silliest new game show', Byrne – as 'the undisputed king of live TV' – was accused of 'wasting his undoubted talent on this chunk of trivia.'[25] Some brief engagements with BBC Radio were to follow, and a quiz show, *Jackpot*, on RTÉ,[26] after

---

[21] Gay Byrne, quoted in Ryan Tubridy, *The Irish Are Coming* (William Collins: London, 2013) p. 62.

[22] *Ibid.*, p. 60.

[23] 'I'm a little worried about Elvis', Gay Byrne in the *RTV Guide*, 22–28 April 1963.

[24] 'Gay Byrne's punk radio: I'd say we're down to about 300 doddering old fools', *Irish Times*, 4 December 2013.

[25] *Irish Press*, 7 February 1962.

[26] Byrne was to later host another similarly styled game show, *Who Wants to Be a Millionaire?*, on RTÉ television from 17 October 2000 to 29 March 2002.

which he finally landed his defining role as presenter and producer of *The Late Late Show*. At various times, two other Irish
presenters – Frank Hall and Bunny Carr – tried without success
to adapt their individual but established hosting styles to the
show, but it was ultimately Byrne who made it his own.

From 1962 to 1999, Byrne maintained what appeared to be
an effortless grip on the live talk show, both on radio and on
television. Was he a missionary or simply a talented broadcaster? Either way, he had no hesitation in pushing boundaries
to make entertaining television. Viewers watched in their thousands – at times complicit, outraged, scornful or fascinated – as
Byrne, albeit unintentionally, shaped and challenged viewers'
assumptions on any number of issues, from Travellers' rights
to legislative equality for homosexuals to the bloodied North
and the blight of institutionalised paedophilia. According to
novelist Colm Tóibín, 'his talent was in knowing how fast the
pulse of the country was beating and in knowing whose pulse
he should be taking.'[27]

Byrne's ability to monitor the heartbeat of the Irish nation was
evidenced in the fact that, after just three years of *The Gay Byrne
Hour* he received a Jacob's Award, the highest honour at that
time in the Irish radio industry. The programme was re-titled
The Gay Byrne Show in 1979, and it began modestly with music,
greetings and light-hearted interviews.[28] Then the letters from
listeners started to come, increasingly sad and more despairing.
Byrne would read them aloud in the serious or funny voices he
was known for and turn them into a national debate.

The Gay Byrne Show gradually became the talking point of its
day, reflecting or creating the pulse of the nation. And the nation
was pulsating to a new rhythm in the 1960s. Beatle mania was
replacing the showband era, and young, idealistic emigrants
were returning to Ireland, mostly from Britain, bringing with
them a new-found confidence and a desire for change.

---

[27] Colm Tóibín, 'Gay Byrne: Irish Life as Cabaret', *Crane Bag*, Vol 8. No. 2, p. 65.
[28] Michael Talty, Assistant Librarian and Archivist at RTÉ, in conversation with
the author, 11 June 2014.

Alongside this new breed of returned emigrants were the first promoters of television in Ireland. This latter group shared a common desire that television should, like radio, become an instrument for cementing the nation together. More traditionalist thinkers, including then President Éamon de Valera, feared the onslaught of this new medium, considering it a force that could rupture an intact homogenous culture. This belief prompted the rather prescient de Valera to claim in a speech on the opening night of the new television service that, in time, television viewing could lead to 'demoralisation and decadence and disillusion.'[29]

By the time it was officially launched in Ireland in 1962, the State television service, RTÉ, had been liberated from the shackles of the Civil Service. It had become a semi-state company, answerable indirectly through an Authority to the Government. In the newer dispensation, greater freedom of expression became possible. The legislation that created RTÉ Television was modelled closely on the BBC Charter. With it, came BBC management and trade-union structures. For the first time in Irish broadcasting, salaries and fees rose to a high level, a level that was nevertheless still well behind those of the BBC and ITV. However, they were sufficiently attractive to cause a nationwide stampede of people wanting to become involved in the glamour of television and to lure many away from the traditional show business and newspaper industries.

Into this atmosphere of new-found freedom, rising salaries, lucrative contracts and trade-union power, came *The Late Late Show*, and Gay Byrne entered the socio-political life stream of the country. Certainly, no one could have foreseen that a production of RTÉ's light entertainment department – a mixture of music, song and chat – would develop into a show that took the country by the ears almost from its first night and made ripples in the body politic more consistently and more dramatically than any other show in the history of Irish broadcasting.

---

[29] President Éamon de Valera's opening address to launch the new television station on New Year's Eve, 1961.

The Late Late Show is still a central plank of RTÉ's weekly television schedule. The first show with Gay Byrne as host was always intended to be a leap into the dark. Its display of lights and camera, its mix of light and serious topics, and its policy of allowing ordinary people to tell their extraordinary tales were entirely original in concept, primarily because Irish audiences were, and still are, very different to non-Irish audiences in their expectations of what a talk show should provide.

The Late Late Show was then, and is still to a certain extent, unique. It does not fit into that strict opposition between information and entertainment. In *The Late Late Show*, elements of, for example, the game show and the current-affairs programme converge. The programme's debates in its earlier years made established power accountable to personal experience, providing the opportunity for legitimisation through public expression. Back then, it teetered on the brink of approbation and public outrage, with stories of bishops and nighties, debates on the Irish language, sex, religion and politics all thrown into a cauldron masterfully stirred and directed by Gay Byrne, the amiable host of the manor and the ringmaster of a bizarre range of controversies that would reflect the anomalies at the heart of Irish life.

In the early years of his television and radio programmes Byrne claimed he knew he was going to be thoroughly detested by a large section of the Irish people for speaking about things 'they had never spoken about before and never heard spoken about.'[30] He was aware from the outset that life would not be easy as a talk-show host in a small, conservative country, where few wished to scratch beneath the surface of Irish life.

And so it was on 2 July 1962 that Byrne commenced his role as host of Ireland's – and Europe's – longest-running television talk show,[31] a role that would bring him into direct conflict with outraged viewers and the Catholic Church alike. His task of bringing oftentimes uncomfortable issues to public attention was bound to elicit much controversy and criticism. More

---

[30] Oliver O'Donohue, *Interviewers Interviewed* (Mercier Press: Dublin, 1996) p. 71.
[31] *Guinness World Records 2015.*

significantly, Byrne's genial charm and avuncular presence would belie his ability to probe and pursue a reluctant interviewee with unabated steeliness until they made a revealing confession that would ultimately set the nation talking.

2

From the Nightie to the Naughty: The Early Years of *The Late Late Show* 1962–1972

Launch of *The Late Late Show*

When *The Late Late Show* first aired on 2 July 1962 the press did not know quite what to make of it. *Dublin Opinion*, an influential magazine of the period, denounced the fact that Irish television was an overspill of British television and was already a considerable diversion away from the native, oral traditions of Ireland, exemplified by the hearth-side storyteller.[1] The first four weeks of the show were not well received due to a lack of advertising and the fact that the viewing public had anticipated a television variety show rather than a talk show. The first guests on the first episode were TV critic Ken Grey, Count Cyril McCormack (son of the great Irish tenor), a rather eccentric jazz pianist, George Hodnett, and Harry Thuillier, an Irish broadcaster and former Irish Olympian fencer, none of whom were household names.[2] The show's mixture of serious and casual

---

[1] *Dublin Opinion*, 4 August 1962. (*Dublin Opinion* was an Irish satirical magazine, which was launched on the eve of the Irish Civil War. It was published monthly from 1922–68 and was edited by the cartoonist Arthur Booth.)

[2] Gay Byrne with Deirdre Purcell, *The Time of My Life: An Autobiography* (Gill & Macmillan: Dublin, 1989), p. 197.

panellists and guests, its studio audience, and its ability to shift, chameleon-like, from light to serious topics with obvious ease, made the general media uneasy. Little by little, however, the mood of the press changed, and it was generally deemed to be a success.[3]

The Late Late Show was dreamed up by producer Tom McGrath, who had worked as a floor manager at CBC in Toronto and was hugely impressed by the format of *The Tonight Show*, then hosted by Jack Parr and later by Johnny Carson. McGrath returned from Canada and went to RTÉ with the intention of creating a similar style talk show, with American Burt Budin as director. It was envisaged as a cosy fireside chat, employing the lexicon of de Valera's Ireland, with Byrne as the young host, chatting with a panel of regular guests who were perceived as representative of the typical Irish family. These included part-time model and girl-next-door Verona Mullen, Professor Liam O'Bríon as the father figure, and comedian Danny Cummins, who was 'the messer, the scamp who would stir things up.'[4] There was also writer and polemicist Ulick O'Connor, who, along with his sparring partner Denis Franks, a rather posh-voiced actor of Polish–Jewish decent, engaged in many heated political debates, in addition to any other visitors who might drop in to sing, dance or just talk. The show also had a resident band, a trio led by Noel Kelehan and fronted by singer Frankie Blowers.

Soon *The Late Late Show* became the national forum. It aired from 10.30 p.m. until late on Saturday nights, and many tuned in to see what was happening. A main strength, which no longer exists as part of its format, was its refusal to reveal in advance what was being planned for that night's programme. This meant that Byrne, particularly in the early days, had to live dangerously, never knowing who might pop out of the audience and deliver a broadside.

---

[3] *RTV Guide*, 12 October 1962.
[4] Byrne and Purcell, *op. cit.*, p. 167.

This was, after all, the 'swinging sixties', an era of hope, optimism and change. This decade was a time of Flower Power, the Beatles and the Rolling Stones. It was a period of sexual freedom for some. It was the time of the first space docking by US astronauts, the Vietnam War and Martin Luther King's great dream. Ireland was becoming increasingly prosperous, and it was unlikely that the country would remain unaffected by the acceleration of change from both within its boundaries and without. However, some were tempted to attribute the changing Irish attitudes to the sole influence of television. Equally, there were people who credited *The Late Late Show* with an inordinate responsibility for these changes. The more lucid view is that the show provided a conductive milieu into which those changes could be presented to, and challenged by, Irish audiences.

The 26-year-old Gay Byrne was described by Pan Collins, the show's first researcher, as 'a bright and sassy disc jockey, sometime newsreader and occasional continuity announcer.'[5] Byrne perfectly reflected the optimism and vigour of the younger generation of 1960s Ireland. He seemed to be a truly Irish version of John F. Kennedy. He was considered charming, sophisticated and worldly-wise. He had made it in England with Granada Television and the BBC, yet he was loyal to his roots and wanted to come home. He could talk comfortably and on equal terms with suave foreigners, yet he remained as intrinsically Irish as his audience. It was for these reasons that the youthful Byrne was chosen by RTÉ's first controller of programmes, Gunnar Rugheimer, to host the key Saturday night spot when the show began a regular late time slot on RTÉ in October 1963.

However, Byrne was also contracted to the BBC's new station, BBC2, where he presented a live Saturday afternoon two-hour talk show called *Open House*. His arduous weekly dash from Heathrow to Dublin meant standby presenter Ronnie Walsh filled in if his flight was delayed. This unreliability led Rugheimer to replace Byrne with Frank Hall for

---

[5] Pan Collins, *It Started on The Late Late Show* (Ward River Press: Dublin, 1981), p. 62.

the 1964 season. However, Hall's tenure as host was unsuccessful, heralding the return of Byrne in January 1965. Byrne returned as both presenter and producer, giving the show an edgier feel and content, which at times was a 'double-edged weapon',[6] such was his level of responsibility for the success of the programme.

Yet, much of the programme's impact in its earlier years is also attributable to the diverse and talented pool of researchers who worked with Byrne. In the late 1960s, these included 'the keen and incisive'[7] John Caden, who would later produce *The Gay Byrne Show*; the 'mercurial'[8] political animal Vincent Browne; Myles McWeeney, who loyally served for seven years; and Oliver Donoghue, who came up with the unique idea of the all-Traveller show, starring the much-loved Granny Connors. Joe McAnthony, June Levine and Colette Farmer were also there in the early years, with Pan Collins remaining the one constant.

The Late Late Show was popular because it was lively. It began very much in the mould of the language and imagery of de Valera's protectionist culture, but soon abandoned this restrictive ethos to gradually become modern and post-protectionist in style. The show revelled in the newness of television, paradoxically combining a home-spun intimacy with the display of studio technology. Byrne himself would call the shots at times, as evidenced in his catchphrase 'Roll it there, Colette', as he issued commands for a video to be played. All these aspects of the show gave it a place in Irish life not unlike that of the provincial newspaper: people watched it because they were afraid they might miss out on something.

The ideas and opinions aired on the show were challenging in their openness and in their candour. *The Late Late Show* appeared to operate outside the grammar of established values and was to become at once an outlet for popular impatience and

---

[6]   Gay Byrne, in interview with Olivia O'Leary on RTÉ Radio 1, 5 December 2000.

[7]   Collins, *op. cit.*, p. 64.

[8]   *Ibid.*, p. 65.

an example of what it might be possible for an outward-looking Ireland to achieve.

Yet, the success of the show greatly depended on Byrne's personality. Right up until his retirement from the show in May 1999, it was his persona that acted as a fulcrum around which the entire programme revolved. He was at the centre of every opinion generated, every action initiated and every myth perpetuated. Former *Irish Times* television critic Ken Gray, who was a guest on the first ever episode of the show, referred to Byrne in the 1960s as 'the great window-opener' who ensured the show's success by running into trouble with the Establishment.[9] Byrne's unique broadcasting style was also a contentious issue for many.

Yet, in effect, it was just two aspects of his personality that were particularly important for his broadcasting skills. The first was that he was an actor at heart – the funny faces that he pulled, the comical voices he adopted, and his eagerness to get involved and to raise a few laughs from his audience were all part of his persona. These characteristics led to an acceptance of the more unpalatable aspects of the show. A difficult item would be followed by a song and a lighter topic after the commercial break.

The second aspect of his personality, which was important for his professional achievement generally, was the nature of his life, the fact that his personal odyssey had paralleled that of the national epic, with the same serpentine currents of hope and despair.[10] He was brought up in a sheltered, frugal, quasi-conservative but tolerant family environment. He was inculcated by the Christian Brothers with the values of piety and hard work, but he did not subscribe to the cult of patriotism that they espoused. His family background taught him to accommodate diversity. He had emigrated in the 1950s and returned in the 1960s, getting richer as the country got richer.

---

[9]   Ken Gray, 'First guest on the first Late Late Show', *Irish Times*, 4 July 1987.

[10] Fintan O'Toole, *A Mass for Jesse James: A Journey Through 1980's Ireland* (Raven Arts Press: Dublin, 1990), p. 170.

The dichotomous nature of Byrne's personality was best articulated by journalist Fintan O'Toole over a decade ago when he said that Gay Byrne, 'like his country, is both traditional and modern, both conservative and liberal, both Catholic and materialistic.'[11]

This contradictory persona was to become less acceptable in the Ireland of the 1990s. However, at the height of the show's success in the 1960s and 1970s, Byrne's abandonment of the cosy fireside chat and his willingness to assume the role of devil's advocate for social reform in a tiny conservative island was to bring a level of controversy hitherto unknown to Irish television. Complacency turned to shock for many who watched as he presented a variety of socially contentious issues and raised questions which were taboo in Irish society.

In the early years of the show, Byrne was generally perceived to be progressive without being threatening, and candid while still remaining within the parameters of what the Irish considered 'decency'. His greatest talent lay in his ability to measure the pulse of the community and to ascertain whether or not it was ready to deal with a specific issue at a given time. Byrne wanted to 'reflect what people are ready to talk about, sometimes slightly in advance of public discussion.'[12] He has himself stated that 'one of the great strengths of *The Late Late Show* has been its willingness to deal with new, even frightening ideas.'[13]

He Wants 50 Irish Bunnies[14]

The notion of *The Late Late Show* as a catalyst for change in Irish life is a contentious one. In its earliest years, the show did act as a significant barometer of social transformation, by virtue of the diversity of opinions aired on the show. Inadvertently,

---

[11] *Ibid.*, p. 171.

[12] Gay Byrne, *To Whom It Concerns: Ten Years of the Late Late Show* (Gill & Macmillan: Dublin, 1972), p. 152.

[13] *Ibid.*

[14] 'He Wants 50 Irish Bunnies', *Evening Press*, 27 January 1966.

however, it also soon became an agent of controversy, beginning in earnest in 1966 as a result of the furore caused over
Playboy's London representative, Victor Lownes, and his quest
for 'Irish bunnies', an incident highlighted in the 1997 State
Papers in almost humorous detail.[15]

The controversy began as a result of unfounded reports that
Byrne intended to bring on a 'Bunny girl' from the Playboy
club in London. Victor Lownes further fuelled the controversy
by issuing a press release stating that the purpose of his visit
to Ireland was to recruit Irish girls for Hugh Hefner's Playboy
clubs.[16] With so much adverse publicity prior to the show and
mounting pressure on it to respond, RTÉ eventually announced
that it had not been aware of the nature of Mr Lownes's visit.
When it became apprised of the matter, it was considered necessary to withdraw Lownes's invitation.

But Catholic Ireland would not be silenced. RTÉ's Written
Archives contain a letter from a bank manager in Sligo to the
Director General of RTÉ, Kevin McCourt. He complained that
Byrne was 'permitting obscenities that are unheard of in normal
Irish society' and believed the 'time had come when the public
should be assured that definite action has been taken to prevent
the recurrence of such scandalous incidents.' The bank manager – a position that commanded much respect and wielded
much authority in 1960s Ireland – went on to demand that if
Byrne could not be controlled, there could be 'no option' but to
have the show 'withdrawn completely'.[17]

More formidable dissent was still to come in the form of
Dr John Charles McQuaid, Archbishop of Dublin and Primate
of Ireland, a man intent on ruling over 'the sea of Dublin'.[18]

---

[15] Ryle Dwyer, 'Media breaks thin blue line between Church and State', *Irish
Examiner*, 4 January 1997.

[16] *Ibid.*

[17] Dublin Diocesan Archives: McQuaid Papers, Sean Foran to Kevin McCourt,
copy to Archbishop McQuaid, 31 March 1966, quoted in Dermot Ferriter, *Occasions of Sin: Sex and Society in Modern Ireland* (Profile Books: London, 2010), p. 376.

[18] Louis Fuller, *Irish Catholicism Since 1950: The Undoing of a Culture* (Gill &
Macmillan: Dublin, 2002), p. 139.

McQuaid also wrote to Kevin McCourt regarding the 'bunny man'. McCourt issued a solicitous but measured response to 'His Grace, the Most Rev. Dr John Charles McQuaid':

> Your Grace,
>
> I knew of that 'bunny' man and thus had his intended appearance cancelled immediately when the intention to invite him came to my notice. Not infrequently to my frustration, I cannot be the policeman of all I want and still manage a large and complex organisation … I am greatly strengthened in my concern to do justice in this field by Your Grace's guidance and understanding.[19]

Public outcry abated temporarily, but no sooner had Catholic Ireland escaped the bunny girls when, less than a month later, *The Late Late Show* was again embroiled in controversy, in an incident which has become part of Irish folklore.

The Bishop and the Nightie

> The brouhaha that has followed Mr Byrne's entry to the world of ladies' nightwear is something else altogether.[20]

Referred to by *The Irish Times* as the 'Bishop and the Nightie' incident,[21] the programme had a segment imitating *The Newlywed Game*, an American television game show. This involved a husband and a wife being asked the same questions separately to see how closely their answers compared.

During the game, played with audience participation, a man was asked what colour nightie his wife wore on their wedding night. He replied that it was 'transparent', eliciting huge

---

[19] From Kevin McCourt to Archbishop Charles McQuaid, 15 February 1966, Diocesan Archives (DDA), Archbishop Charles McQuaid Papers (xxv1/9/2/1999).
[20] 'An Fear Sin—will never be a Handley', *Irish Press*, 19 February 1966.
[21] O'Toole 1990, *op. cit.*, p. 170.

guffaws from the audience.[22] When asked the same question, his wife answered that she could not remember and that maybe she had worn none at all, a response which was to cause huge controversy.

Until the arrival of *The Late Late Show*, matters of such personal intimacy were virtually unheard of as topics of public discourse. Furthermore, the fact that the comment by Mr Fox on his wife's 'transparent' nightie caused no public outrage manifests the gendered nature of Irish culture of the time. In 1960s Ireland it was not entirely condemnable for a man to make comments, albeit unintentionally, of a sexual nature. Mrs Fox's comments, however, were deemed unacceptable utterances from a woman, moreover a woman who on first encounter had appeared wholesome and content. In an earlier question, Byrne asked her which of three holidays she would choose if money were no object: two weeks in Spain, a trip to New York (enormously costly at that time) or a cruise down the River Shannon. She chose the cruise down the Shannon, proving herself to be a homely sort of woman. Such a persona was seemingly at odds with her more worldly response regarding her wedding night. Candid comments on sexual matters, especially by a woman, were simply not the norm on Irish television, irrespective of how light-hearted the context.

Such a remark on UK television would have been perceived as tacky or tasteless. To Byrne, it was merely light-hearted, if slightly risqué, banter. To the Bishop of Clonfert, the Most Reverend Dr Thomas Ryan, it was 'most objectionable' and 'completely unworthy of Irish television'.[23]

He was so outraged he issued an immediate statement to the *Sunday Press*, which gave it front-page treatment the following morning. The Bishop, in his sermon at eight o'clock Mass at St. Brendan's Cathedral in Loughrea, urged his congregation to register its protest 'in any manner you think fit, so as to show the producers in Irish television, that you, as decent Catholics,

---

[22] *The Late Late Show*, 1 February 1968.
[23] Byrne and Purcell, *op. cit.*, p. 74.

will not tolerate programmes of this nature.'[24] Such speed of action propelled the whole affair into the national arena. Byrne himself professed amazement at the furore and initially thought it was all a joke.[25] When forced to make a public apology, he stated, 'It has never been our intention that viewers would be embarrassed by the programme … Bearing in mind, that it is an ad lib, late night show for adult viewing.'[26]

One of the behind-the-scenes movers in this incident was once again the Archbishop of Dublin, Dr John Charles McQuaid. He had a keen interest in broadcasting and a heightened aware-ness of the dangers it could pose to his authority. However, 'it was clear McQuaid was reluctant to go public on the issue, for which the Bishop Tom Ryan of Clonfert had found himself held up to ridicule,' for the most part by the media.[27] Once again, he thought it best to write to Kevin McCourt, in a rather peaceable and sympathetic manner. By writing in a personal capacity to McCourt's private address, Archbishop McQuaid was perhaps testing the water to elicit McCourt's response to his not-so-subtle admonishment of Byrne and the questionable content of *The Late Late Show*.

> The questions and answers in the case of a Mr and Mrs Fox were vulgar, even coarse and suggestive … You have not been fairly treated.[28]

The implication here is that McCourt had received unfair criti-cism arising from Byrne's 'nightie' interview with Mrs Fox and now, in the Archbishop's mind, it was time for Byrne to go.

---

[24] 'Bishop calls Late Late Show "objectionable"', *Irish Times*, 14 February 1966.

[25] Byrne and Purcell, *op. cit.*, p. 183.

[26] 'Byrne now realises show was "embarrassing to a section"', *Irish Times*, 15 February 1966.

[27] John Horgan, *Broadcasting and Public Life* (RTÉ: Dublin, 2004).

[28] Archbishop McQuaid to Kevin McCourt, 10 February 1966, quoted in Horgan, *ibid.*, p. 31.

However, McCourt was equally adept at informing McQuaid, his former principal at Blackrock College, just who was in charge. His response to the Archbishop indicated that they shared common ground and he, like McQuaid, did not 'tolerate the tawdry, the deprecation of what I believe to be the inherent good taste of Irish people.'[29] McCourt's diplomatic response to the Archbishop manifests his determination not to brook interference from His Eminence.

Moreover, of the 36 calls received by RTÉ regarding the show, only one was critical of the incident, indicating that the public was unwilling to privately support clerical outrage, even if they were publicly galvanised into action by the might of the crozier. Within 48 hours the affair began to assume proportions of alleged indecency, obscenity and filth as the disapprobation of the Church was filtered through newspaper reports, Church homilies and mass demonstrations of staunchly Catholic organisations, including the Mayo GAA Board and the Meath Vocational Educational Committee. These were joined by the *Catholic Standard* newspaper and the Loughrea town commissioners, with the latter referring to *The Late Late Show* as 'a dirty programme that should be abolished altogether.'[30] The Parish Priest of St. Brigid's Church, Dunleer, Co. Louth, Father Michael McRory, also condemned the show in his sermon that Sunday. He stressed: 'The duty of Catholic viewers to such a programme is clear – they should turn it off.'[31]

One brave dissenting voice was that of Mr Patrick Cahill in Waterford County Council. He asserted at a council meeting that he saw nothing objectionable in the programme but was shouted down by the majority of his county councillor colleagues, including one Mr M. Galgey, who stated, 'If … [Bishop Ryan] thought it suitable to criticise *The Late Late Show* … he was quite right to do so in his capacity as spiritual director of

---

[29] *Ibid.*

[30] Byrne and Purcell, *op. cit.*, p. 171.

[31] 'Brouha on the Late Late Show', *Cork Examiner*, 15 February 1966.

the people, particularly the young.'[32] Mr Galgey further high-lighted the absolute deference to the clergy at that time when he insisted that 'it was not up to the County Council to criticise the Bishop.'[33]

In the much more tolerant milieu of twenty-first century Ireland, this incident may now seem trivial and almost laughable. Indeed an editorial in *The Irish Times* just days after the incident was, as Byrne himself put it, 'toffee-nosed and amusing and right.'[34] The article praised the BBC, which, unlike Teilifís Éireann, provided programmes that enabled the English to laugh at themselves, their public figures, and the state of the world in general. The article ended with the claim that 'a lapse of taste has been treated as if it were an outrage to morals.'[35]

Nonetheless, not to be outdone, Bishop Ryan insisted that he had been 'inundated' with calls to congratulate him on his stand in speaking out against an 'objectionable show'.[36] But contrary to his belief that he had the support of the majority of the people of Ireland, just seven letters on the issue were sent to *The Irish Times*. Stephen Barrett, TD, pointed out that 'a large number of viewers do not share Mr Byrne's morbid curiosity in regard to the colour of Mrs Fox's honeymoon nightie' and went on to remind Gay Byrne that many of his viewers 'are grown-up and Mr Byrne should attempt to reach their stature.'[37] The remaining six letters displayed an inimitable Irish humour, such as that from a reader who wrote:

It should be recognised that night attire is not in use throughout the world. Many of my male friends go to bed in the raw. In West Cork they wear corduroys.[38]

---

[32] *Ibid.*

[33] *Ibid.*

[34] Quoted in Byrne and Purcell, *op. cit.*, p. 162.

[35] *Irish Times*, 15 February 1966.

[36] *Evening Herald*, 14 February 1966.

[37] *Irish Times*, 17 February 1966.

[38] *Ibid.*

This 'Bishop and Nightie' incident is of significance in that it reveals the power and the pace with which the Catholic Church sought to harness and direct public opinion at that time, while simultaneously providing a glimpse into the gradual dismantling of that power. The diversity of opinion generated by the incident also makes it noteworthy. There was not total acceptance of the moral degradation of the event as viewed by Bishop Tom Ryan of Clonfert. From the letters sent to the press, it is clear that the public perceived the incident as tasteless and lacking in decorum rather than sexually or morally offensive.

Nevertheless, the incident does reflect popular culture at that time. Many Irish people accepted a certain status quo with an almost total lack of questioning. Even if in the privacy of their own homes they may have found the incident amusing, many members of the public assumed very different positions when the voice of the Catholic Church was raised in condemnation. It was still customary in 1960s Ireland to pay respect to that voice. Thus, if a bishop was critical of an incident that originally seemed inoffensive, the matter would be reconsidered in a new light, with support for the Church's stance coming from institutions, town councils and educational bodies the length and breadth of the country.

Conversely, the students of Trinity College cared little for the disapprobation of the Catholic Church. They found the whole incident farcical. They allied themselves against what they referred to as the Bishop's 'absurdity',[39] and it was rumoured that they were planning a parade, with students dressed in white nightdresses in protest. This was called off, however, on the Monday following the controversial programme, after 'a fawning apology' came from Byrne.[40]

Years later, in his autobiography, Byrne stated how appalled he was that so many people in responsible positions, who must have known they were right regarding the absurdity of the whole incident, 'allowed themselves to be placed in a one-down

[39] 'The Bishop and the Nightie', *Irish Times*, 19 February 1966.
[40] *Ibid.*

situation,' because they feared the wrath of the Church, adding '… and I include myself in that criticism.'[41]

Journalist Gene Kerrigan makes the point that *The Late Late Show* was, in effect:

> … articulating the subtle and not so-subtle changes through which the country was going. We were talking in different ways and about different things. The old subservience and automatic reverence [to the Catholic Church] was going.[42]

The Late Late Show can be credited with introducing a public forum where the values and beliefs that dominated Irish society were challenged and held up to public scrutiny. It is all too easy for those of us living through the media-saturated Ireland of the new millennium to dismiss the importance of the show as a microcosm of the sweeping changes taking place in de Valera's Ireland. Before the emergence of such a talk show, these changes were hidden from public scrutiny by countless lists of taboos that curtailed freedom of speech and diversity of opinion. Byrne and his production team used the television medium to publicly examine and challenge the nature of Irish society and, in essence, put a mirror up to the face of the country to reflect the transformations taking place. By doing so, Irish people were forced to face up to themselves.

Nevertheless, the openly confrontational style of *The Late Late Show* was at odds with the Catholic Church, and this would not be the end of the clashes between the two. The Church feared not only *The Late Late Show*, but the power and influence of television itself. State Papers from 1967, released in January 1998, reveal the disproportionate level of indignation caused by Byrne.[43] Not only had the show angered Irish

---

[41] Byrne and Purcell, *op. cit.*, p. 195.

[42] Gene Kerrigan, 'The night the Late Late almost sank', *Sunday Independent*, 5 January 1997.

[43] State Papers, National Archives of Ireland: Archives of the Irish Government, 1922–75.

politicians and bishops, but it had also caused disquiet within the British establishment. The British Ambassador, Sir Andrew Gilchrist, accused the young broadcaster of organising controversial programmes to 'publicise himself' without 'a due sense of responsibility towards the community.'[44]

The State Papers make reference to a complaint to the Government regarding Byrne's interviewing of suspected members of the Irish Republican Army – Cathal Goulding and Richard Behal – on *The Late Late Show*. The Ambassador stated that he had personally received several complaints regarding the interview, including one from Princess Margaret's relatives in Ireland. A Government official at the time told the Ambassador 'of the delicate nature'[45] of the problem of seeking to influence what was put out by RTÉ and doubted whether anything could be done about the matter.

The difficulties of controlling a monolith like RTÉ, or indeed television in general, is one which many sociologists, in their research on television, have a certain sympathy with. They believe the influence of television is so significant that institutions such as Church and Government have much to fear from the adverse influence of unsympathetic television portrayals. As a debasing cultural force, television is potentially lethal, claims sociologist Richard Collins. Almost three decades ago he accurately pointed out that monitoring the content of television in the interests of the national community was vital in order to resist what he termed 'an alien tide of kitsch'.[46]

For many, *The Late Late Show* did bring this 'tide of kitsch'. Throughout the 1960s, it continued to cause outrage. Government State Papers from 1966 reveal that a Galway doctor dispatched a long telegram to the Taoiseach, demanding an immediate end to *The Late Late Show*:

---

[44] *Ibid.*

[45] DDA, Archbishop McQuaid Papers, Dublin Diocesan Office, Glasnevin (xxv1/9/3/98).

[46] Richard Collins, *Culture, Communication and National Identity: The Case of Canadian Television* (University of Toronto Press: Toronto, 1990), p. 10.

Gay Byrne must go. I find him utterly out of sympathy with the great majority of my own people ... He must be suspended for one month and then we will give him another job where he will learn to align himself with the thoughts and feelings and with the majority belief of my own dear country north and south.[47]

The patriotic tenor and tone of this letter reveals once again the hierarchical nature of Irish society at that time. At the higher echelons were the clergy, followed by respected professionals such as doctors, bank managers and teachers, each of whom saw their role as custodian of public morals intrinsic to their chosen profession.

This call to arms in defence of Irish morality, imbued with a strong sense of Catholic, nationalistic fervour, surfaced once again in an incident involving a young Trinity College student and part-time playwright named Brian Trevaskis, who appeared on *The Late Late Show* in 1966. It is important to note that, at that time, Archbishop Charles McQuaid had attempted to protect Irish Catholic students from the 'godless' institution that was Trinity by imposing a ban preventing Catholics from attending the university. Trevaskis's appearance as a panellist on the show sparked another sense of outrage on issues as diverse as those relating to freedom of speech and the entrenched perceptions of many Irish people regarding students who attended Trinity College Dublin.

The Brian Trevaskis Affair

When Brian Trevaskis made his first appearance on Irish television as a guest on *The Late Late Show*, ostensibly to discuss the craft of playwriting, he waded into a whole herd of sacred cows. He began by describing Galway Cathedral in the west of Ireland as a monstrosity. He then condemned the Irish educational

---

[47] Broadcasting Complaints, S593: Television Programmes on RTÉ, former State Paper Office, Dublin Castle (now in National Archives), 1966.

systems and Ireland's interpretation of Christianity. Further-more, he accused the nation of having failed to fulfil even one of the provisions drawn up by 1916 Republican martyr Padraig Pearse. Without a pause, Trevaskis also admonished roundly both their Graces the Archbishop of Dublin and the Bishop of Galway, questioned the value of the Irish language and inferred that the Christian Brothers were overfond of the cane. This was quite a mouthful, even for a show which by then had gained a reputation for controversy.

As expected, the show was attacked by the Church. The *Irish Catholic* newspaper accused *The Late Late Show* of providing a soapbox for liberal idealists.[48] Protests were made by Galway County Council, Limerick Corporation and Carlow County Council regarding Trevaskis's remarks on the show. At a meeting of the Galway County Council, Senator Mark Killilea, Chairman, said that if *The Late Late Show* could not change and produce something that could be enjoyed, 'then the quicker it can be dropped the better.'[49] Carlow County Council held an hour-long discussion on the matter and decided to send a resolution to the Minister and to the Director-General 'vehemently protesting against attacks on the hierarchy and asking that the show be drastically reformed.'[50]

The man who made the proposal, Councillor Paddy Cogan, said that in his opinion there was an organised plan to vilify the bishops, and he suspected the work of 'an advance guard of Communism'.[51] One of his colleagues, Councillor Kathleen Brady-O'Neill, said that the councillors were simply branding anyone who said anything out of the ordinary as communists and insisted she was 'a good Catholic and no Communist,' adding, 'I do not condone any personal insult to the Bishop of Galway, but we must not be too sweeping in our condemnations.'[52]

---

[48] Quoted in Byrne and Purcell, *op. cit.*, p. 112.
[49] *Irish Times*, 14 February 1966.
[50] *Ibid.*
[51] *Irish Times*, 15 February 1966.
[52] *Ibid.*

Trinity College took exception to the fact that the Bishop of Galway was not surprised that a student of Trinity College would call him a moron. Was there an intimation of old historical prejudices being unearthed? The following comments from the Deputy President of Trinity College Students' Representative Council seem to suggest that this was indeed the case:

> I am disappointed that the Bishop accepts without surprise the term 'moron' from heirs to Berkeley, Swift, Goldsmith, Burke, Yeats and so many other noble Irishmen, and I am incensed that His Lordship should throw salt in old wounds and attempt to doubt the genuine affection and respect that exists between the students of TCD and the Irish people.[53]

Letters to *The Irish Times* referring to Trevaskis clearly reveal anti-British sentiments. The fact alone that Trevaskis was attending Trinity College attracted the following negative comments:

> His one distinction is that the British Government is paying his way through Trinity College ... plainly he was known to his sponsor as an iconoclast and in this Christian country had no right to be invested with the right of free speech on Telefís Éireann.[54]

Once more, simply because he was a student of Trinity College, Trevaskis was referred to by another letter writer as an 'axe-grinding egotist'. The writer further maintained that Trevaskis knew no more about the architectural merits of Galway Cathedral 'than I do about taming a ferocious grasshopper.'[55] Those who wrote in support of Trevaskis generally chose to do so on the grounds that everyone is entitled to freedom of speech. One reader wrote that: 'You either have free speech or you don't,'

---

[53] *Irish Times*, 14 February 1966.
[54] *Irish Times*, 20 March 1966.
[55] *Ibid*.

and suggested that Brian Trevaskis certainly had not over-stepped the bounds of public decency in saying what he said. Instead, the person claimed:

> This young man had the courage of his convictions, and had the courage to say what he thought in the most public possible way. More power to his elbow.[56]

In an editorial on the controversy, *The Church of Ireland Gazette* stated that Gay Byrne 'deserves the best thanks of the Irish people for a courageous and sagacious blow struck for freedom of speech,' while acknowledging that 'while striking that blow, it is wholly regrettable that an insult was offered to the Roman Catholic hierarchy.'[57]

An apology was issued by the then Director General of RTÉ, Kevin McCourt, regarding the comments made by Trevaskis. In the midst of it all, Trevaskis let it be known that he wished to reappear on the show the following weekend to apologise to the Bishop of Galway. Once again, Archbishop McQuaid wrote to Kevin McCourt to express his disquiet regarding the 'scandalous' content of *The Late Late Show*, urging McCourt to assert his authority when dealing with Byrne and his team. It is worth quoting almost the entire contents of McQuaid's letter with a view to highlighting the level of controversy that *The Late Late Show* provoked and the level of distaste with which Byrne was viewed by the 'Catholic majority' at that time:

> Dear Mr McCourt,
>
> I am of the opinion that the further appearance of Mr Trevaskis on television, whether for the purpose of apologising or not, would be most unwelcome to the Irish people. It is respectfully suggested that you use your

---

[56] *Irish Times*, 13 April 1966.
[57] 'TÉ [Teilifís Éireann] show is praised by Church journal', *Irish Press*, 16 April 1966.

authority to ensure that he does not appear again and, furthermore, I think you should adopt some system whereby you could supervise, personally, the selection of the speakers to the panel.

It is strongly felt by many people down here that Gay Byrne should make a public apology for allowing so many of the panel whose philosophy of life and ideas are alien to Irish, and especially Irish Catholic, traditions. I refer in particular to the attempts to publicise 'Bunny' girls, hypnotism, pornographic literature, as well as permitting obscenities that are unheard of in normal Irish society.

In view of the many previous occasions on which there was cause for complaint, I think something more is now required than a mere apology. I am inclined to doubt the good faith of a person who has apologised on several occasions but has now permitted similar unpleasant incidents.

What I cannot understand is that in almost every show panellists appear who are loud in their voicing of anti-Irish sentiments and in trying to propagate notions which are confined to but a very small minority, without any regard for the normally accepted ideas on Ethics, Religion and Art.

… The time has come when the public should be assured that definite action has been taken to prevent the recurrence of such scandalous incidents, and if that cannot be done there can be no option only to have the show withdrawn completely.[58]

In spite of the personal and excoriating tone of McQuaid's letter, McCourt appears to have taken little action to prevent

---

[58] Archbishop Charles McQuaid to Kevin McCourt, 31 March 1966, DDA, McQuaid Papers (AB8 (XXV1)).

Trevaskis's reappearance on the show. Trevaskis apologised for calling the Bishop a moron, before adding that while the Bishop of Galway, Dr Browne, might know the meaning of the word moron, it was unclear whether he understood the true meaning of the word Christianity. And so began round two of a controversy that saw clergy members and county councillors deliver dire warnings and outraged attacks to the community and the Church congregation in equal measure, eventually bringing a response at Cabinet level. The Minister for Posts and Telegraphs, Joe Brennan, wrote to Eamonn Andrews, Chairman of the RTÉ Authority, on 30 March 1966. It could be argued that what mattered was not so much what Trevaskis had said but that Gay Byrne had defended his right to say it, as is evident from the following letter from Brennan:

> I must take exception to the view expressed last Saturday night by the compère when he implied, or indeed, explic- itly stated that anybody is free to say anything they like on the programme. We must guard against providing a forum for every crank to vent his grievance, and the first step towards exercising this type of control I have in mind would be keeping the irreverent likes of Trevaskis off the show. If this programme is allowed to develop along the lines on which it is moving in recent times, it would be better it were taken off the air.[59]

Andrews replied on 6 April. Tactfully, he said he shared Bren- nan's concern about complaints and suggested that Brennan himself must have hosted hostile meetings 'where I am sure you have invited freedom of expression.'[60] It is clear that Andrews was not to be dictated to. Both he and Byrne were professional broadcasters willing to reflect the mood of change in Ireland. They and the generation they represented would set the limits to discussion, not Ministers or members of the Church hierarchy. It

---

[59] Broadcasting Complaints, S593, *op. cit.*
[60] *Ibid.*

was this belief in the freedom of expression for each individual, along with the understanding that certain sectors of Irish audiences were no longer automatically reverent to the opinions of the Establishment, which led Andrews to further suggest in his letter to Minister Brennan:

> It would be a great pity for broadcasting if such external pressures were ever applied to an authority such as ours that any programme had to be removed. A live programme with a good record of information and entertainment for the great bulk of the country's population is a rarity in broadcasting and should be nurtured now that we have it established.[61]

This resistance to frank talk in public formed the genesis of a critique of RTÉ's programming policy in the form of the 1969 book by Jack Dowling, Lelia Doolin and Bob Quinn called *Sit Down and Be Counted*.[62] In the book, news and current affairs were also cited as hotbeds for controversies. Nevertheless, in the 1960s it was not these programmes that provoked a passionate response from viewers. Most of the overt controversy was centred on *The Late Late Show*. The Brian Trevaskis incident and the 'Bishop and the Nightie' affair combined to crystallise the polarised viewpoints that existed in Irish society. It was those who deemed the show unrepresentative of Irish life who mobilised themselves most formidably, and questions were raised about the format of the show. Its tenor was also put under scrutiny. Was it a serious discussion programme or a light-hearted entertainment show? If the latter were true, then it should observe certain rules such as impartiality and a structured approach. There were suggestions that radical opinions such as those aired by Trevaskis should not be permissible on the programme, but opinion polls taken shortly after his appearance on the show revealed that as

---

[61] *Ibid.*

[62] L. Doolan, J. Dowling and B. Quinn, *Sit Down and Be Counted: The Cultural Evolution of a Television Station* (Waterloo Publications: Dublin, 1969).

many as 50 per cent of those surveyed agreed with the views he had expressed.[63]

In 1968, less than two years after Trevasksis's appearance on the show, a simmering anti-RTÉ undercurrent in clerical circles was brought to light. This took the form of a letter from 'a group of priests' in Dundalk to the Archbishop of Dublin, Dr John Charles McQuaid. They asked:

> Do our esteemed leaders have any idea at all of the harm that is being done to the Catholics of Ireland by the anti-Catholic, anti-Irish propaganda of *The Late Late show*? Surely the time is lamentably overdue for responsible leaders to see to it that the suave Mr Byrne be prevented from providing a platform for the vermin of England, France, USA or anywhere such vermin can be picked up.[64]

But Byrne and his production team would not be silenced by 'this group of priests' or any other dissenting voices. It was now clear that the show had stepped up a gear in allowing representation to diverse viewpoints. Its ultimate strength lay in its lack of structure. Moreover, its accommodation of adversity, its impromptu nature and its utter lack of predictability all made the show impossible to miss. The topics discussed on the show were the topics close to the heart of the nation and reflected contemporary Irish culture. The Church was criticised, and guests spoke about sexual and moral issues. Viewers were delighted, and they were outraged. They could revel in the programme, or they could switch it off, but it was difficult to turn off *The Late Late Show*. It was, for many, just too unpredictable, with a constant energy facilitating a freedom of speech.

Throughout the 1960s, Byrne also presented a number of sponsored radio programmes on Raidió Éireann, including what we would now call 'infomercials' on items such as 'menswear bargains in the New Year's sale', where men's overcoats

---

[63] Figures quoted in Byrne and Purcell, *op. cit.*, p. 113.
[64] Horgan, *op. cit.*, p. 62.

would provide 'warmth, style, value and class'.[65] These light, sponsored radio items were in sharp contrast to the content of *The Late Late Show*, where viewers were exposed to a diversity of subjects, many of them disconcerting.

Some of the more provocative and influential discussions on *The Late Late Show* included the 1965 debate on the Irish language. This was a real turning point for the show, and it certainly broke new ground. For the first time ever a Government organisation was being used as an instrument to allow anti-Irish language lobbyists to strike out at some of the most sacred of sacred cows. The Church's ban on Catholics attending Trinity College was discussed on the show in March 1967,[66] and because the timing was right, the piece was instrumental in highlighting the fact that the ban was outmoded. The ban was later revoked in 1970.[67] With the passing of the decade, the Irish viewing public grew more accustomed to public debate. As the nation's horizons broadened, dissension became more infrequent.

All Kinds of Everything

By 1970, Ireland was experiencing an era of profound change, much of which was shaped and debated on *The Late Late Show*. In January 1970, Dr Thekla Beere was appointed to chair the Commission on the Status of Women, kick-starting a decade which would see women's rights pushed to the forefront of political debate.[68] That same year, Ireland won the Eurovision Song Contest for the first time, with the winning song, 'All Kinds Of Everything', sung by 17-year-old Derry girl Dana.[69] This event made way for Ireland's hosting of the competition, in full colour, in April 1971, the same year that members of the

---

[65] 1966 sponsored programme on Raidió Éireann, presented by Gay Byrne.

[66] *The Late Late Show*, 3 March 1967.

[67] John Cooney, *John Charles McQuaid: Ruler of Catholic Ireland* (O'Brien Press: Dublin, 2009), p. 78.

[68] Diarmaid Ferriter, *Ambiguous Republic: Ireland in the 1970s* (Profile Books: London, 2012), p. xiv.

[69] *Ibid.*

Irish Women's Liberation Movement (IWLM) brought contraceptives into the Republic from over the border in Northern Ireland, an act of protest against the laws prohibiting their use and importation.[70]

The IWLM, along with legal rights campaigner and Ireland's future first female president Mary Robinson, harnessed support for women's right to equal pay to ease the way for the introduction of more reliable forms of contraception. Changes were also occurring in the North of Ireland. On 30 January 1972 (thenceforth known as Bloody Sunday), violence escalated in the region when thirteen unarmed civilians were shot dead in Derry by British paratroopers.[71]

On *The Late Late Show* this change was reflected in the meticulously thought-out showpieces of political debate that occurred in the early 1970s. The programme reflected a culture that was changing rapidly, and at times it helped to accelerate this change. In 1970, when author and paraplegic Christy Brown used the 'F' word on the show, only two complaints were received, contrasting significantly with the volume of complaints elicited by Trevaskis's comments just five years previously. According to *The Irish Times* this was 'a moment of television history'.[72] The paper asked whether the muted reaction to Brown's expletive was due to him being 'a cripple who had overcome most magnificently his terrible handicaps.'[73]

As ever balancing the more controversial elements with light entertainment, the 'world's longest-running commercial',[74] *The Late Late Toy Show*, was inaugurated by Pan Collins in 1971 and remains an annual feature of the show to this day.

But an overall review of the content of *The Late Late Show* from 1962–72 shows that it reflected Ireland's readiness for the sexual and cultural diversity which existed within and without

---

[70] *Ibid.*, p. xvii.

[71] *Ibid.*, p. xix.

[72] 'On the offensive', *Irish Times*, 1 June 1970.

[73] *Ibid.*

[74] Collins, *op. cit.*, p. 73.

its shores. The appearance on the show in March 1971 of representatives from the newly established IWLM propelled the organisation to national attention. One of the founders of the Movement, journalist Mary Maher, confessed herself surprised at the level of reaction the interview provoked. In an article in *The Irish Times* she elaborated on the IWLM's appearance on the talk show and maintained that the organisation had more 'recruits than any other civil rights movement of its time.'[75]

Another founding member of the Movement, journalist Mary Kenny, believed Byrne had the 'instinct' that things were changing in Ireland, and he had the ambition to be the propeller of that change.[76] By grasping the women's liberation 'story', Kenny believes Byrne was aware of its potential to have people 'gasping with shock in their armchairs.'[77] An interesting personality trait of Byrne's – which would later evoke criticism in his interview with Annie Murphy, the former lover of Bishop Eamon Casey[78] (discussed in Chapter 5) – is Kenny's observation that Byrne was not the kind of man who would feel comfortable around women who were too 'forward'. She recalls seeing him 'recoil in aversion' when author Edna O'Brien began to act flirtatiously with him.[79]

Former *Late Late Show* researcher June Levine has also spoken of Byrne's attitude to a certain type of female personality. She reveals that in her role as a researcher on the show, she was always on the lookout for female guests 'who reminded him of the women he liked, such as Emer Bowman (a friend of the Byrne family); his beautiful and perfect secretary, Maura Connolly, and his wife, Kathleen Watkins, multi-talented and maternal.'[80]

---

[75] 'Women's Liberation', *Irish Times*, 9 March 1971.

[76] Mary Kenny, in a letter to the author, 10 January 2012.

[77] *Ibid.*

[78] In 1992 it was revealed that the Bishop of Galway, Eamon Casey, had fathered a child with American divorcee Annie Murphy. Casey's subsequent resignation from his role as bishop is seen as a pivotal juncture in highlighting the diminution of Church power in Ireland.

[79] Mary Kenny, *op. cit.*

[80] 'Gay the Ayatollah the Late', *Irish Independent*, 7 December 1982.

Journalist and feminist Nell McCafferty recalls meeting Byrne, 'the first male they had to make a case to,'[81] regarding the upcoming appearance of members of the IWLM on the show. According to McCafferty, Byrne 'knew nothing of feminism'[82] but had agreed to the meeting at the request of the show's researchers Pan Collins and June Levine. As the IWLM's manifesto *Chains or Change?* was explained, Byrne, according to McCafferty's recollections, sat 'bemused'.[83] This particular episode of the show, hosted temporarily by broadcaster Marian Finucane, was entirely given over to the issue of feminism and had an all-female panel, until Garret FitzGerald, the leader of opposition party Fine Gael, came on. Mary Kenny recounts her memories of the event:

> It was one of the first times we had the opportunity to speak about this new wave of feminism in the public realm. But halfway through the programme, Gay Byrne had suddenly announced that Garrett Fitzgerald had been sitting watching the show at home and had been so engaged by the subject that he asked if could come and join us, and Gay had eagerly agreed. The announcement was greeted by a sustained audience response: 'You're hijacking our show,' we cried. There was huge resentment and an entirely spontaneous orchestration of booing from the assembled group of women, panel and of Gay and of Garrett, that these two men couldn't have let the women have their say, uninterrupted, without trying to muscle in on the act.[84]

However, there were also those who resented the fact that Byrne had allowed the 'shrill chorus from the Women's Lib on *The Late Late Show* for a romp,' and even the suggestion that 'the

---

[81] Nell McCafferty, in an interview with the author, 7 February 2012.

[82] *Ibid.*

[83] *Ibid.*

[84] 'A self-professed feminist who was devoted to women in his life', *Irish Independent*, 20 May 2011.

time had come to apply the brakes.'[85] Once again, Byrne was damned if he did and damned if he didn't.

Nell McCafferty was to feature again on the show, along with June Levine and others, in 1971, as part of the 'Contraceptive Train', a group of women who carried bags of condoms from Belfast to Dublin on a train in protest at Ireland's strict anti-contraception laws.[86] The whole issue of contraception was to prove divisive. On an episode of *The Late Late Show* over two years later, the topic of family planning evoked a very negative response, largely, it has to be said, from men, as well as criticism of Byrne regarding his handling of the issue. Letters to the *Irish Press* newspaper were critical of Byrne's apparent bias and liberal attitude to contraception, as the following samples demonstrate:

> Having watched *The Late Late Show* and the discussion on contraceptives, I was amazed with the attitude adopted by Gay Byrne … For a person in his position, which brings its own responsibilities, he should obtain some knowledge and advice from the proper channels …[87]

> It would appear that Gay Byrne does not show much concern for future parents and leaders of our country.[88]

> Looking at Gay Byrne on *The Late Late Show* of November 26, I can't figure out why he dressed it up as a debate at all. His window dressing was superb. It is very much to his credit that he gave the progressive contraceptionists plenty of scope and valuable help.[89]

---

[85] Letters to the Editor, *Irish Times*, 9 April 1971.

[86] Contraception was illegal in Ireland until 1980. Thomas Ryan, Bishop of Clonfert, referred to the actions of IWLM as 'an assault on the Catholic heritage of Ireland on the pretext of civil rights, conscience and women's liberation,' quoted in *Field Day Anthology of Irish Writing* (NYU Press, 2002), p. 200.

[87] Letters to the Editor, *Irish Press*, 3 December 1973.

[88] *Ibid.*

[89] *Ibid.*

The newly coined phrase 'progressive contraceptionists' further highlights the diversity and depth of opinion on female reproduction prevalent in the country at that time, an issue which everyone had a view on. According to Mary Leland, one of the contributors to the pioneering 'Women First' page in *The Irish Times*:

> The sacredness of the female reproductive system vanished forever with the publication of *Humanae Vitae* [Pope Paul VI's 1968 encyclical on the regulation of birth control]. From there on ovaries, wombs and menstruation became acceptable items of popular as well as clerical obsession.[90]

Rather unexpectedly, another area of 'clerical obsession' was the issue of divorce. In early 1972, *Late Late Show* panellist Father Fergal O'Connor openly criticised the Catholic establishment for disallowing divorce,[91] a topic later returned to in 1986 when the show featured a special episode on the issue in the form of a mock court trial, with a full complement of senior and junior counsels as well as a judge.[92]

Almost a decade after the show began, *The Late Late Show* had evolved into a unique example of a talk show that furtively extended its brief to include current affairs, a charge that was also levelled against *The Gay Byrne Show* in 1975.[93] But Byrne himself had never perceived the show as mere entertainment; instead he viewed it as a forum for national debate, a form of 'town hall of the air'.[94] In the earlier days he had tried to extend the brief of the programme to embrace current affairs and wanted politicians to appear on the show.

Media academic and author John Horgan recounts how Byrne telephoned the Secretary of the Department of the Taoiseach to

---

[90] Mary Leland, 'Father Marx and Abortion' in *Changing the Times: Irish Women Journalists 1969–1981* (The Lilliput Press: Dublin, 2003), p. 142.

[91] *The Late Late Show*, 18 February 1972.

[92] 'Late Late Special on divorce sure to top TAM ratings', *Irish Press*, 20 June 1986.

[93] Horgan, *op. cit.*, p. 145.

[94] Byrne and Purcell, *op. cit.*, p. 185.

ask if the Taoiseach would meet with him to discuss ministerial participation in the show. Byrne informed the Taoiseach that he hoped to get away from 'the present light entertainment type of programme and to turn it instead into a programme in which matters of public interest would be discussed in a serious manner.'[95] Byrne had previously made informal approaches to three ministers, Charles Haughey, George Colley and Donagh O'Malley, the latter of whom indicated his willingness to participate should the Taoiseach be in favour of such a move.

However, reaction was swift and unambiguous. Following a Government meeting, Taoiseach Jack Lynch told his departmental secretary that he did not approve of ministers going on *The Late Late Show*. He stressed that there was already a provision for political programmes and, therefore, there was no need for a meeting with Gay Byrne. The whips of all political parties took grave exception to Byrne's request and told RTÉ journalists at a meeting at Leinster House in 1972 that 'they deplored the fact that RTÉ should vilify and ridicule politics and politicians in shows like the *Late Late*.'[96] Byrne was censured by the Director-General of RTÉ, Kevin McCourt. Nonetheless, he remained mindful that *The Late Late Show* was the perfect vehicle to show how good an interviewer he was, 'without having the strictures of the more formalised current-affairs programme situation.'[97]

By the end of its first decade, priest, playwright and *Radharc*[98] filmmaker Desmond Forristal reckoned that *The Late Late Show* 'had probably done more than any other single factor to form the national consciousness on a hundred different topics.'[99] Yet, few could have predicted that just around the corner,

---

[95] Note to Taoiseach, quoted in Horgan, *op. cit.*, p. 52.

[96] Horgan, *op. cit.*, p. 52.

[97] Byrne 1972, *op. cit.*, pp. 20–21.

[98] *Radharc* was an Irish documentary film series broadcast by RTÉ Television from 1962–96. It was funded by Archbishop Charles McQuaid, who at times was unhappy with the pioneering and excavating view of Irish life and clerical influence caught on camera by McQuaid's appointee as head of the film unit, Fr Joe Dunn.

[99] Desmond Forristal, 'The Late Late Show', *Furrow*, 23 October 1970.

in February 1973, a 'housewives' choice' radio programme, *The Gay Byrne Hour*, would begin broadcasting. This would evolve into a public confessional, a form of 'talking cure' for the Irish nation. Broadcast daily from Monday to Friday, with Byrne as presenter, the radio programme would prove every bit as controversial as its television counterpart.

3

All Human Life: The Birth of *The Gay Byrne Show* and 21 Years of *The Late Late Show*

Simultaneous to his role as television host, Byrne also presented the popular radio programme, *The Gay Byrne Show*, originally called *The Gay Byrne Hour*. The poet Brendan Kennelly once referred to Byrne as the 'comforter of the afflicted and afflicter of the comfortable.'[1] He believed Byrne's radio show had all the hallmarks of an open university because it aired on radio subjects that were furtive and normally hidden in Irish life. Moreover, Byrne's searing, albeit affectionate, gaze on all aspects of Ireland's culture, alongside his unique veneration of the Irish 'mammy', whose thoughts and concerns he seemed to value and understand, made his show a central conduit of Ireland's social history for over two decades. To add to his influential position, Byrne was also host of both the Rose of Tralee and the Calor Kosangas Housewife of the Year competitions, all of which further endeared him to female audiences nationwide.

The Housewives' Choice

In 1973, when *The Gay Byrne Show* began life as *The Gay Byrne Hour*, little did the show's creators realise that a one-hour radio

---

[1] *Irish Independent*, 1 September 1990.

programme targeted at women in the home would evolve into an oftentimes painful and revealing journey through popular Irish culture or that it would continue for almost three decades, ultimately setting the template for the radio talk-show genre.

It is hard to imagine now the impact of *The Gay Byrne Show*. It aired at a time in Ireland's cultural history when merely broadcasting social and personal relationship problems was in itself a socially revolutionary activity. What was needed at that time was to get people to stop brushing reality under the carpet and to start talking about issues such as domestic violence, single parenthood, adoption, bad marriages, sexuality, infidelity, religion and hypocrisy. All of these issues formed a major part of the early years of the programme and were central to its unintentional role as a conduit for change in Irish life.

Before the advent of *The Gay Byrne Show*, afternoons were silent on RTÉ radio, with many Irish people tuning into the BBC for light relief. The 1960s had witnessed attempts to prise open Irish society, yet the 1970s still bore the legacy of conservatism and censorship. For women in particular civil freedoms were few. It was illegal to divorce, women couldn't sit on a jury, access to contraception was prohibited and, once married, women were obliged by law to give up their jobs.[2] To the young Julie Parsons, newly arrived from New Zealand and later a producer on *The Gay Byrne Show*, Ireland was 'a frightening place – dark, dull and grey, overwhelmingly dominated by the Catholic Church, with people stopping in the streets to bless themselves when they heard the Angelus bell.'[3]

From the beginning, *The Gay Byrne Show* had a captive audience of housewives who were content to listen to 'Gaybo', the 'nice, safe, conservative man, the upwardly mobile son every mother wanted to have.'[4] The show started out quite straightforward in its approach, focusing primarily on music and

---

[2] The 'marriage bar' was repealed in 1973.
[3] BBC Radio 4 documentary, *A Cup of Tea, a Sticky Bun and an Hour of Gaybo*, presented by Fintan O'Toole, 8 January 2003.
[4] *Ibid.*

requests, interspersed with colourful and innocuous anecdotes. It had a mystery sound, people doing press-ups in studio and, in the words of novelist Colm Tóibín, 'it was never strident or political, except in the area of consumer rights,'[5] an area that will be assessed later in this chapter.

The MORI[6] poll, which appeared six months after the show began, showed that it had caused the biggest shift in radio listenership patterns in Ireland since radio began. According to Byrne in his autobiography, *The Time of My Life*, the most extraordinary thing about *The Gay Byrne Show* was that it took off from day one:

> It must be remembered that until we came on there was little of interest on Irish radio. Morning radio was pretty dull stuff, and the ground was fertile. The listenership graph shot up immediately, and the amazing thing is that for 17 years it has remained constant, despite all the additional competition from pirates, Radio 2 [now 2fm], and morning television.[7]

Similar to *The Late Late Show*, which began life as a cosy fire-side chat of summer filler, Gay Byrne's radio show started with bits and pieces of chat and music and acted as a last port of call for listeners searching for everything from parts of washing machines to ancient gramophone records to pieces of china. In essence, the show filled 'a gap that had not been filled on RTÉ Radio.'[8]

The audience reaction was swift and favourable. The Irish public wanted more. According to Byrne:

[5] Colm Tóibín, 'Gay Byrne: Irish Life as Cabaret', *Crane Bag*, Vol. 8. No. 2 (1984), p. 66.
[6] MORI Ireland is a market and public opinion research agency operating across Ireland.
[7] Gay Byrne with Deirdre Purcell, *The Time of My Life: An Autobiography* (Gill & Macmillan: Dublin, 1989), p. 242.
[8] Desmond Fennell, 'The Perfect Day', *Irish Press*, 31 March 1973.

Usually the criticism of radio programmes that feature music is that there is too much talk. With us, the opposite was the case. The criticisms focused on the fact that there was too much music and that there should be more talk, more interviews, more letters read, more telephone calls. This was unusual.[9]

From the very beginning, Byrne was the housewives' first choice, even when it came to promoting tea. In 1978, when RTÉ refused to allow Byrne to continue to advertise Twinings Tea, Managing Director of the company Mr Pat Nolan pledged that 'if we can't have Gay to reach the housewives then we will go to them ourselves,'[10] thus launching the first door-to-door campaign by the company.

However, as the 1970s drew to a close and the turbulent 1980s fast approached, *The Gay Byrne Show* became much bolder in its style of programming. There are many reasons attributed to this change in direction. The show, with its familiar 'Tico's Tune',[11] had moved from a one-hour to a two-hour slot, allowing for a more diverse range of content. Allied to this was the fact that the country had embraced telephone technology almost overnight, allowing for immediate listener access to the programme. More important, however, was that a new producer, John Caden, had come on board since 1979, taking over from Billy Wall. Caden was an altogether more 'restless, searching and more politically minded character than Byrne.'[12] Nevertheless, both were primed to move *The Gay Byrne Show* to the centre of Irish life, and 'the audience was now able to talk back.'[13] With a two-hour slot, both Byrne and Caden saw the opportunity to dig deep beneath the surface, and soon the floodgates opened as a mirror was held up to the darker side of Irish life.

---

[9]   Byrne and Purcell, *op. cit.*, p. 170.

[10] 'RTÉ storm over tea advertising', *Irish Press*, 29 June 1978.

[11] 'Gaybo's Early Early Show', *Irish Times*, 9 October 1984.

[12] BBC Radio 4 documentary presented by Fintan O'Toole, *op. cit.*

[13] *Ibid.*

By being the first radio programme in Ireland to use the medium of the live telephone call as the central core of a discussion,[14] the show was now garnering audiences of eight hundred thousand each day. The partnership of Caden and Byrne was a unique one. They were born within a few hundred yards of each other, just north of the Grand Canal in Dublin. According to a political correspondent in the *Irish Independent*:

> In outlook and temperament Byrne and Caden seem superficially unalike; Byrne has no political convictions, at least none which are discernible, except for an admiration for those elements in Fianna Fáil and Fine Gael that represent the go-getting middle-class values and the decencies of the bourgeoisie. Caden's politics are those of the socio-economic stratum just below the one into which he was born.[15]

Byrne's radio show was not afraid to challenge the autocratic authority of Church and State. Not that Byrne himself was hostile to the authority of the Church and politicians – quite the opposite. He has publicly declared his admiration for the late Archbishop of Dublin and Primate of Ireland, Dr John Charles McQuaid, and for politicians such as Éamon de Valera and Seán Lemass. Indeed, his loyalty and admiration for former Taoiseach Charles Haughey was still very evident in 1998 at the farewell party held to mark Byrne's departure from radio. Despite the fact that Haughey was the subject of a slew of judicial tribunals, Byrne insisted that he sit at the top table with him as one of his invited guests. As journalist Nell McCafferty recounts, 'At a time when no one would touch Charlie Haughey with a barge pole, Gay Byrne remained loyal.'[16]

---

[14] Gay Byrne, in interview with Olivia O'Leary in 2001 for the RTÉ radio series *In My Life*, says he was the first to use telephones live on air in 1969 when callers phoned in to comment on the first moon landing.

[15] 'He's a window-dresser not a salesman when he presents mirror-image of the Irish', *Irish Independent*, 25 February 1984.

[16] O'Toole, *op. cit.*

In a similar fashion, listeners remained steadily loyal to Byrne throughout the first ten years of *The Gay Byrne Show*, in part because his was the only talk show on the air in Ireland at that time. Furthermore, in 1978 he began a 17-year reign as annual host of the Rose of Tralee, a festival at times ridiculed as an archaic beauty pageant, yet now very much part of Ireland's social history since its inception in 1959. Byrne's endorsement of the festival's role as a clarion call to the Irish diaspora, and his insistence that RTÉ, the State broadcaster, televise the show live, earned him a Jacob's Television Award. Since 1978, the show has recorded very high ratings for a home-produced programme.

In stark contrast to this wholesome veneration of Irish womanhood, in particular the nostalgia for those who had emigrated, Ireland was experiencing a period of immense social change. High unemployment dominated the national agenda. By 1980, hundreds of thousands of PAYE workers marched to demand tax reforms, making it the biggest demonstration of organised labour in the history of the Irish State. In 1983, unemployment was at 17.5 per cent and inflation was running at 12 per cent.[17] In the mid-1980s, emigration reached a second wave, peaking in the period between 1987 and 1990, when an estimated 228,220 people left Ireland.[18] In fact, many graduates were encouraged to emigrate by former Fianna Fáil Minister Brian Lenihan (Snr), who advised that they could always return to Ireland with the skills they had developed abroad. He infamously commented, 'After all, we can't all live on a small island.'[19]

National politics, such as 'The Troubles' in Northern Ireland, also topped the news agenda in the early 1980s, with an Anglo-Irish Intergovernmental Council formed to negotiate peace between the two governments. Byrne's treatment of the thorny issue of the North was a bone of contention for some. In 1976, a letter writer to the *Irish Press*, commenting on a panel

---

[17] 'No, we're not going back to the 1980s', *Sunday Business Post*, 29 June 2008.

[18] www.emigrantadvice.ie, 2008.

[19] Brian Lenihan (Snr) quoted in 'Goodbye all over again', *Irish Times*, 1 January 2009.

discussion on the North that had taken place on *The Late Late Show*, believed that 'when it came to politics, and especially Northern strife, Gay Byrne was as transparent as a clear glass.'[20] The letter writer suggested that Byrne 'was out of his depth in all of the facts of the Northern struggle.'

Byrne was also accused of 'providing a platform for fascism'[21] in his interview with Tory MP Mr Patrick Cosgrave in March 1980. Mr Cosgrave, a close associate of then Prime Minister Margaret Thatcher, was interviewed by Byrne in London, in a pre-recorded section of *The Late Late Show*. Mr Gerry Flanagan, a Fermanagh man, commented on the segment that Mr Cosgrave 'was allowed to voice reactionary personal opinions about Northern Ireland without any counterbalancing view.'[22]

Controversy on *The Gay Byrne Show*

Yet, to his critics, Byrne's persona on *The Gay Byrne Show* appeared more challenging and, at times, more combative than the personality he evinced on *The Late Late Show*. This ability to stir up reaction was in evidence as far back as 1973, when Byrne stated that the records of most Irish singers of popular songs were 'crap'. According to the radio critic of *The Irish Times*, 'it was a vulgar but accurate description of the sort of stuff you hear too often on Radió Éireann.'[23] He believed Byrne was 'perfectly right' not to play Irish singers, an issue of some disquiet for the Irish Federation of Musicians who surveyed Byrne's radio programme, revealing that out of the 202 records he played during the month of April 1973, only 14 were Irish.[24]

Paradoxically, on *The Late Late Show* it is possible to chart much of Ireland's musical talent from the 1960s through to

---

[20] 'North and the Late Late Show', Letters to the Editor, *Irish Press*, 15 January 1976.

[21] Similar opposition was made to Byrne's comments on the issue of Northern Ireland on *The Gay Byrne Show* (discussed in Chapter 6) and in the *Irish Press*, 15 January 1976.

[22] 'Late Late "a platform for fascism"', *Irish Press*, 11 March 1980.

[23] 'Bully for Gay', *Irish Times*, 22 October 1973.

[24] *Ibid.*

the subsequent decades by merely trawling through the range of performers who started out on the show. *The Late Late Show* celebrated established Irish showbiz acts such as The Dubliners, Christy Moore, Sharon Shannon, Mary Black and many more. Other acts that made it onto the programme did so in a circuitous fashion. Maura Connolly, Byrne's personal assistant for over 30 years, and instigator of the line, 'There's one for everyone in the audience,' recalls how U2 made it onto the show:

> My sister worked with an American-based company where she met Larry Mullen. She said there's this guy and they have a little band and he plays the drums and you should see them some time.[25]

U2 was to tread a well-worn path onto the show and would later become synonymous with the programme, with drummer Larry Mullen and frontman Bono presenting Byrne with a Harley-Davidson motorbike on the final episode of the show in May 1999. When Bob Geldolf, the lead singer with The Boomtown Rats, made his debut on the show in the late 1970s, he shot straight from the hip when Byrne asked him what motivated him to get involved in the rock-and-roll scene. 'He said that he wanted to get rich, famous and get laid and that he would do it all within a year,' remembers Maura Connolly. 'And Gay said, "Right, if you're rich and famous – whatever about being laid – within a year, we'll have you back again," and we did.'[26]

However, far from the celebrity guests on *The Late Late Show*, it was the issues concerning family and domestic dynamics that really energised many listeners of *The Gay Byrne Show*. Initially, the programme's production team was very much aware that Irish listeners were slow to pick up a phone for fear of being recognised. Therefore, at the beginning of John Caden's tenure as producer, he orchestrated callers on the line to generate discussion and 'commissioned' letters to set public debates in

---

[25] *RTÉ Guide*, 14 May 1999, p. 11.
[26] *Ibid.*

motion.[27] This has always been widely disputed by Byrne,[28] and it is clear that within a short space of time, researchers were led by the stream of increasingly articulate letters from listeners that arrived in their hundreds each day.

When Caden became the producer of the show, he felt his remit was to 'challenge the powerful' and to make the show 'a platform for change'.[29] Colm Tóibín, in a wide-ranging article on Gay Byrne, talks of the team element in Byrne's work on the radio show.[30] He points to June Levine in particular as bringing the focus of attention on the women's movement and mentions Vincent Browne, who worked as a researcher on the show, with regard to issues surrounding the problems in the North when they were at their height. Other producers and researchers during the earlier years of the show included Rocky de Valera, Tony Boland, Billy Wall (later head of 2fm), Lorelei Harris, Julie Parsons, Carol Louth (who later worked with Marian Finucane on *Liveline*), and Philip Kampf (who later devised the popular RTÉ programmes *The Lyrics Board* and *Operation Transformation*).

There were others, too, who bought a real dynamism to the programme and contributed to its enormous impact, among them Alex White (producer of the show after Caden and later appointed a Junior Health Minister in 2012), Anne Marie Hourihane, talented reporters Ann Walsh and Joe Duffy, and film reviewer Maura Clarke.

The show is credited as the first to discuss in explicit detail the then controversial issue of AIDS in the early 1980s, with Dr Austin Darragh and Dr Darren Friedman as guests. Ironically, the moment that resonates most with Irish viewers from this time is when Byrne, on *The Late Late Show* in 1982, placed a condom on his middle finger, another signifier of the potency of the visual medium of television.

---

[27] 'Letter-prompt claim "amazes" Gay', *Irish Press*, 5 July 1993.

[28] On 2 September 2011, Byrne further vehemently denied all claims of letter writers being paid to write letters to his morning show.

[29] John Caden, in interview with the author, 8 September 2007.

[30] Colm Tóibín, 'Gay Byrne: Irish Life as Cabaret', *Crane Bag*, Vol 8. No. 2, p. 65.

Even so, there were many controversial moments on the radio show, many of which went unchecked and uncommented upon by the media. For example, Senator David Norris, a former guest on the programme, recalls a segment in which Dr Austin Darragh, a regular contributor to the show, insisted he could identify gay people by their urine. Norris felt this topic was uniquely hilarious, but the segment was moderated by Byrne in an extremely professional manner.[31]

Fifty Shades of Gay

Throughout the 1980s, Byrne incurred the wrath of politicians, Gaeilgeoirí[32] and feminists, but his core audience – the house-wives – couldn't wait for their husbands to leave for work so that they could engage in public intimacies with Gay Byrne. Among the most successful items on his radio show have been accounts of extra-marital affairs, sexual difficulties and a filthy husband with putrid underwear, as well as a range of other intimate problems, including frigidity and the sheer loneliness of marriage.

In spite of his legions of female followers, some women who have worked with Byrne have been irked by his casual assump-tion of male authority, an aspect of his personality explored later in this chapter. Listening to his radio programme, it is evident that he believed a woman's most important place was in the home. While his female co-workers may have struggled with this attitude, many of his followers found it most reassuring. In a society where the housewife was forced to play a Cinder-ella-type role in an increasingly media-orientated world where career women were overtly praised, Byrne turned the spotlight on the Cinderella. He acknowledged her needs, her emo-tions and her ideas. Throughout the 1980s, mothers – referred to with deference and intimacy as 'mammies' – and loving sons were exalted on the show. Mammies, and in particular

---

[31] David Norris, in interview with the author, 22 March 2012.
[32] Irish speakers.

work-in-the-home mammies, made up an estimated 70 per cent of the show's listenership. Byrne became an extension of the matriarchal family. He was Ireland's 'Uncle Gaybo', even referring to himself as such.

Byrne was the mainstream of mainstream Ireland, accepted as a father confessor to the nation's mothers, and beloved as every mother's favourite son. His ability to straddle these diverse roles could perhaps be due to the formative influence of his own mother, who he has described as 'a tough nut but very fair woman' who 'coaxed and domineered us into doing better.'[33]

In former researcher Alice O'Sullivan's compilation of the best bits of *The Gay Byrne Show*, she says she believes Byrne touched people in areas of their lives that no one else could touch. She recalls in particular his ability to elicit intimate information without ever displaying a hint of voyeurism or sensationalism, citing his interview with Maria, a middle-aged woman who discovered that her husband of 27 years was having an affair, as an example of this.[34] Language such as 'distant in the bedroom' cut to the heart of Maria's disclosure that the man she loved so desperately had abandoned her for a business colleague in her thirties. Listening back to these painfully revealing interviews, Byrne's ability to monitor the pace of an interview displays his mastery of the confessional radio genre. When 'Ann', a 22-year-old mother of two with AIDS spoke on air of her anguish of spreading the disease to her children and her partner, Byrne held her hand and stroked her cheek. This was a very moving gesture at a time when many people believed that any type of physical contact with a victim of AIDS could spread the virus.

Unmarried Mothers

On *The Late Late Show* in 1975, Byrne highlighted the issue of unmarried mothers when he interviewed single mother Maura

[33] Byrne and Purcell, *op. cit.*, p. 56.
[34] Alice O'Sullivan, in interview with the author, 3 November 2011.

O'Dea (who later formed Cherish, a support group for unmarried mothers). O'Dea (later Richardson) had opted to keep her child, and her appearance on the show helped to generate public debate on the unspoken issue of unmarried mothers and deserted wives. Though the Unmarried Mothers Allowance had been introduced in 1973 and the Deserted Wives Allowance in 1970 (now the One-Parent Family Payment), O'Dea spoke of the obstacles which still remained in the paths of single mothers following the introduction of the Allowance and the ambivalence of Irish society towards single mothers.[35] This was evident in opinions expressed in letters to the editor of the *Irish Press* in 1973, one of which supported equal pay for men and women but suggested that 'less attention should be paid to the immaculate unmarried mothers and more to the needs of mothers of families bearing the burdens of honest wedlock.'[36]

The stigma of bearing a child out of wedlock was also part of Alice O'Sullivan's five-part series of *The Gay Byrne Show* highlights. Here, a very moving letter from a woman named Margaret stands out due to its poignancy.[37] Margaret's letter tells of how, many years earlier, she was shunned by her boyfriend's parents because a relative of hers from a previous generation had been an unmarried mother. Such was the stigma associated with her relative's behaviour that it had carried on into the next generation. Her boyfriend, unable to withstand his parents' prejudice, simply emigrated to London, leaving Margaret behind. In 1983, when Byrne read this letter aloud on air, this man, now in his 60s, had never married and, according to the letter, still asked after Margaret when mutual acquaintances bumped into him in London.

Another compelling letter from a 26-year-old woman was referred to by Byrne as 'the saddest I have ever read.'[38] The young

---

[35] *The Late Late Show*, 11 April 1975.
[36] Hilda Tweedy, Rosaleen Mills and Hazel Boland, Letters to the Editor, *Irish Press*, 5 November 1973.
[37] *The Best of 26 Years of the Gay Byrne Show*, 7 April 1999.
[38] *Ibid.*

woman in question had been molested at the age of 11, and for over two years she believed she was pregnant. She explained in her letter how, between the ages of 12 and 14, she always carried a penny,[39] a towel and a brown paper bag with her wherever she went. The penny was for the public toilets, the towel was to clean up after her, and the brown paper bag was to dispose of the baby once she'd given birth. The letter writer spoke of her deep anger at her Catholic upbringing and felt that she and many others were 'sad victims of the Catholic Church'.[40]

It is clear that Byrne never flinched from airing viewpoints critical of the Church. Perhaps unintentionally, and yet in an almost subtly subversive fashion, his radio show helped to articulate and challenge a hitherto silenced and uncharted discourse on Ireland's Catholic legacy.

The Lighter Side of *The Gay Byrne Show*

Though it is important to underline the impact of the radio show as the template for talk radio in Ireland, *The Gay Byrne Show* itself was quintessentially playful and light-hearted. Humorous items that stood out in the show's earlier years include a classic sketch regarding a 'dead dog' licence and a very popular Christmas cake recipe, during which Byrne appears to have added too much whiskey to the mixture![41] Another classic example is the story of a lady who wrote to Gay to tell him how, in a gesture of love, she had tried to send her used underwear to her husband, who was working temporarily in America. Her husband had failed to receive her loving gift, however, and in her letter, read aloud on air by Byrne, she publicly demanded the return of her underwear, which she believed was being held in the sorting office in Dublin.[42]

---

[39] Old Irish coinage worth approximately 2 cent.

[40] Rebroadcast on *The Best of 26 Years of the Gay Byrne Show*, 6 April 1999.

[41] Available on audio on YouTube under 'Gay Byrne's Christmas Fruit Cake Recipe', accessed 10 April 2014.

[42] *The Best of 26 Years of the Gay Byrne Show*, 6 April 1999.

It was these funny and oftentimes daring segments of the show that helped to amuse and galvanise the nation, while simultaneously highlighting the uniqueness of its remit. Though the programme handled with sensitivity and respect issues of serious import, it was equally at ease within its ambit of generating fun and entertainment. O'Sullivan's compilation of the best bits of the programme also includes a humorous phone-in from disgruntled housewife Dympna from Dún Laoghaire in Dublin.[43] She revealed live on air that she yearned for more romantic presents from her husband. To date she had received a wheelbarrow for her birthday and a two-speed hammer-action Black & Decker drill for Christmas. Her car had recently broken down, and Dympna confided in Gay that she feared she would receive 'a five-litre can of oil' as her next present.[44]

Byrne as Radio Host

Of course Byrne enjoyed Dympna's tale, as it allowed him to indulge his love of acting and his well-honed comedic skills to the full. His multi-layered public persona was vital to the success of *The Gay Byrne Show*. Former producer Julie Parsons has spoken of how working with Byrne was a life-changing experience. It was the best show on the air at that time, and a high standard was expected from each of the researchers. Ronan Kelly and Charlie Bird at various times worked as researchers on the show and share Parsons' view that working with Byrne was a wonderful learning process. Parsons has commented how 'your imagination, your research on each interviewee, was vital to the show's success.'[45] She believed that the juxtaposition of Byrne the performer with the socialist sensibilities of Caden the producer resulted in a wonderfully evocative and powerfully illustrative radio show.

---

[43] *Ibid.*, 7 April 1999.
[44] *Ibid.*
[45] Julie Parsons, in interview with UCC undergraduate student Jennifer Walsh, 12 January 2006.

Although it was the producer's role to come up with ideas for the most riveting radio, it was Byrne who made it human and real. The research team would write material with Gay's voice and mannerisms in mind. He was, according to Parsons, 'a fantastic performer and an actor, and he would deliver it and make it sound spontaneous. It was this ability of his [that] kept his audience captivated and hanging on to every word.'[46]

Parsons also spoke of how the team would decide whether Byrne should read a listener's letter or contact the listener. Would the issue become controversial? If so, would they need a politician or expert in that field to comment? How would the item then be handled to make it more interesting and appealing to listeners? Never was the show driven by its own political or religious agenda, or the personal bias of Byrne or his team, but rather by the necessity of satisfying its listeners. Parsons believes there was a sense of balance in the show, in particular amongst its team. Byrne, she believes, was conventional by nature, but not unadventurous. She herself candidly admits to being a true 1970s feminist, while Caden, she contends, was the antithesis of Byrne. All three reflected to a certain degree the nature of Irish society, which by the 1980s was becoming increasingly diverse. The simultaneous mix of conservative and revolutionary ideas succeeded in making the show not so much a vital catalyst for change in Ireland, but rather a forum that allowed ideas to evolve and subsequently helped 'shape the views of Irish people in their quest for social progress.'[47]

Consumer Issues on *The Gay Byrne Show*

Well before the BBC's *Watchdog* programme (a pioneering consumer affairs TV show),[48] *The Gay Byrne Show* monitored and

---

[46] *Ibid.*

[47] *Ibid.*

[48] *Watchdog* has been running since 1985 on BBC television and has had enormous success in changing consumers' awareness of their purchasing rights. The programme has also been instrumental in forcing changes in consumer legislation and in the operating policies of large businesses.

mediated on consumer issues in a very forthright manner, at times eliciting an impassioned response from listeners. Each week, a 'shopping-basket survey' took place on the show, providing an overview of price trends in supermarkets and local grocery stores throughout Ireland. In 1976, Byrne's weekly shopping-basket run-down led to strong accusations by Fianna Fáil TD Mr Paddy Lalor, who speculated that the 'consistency with which Ben Dunne's[49] cheaper prices were quoted' was due largely to the fact that 'Gay Byrne's wife was the one who did the sponsored programme for Ben Dunne.'[50] In exchanges similar to those you might expect from a B-rated Western, Byrne, not quite with guns loaded, referred to Lalor as a 'rotten sod' and challenged him to repeat his remarks 'outside the Dáil chambers'.[51]

Further controversy raged over the shopping-basket surveys in 1984 when members of the Irish Association of Distributive Trades claimed they were being manipulated by the supermarkets, which were accused of immediately putting up their prices after the surveys were conducted. Byrne dismissed these claims, insisting that he had faith in the housewives of Ireland, who would surely have 'inundated us with calls to the show if the prices in the survey were not exact.'[52] The issue became so toxic that it was soon under investigation by the Dáil Oireachtas Committee. Two supermarket chiefs, Fergal Quinn and Richard Reeves of Quinnsworth, claimed cost factors of the larger stores were not being taken into account in the surveys, while Deputy Francis Fahy, a member of the Joint Oireachtas Committee on Small Businesses, insisted manufacturers would be forced into liquidation if the shopping-basket survey continued on *The Gay Byrne Show*.[53] But continue it did, on the newly extended programme which ran from 9.00 a.m. to 11.00 a.m.

---

[49] The Dunne family own and run the large supermarket chain Dunnes Stores.

[50] 'Lalor's Dáil remark challenged', *Irish Press*, 6 May 1976.

[51] *Ibid.*

[52] 'Gaybo hits back at the shopping survey critics', *Irish Times*, 26 May 1984.

[53] 'Now Fergal Quinn is a Gaybo basket basher', *Irish Independent*, 5 September 1984.

from September 1984,[54] proving once again that Byrne, rather like Margaret Thatcher, was 'not for turning'.

The Radio Phone-In

The Gay Byrne Show differed significantly from *The Late Late Show* in that the latter aspired to challenge and change public opinion, while the former was much more subtle in its approach. It did not set out to intentionally provoke change in the mindset of Irish women but, in hindsight, that is exactly what it achieved. It reached into the hearts and homes of its listeners, using phone-ins to create a forum for debate.

As the technology of the telephone spread vigorously across Ireland in the 1980s, the phone-in became immensely popular with listeners who wanted to air their views. However, as Parsons points out, many people did not realise they were actually on air and, therefore, did not fully comprehend the consequences of their intimate chats with Gay Byrne.[55] Former researcher Philip Kampf also makes this point. He recalls the time when a woman rang the programme to check whether her husband could be gay. He had arrived back from London wearing a T-shirt with the word 'heaven' printed on it, and a friend of hers told her that this was the name of a gay club in London. According to Kampf, 'some people who didn't need to go on radio still did – people always recognise you.'[56]

During the first ten years of the programme, *The Gay Byrne Show* abounded with quirky pieces, such as the humorous 'wanted items' segment, a regular feature on the show. Some of the more bizarre and obscure requests included the Kildare listener who wanted to adopt a grandparent;[57] the wax museum in Dublin which was seeking size 15–22 boots for the

---

[54] 'There's more of Gaybo, basket and all', *Irish Independent*, 6 September 1984.
[55] Julie Parsons interview, *op. cit.*
[56] Philip Kampf, in interview with the author, 20 January 2012.
[57] *The Gay Byrne Show*, 16 December 1986.

figure of Frankenstein;[58] the listener who sought a Cleopatra-oil-combustion chamber;[59] and the US farmer who was seeking an Irish wife![60]

Stories of adventurous Irish travellers were also featured, highlighting what Ireland's first female president, Mary Robinson, would later term 'the diaspora'.[61] Requests began to emerge for someone to take books to São Paulo[62] and Chile,[63] and a parcel to Bhutan.[64] A more sophisticated and self-assured Ireland was in evidence with requests such as 'women's only holiday groups seeking members'[65] and a request for a 'sun-ray lamp'.[66]

Some of the jokes and comments made on the show in the 1980s may now appear old-fashioned and quaint, but they are nonetheless reflective of Ireland's culture at that time. A wonderful example is the following, taken from a show in 1983:

> A gentleman writes from Dublin 9 about dances and women. He also pleads with women who are offered dances by young men. He was at a disco in Dublin. He asked 19 girls to dance. He got 18 refusals. One nice girl danced with him. Even to dance for one song helps a man's pride.[67]

And a response in a later programme:

> A woman caller rings about refusing men during dances. She remembers a fella asking a girl at a dance once and she refused in a very offensive way. He turned to her and said,

---

[58] *Ibid.*, 13 May 1986.

[59] *Ibid.*, 11 October 1988.

[60] *Ibid.*, 15 December 1988.

[61] In her inauguration speech in 1990, entitled *Cherishing the Irish Diaspora*, Ireland's first female president, Mary Robinson, spoke of the diaspora – those 'dispersed ones' who are scattered all over the world due to emigration.

[62] *The Gay Byrne Show*, 3 March 1987.

[63] *Ibid.*, 14 April 1987.

[64] *Ibid.*, 16 November 1987.

[65] *Ibid.*, 3 April 1989.

[66] *Ibid.*, 5 May 1989.

[67] *Ibid.*, 2 December 1987.

'I'm sorry I asked you. You look better in the distance than close up.'[68]

On that same programme, Byrne tells the following anecdote. Although humorous, it nonetheless reflects the sustained interest in the issue of abortion:

There is a story doing the rounds about a girl in Leeson Street nightclub. She meets up with a chap who offers to drive her home. Arrives back at the flat and there's lots of guff from him and wanting to stay the night. She's sobering up at this stage. He asks her how she'd like her eggs in the morning and she replies 'unfertilised'.[69]

Although it was this fluid movement from light to serious issues that made *The Gay Byrne Show* unique, its success also came from its ability to stir up controversy. Take, for example, March 1983, when Irish politicians were up in arms over what they regarded as a 'misrepresentation of their financial situation' on the programme.[70] The Fine Gael deputy at that time, Mr Gay Mitchell, claimed that Byrne had been simply seeking to improve the Television Audience Measurement (TAM) ratings of his show by engaging in controversy. The antipathy of politicians to Byrne was commented upon by journalist John Healy in his popular column in *The Irish Times*, 'Sounding Off', in this instance subtitled 'Waiting for open season on Gay Byrne.'[71] In the piece, Healy makes the point that if Byrne can be allowed to publicly comment on the salaries of politicians, then they too should have knowledge of his income, details of which, at that time, RTÉ was not obliged to disclose:

I return to the matter of Oireachtas Committees ... the real juicy one will be RTÉ ... It is the aim of this committee to

---

[68] *Ibid.*, 17 April 1989.
[69] *Ibid.*
[70] 'TD's furious at Gay Byrne report', *Irish Times*, 3 March 1983.
[71] 'Waiting for open season on Gay Byrne', *Irish Times*, 8 April 1985.

dig deep into the affairs of the station and it is based on a common goal: to take down Gay Byrne. On balance the majority don't like Gaybo and they don't especially like the Gaybo who comments on their salaries.[72]

It was Byrne's absolute refusal to acknowledge any fundamental differences between politicians and other sectors of society, while simultaneously assuming that society should not be privileged with information on his own salary (which was paid by RTÉ, a state-owned public institution), that made Byrne both admired and reviled as a broadcaster.[73] In Byrne's world, respect was apportioned according to one's ability to perform and to entertain. Equally, anything can be said, as long as it was sufficiently 'gripping'.[74] However, the *Irish Press* noted that not everyone was charmed by 'the geniality, the jokes and the involved discussions on *The Gay Byrne Show*'.[75] Yet, because he was presenter of the show and not part of the production team, Byrne could withstand much of the scathing comments from journalists and politicians alike. In contrast, Byrne's attitude and his behaviour on *The Late Late Show,* in his unprecedented role as both presenter and executive producer, was put under intense scrutiny by both the media and members of the RTÉ Authority, whose responsibility it was to safeguard the integrity and content of RTÉ's programme output.

Byrne as *the Late Late Show* Producer

It is significant that for over 33 years, *The Late Late Show* was under Byrne's total control. Moreover, his ad hoc programming policy was partly responsible for the groundbreaking nature of the show. Although the show had a team of researchers and a

---

[72] *Ibid.*
[73] 'The sound of silence', *Irish Times*, 9 September 1989.
[74] *Ibid.*
[75] *Irish Press*, 6 December 1985.

string of producers, Byrne always had the final word. This was crucial to the show's success.

It was in his role as producer that many feel Byrne's real talent lay. Researcher Pan Collins believed his strength lay in his willingness to listen to his researchers and to not expect more from them than he himself was prepared to deliver.[76] It is difficult now to comprehend the level of commitment and organisational rigor required to produce a top-rated show, in addition to being its presenter. From Tuesday to Thursday Byrne would work with his research team on possible items for the show. Then on Fridays, he would work with the show's director and production assistants to decide on the timing for each item, the commercial breaks, the musical inserts, the sound, the lighting, the camera positions, the plotting and planning of an entire show for which he had overall responsibility. To add to the immediacy and energy of the show, Byrne never met his guests in advance, preferring to learn more about them as his audience did. This ensured a natural and more organic conversational tone and style.

Close friend and former work colleague of Byrne's John McColgan, who worked both as a producer and director of programmes in RTÉ in the mid-1970s, believes Byrne ran *The Late Late Show* as 'his personal fiefdom, never allying himself to management and always displaying the strength of an independent producer.'[77]

Pan Collins once commented how the team would deliberately step up a gear to ensure higher audience figures:

Occasionally, at one of our Tuesday morning planning meetings, somebody might say, 'we've been a little bland lately – can't we think of something that would stir it up a little? What's been happening?' If nothing very exciting is going on in this island, one of us may say, 'Well, let's go back to the hardy perennials, there's always good mileage

---

[76] Pan Collins, *It Started on the Late Late Show* (Ward River Press: Dublin, 1981) p. 36.
[77] John McColgan, in interview with the author, 1 March 2012.

in sex, religion, politics and money.' Now which one can we find something fresh in?[78]

Byrne himself has commented on the level of freedom he was allowed in his role as producer, earned perhaps from his early days on Raidió Éireann where he 'came in, non-Gaeilgeoir,[79] non-GAA,[80] playing jazz records' which had been banned in Raidió Éireann for 30 years.[81] According to Byrne, he was 'the antithesis of anything they would have wanted and yet they gave me complete freedom. Although I'm sure there were forces at work behind the scenes trying to put a stop to me.'[82]

Evidence from the minutes of RTÉ Authority Meetings prove that there were indeed many forces trying to stop Gay Byrne. Nevertheless, he held firm in his belief never to impose topics for public discourse that were tasteless or insensitive to the needs of his audience. Former researcher June Levine, in her book *Sisters*, has attributed this stubbornness as quintessential to Byrne's professionalism but also considers it part of his ruthlessness as a producer. Levine felt that Byrne was at times over-demanding of his research team: 'Often he was like a Christian Brother of the nasty type Irishmen have described to me – merciless, unreasonable, and relentless in his attack on anyone who fell short.'[83]

Pan Collins defended this more unsavoury side of Byrne's personality when she commented in 1982: 'If he did not have that ruthlessness the show would not be top of the TAM ratings.'[84] Byrne's former secretary Joan Tuohy has spoken of his 'monumental' temper if a member of the research team had

---

[78] Pan Collins, *op. cit.*, p. 42.
[79] Non-Irish speaking.
[80] The Gaelic Athletic Association (GAA) was founded in 1884 to encourage an interest in the games of Gaelic football and hurling.
[81] Gay Byrne, in interview with Declan Lynch, *Sunday Independent*, 6 October 2013.
[82] *Ibid.*
[83] June Levine, *Sisters* (Attic Press: Dublin, 1982), p. 119.
[84] 'Gay the Ayatollah, the Late', *Irish Independent*, 7 December 1982.

'been slacking or not produced the results expected' by Byrne.[85] There was 'no question of having a quiet word in private with the offender.' Instead the dressing down was 'public and scathing'.[86] Both Tuohy and former researcher Myles McWeeney have spoken of Byrne's meticulous attitude to work, his 'preter-naturally' tidy desk and his 'most retentive memory'.[87]

While he may have been forceful in his opinions behind the scenes, much of Byrne's success as producer on *The Late Late Show* is due to the fact that he appeared to have no entrenched views.[88] Television critic John Boland explores this viewpoint:

> So central was Gay Byrne's presence to the thoughts and feelings of anyone living in Ireland during the latter part of the 20th century that it comes as a shock to realise that there is a whole generation out there – anyone born after 1985 – for whom he's at most a name ... they're living in a country whose attitudes he, perhaps more than anyone else, helped to change. He did this by not having an attitude himself, or a definable one anyway. Yet while no one was ever precisely sure where he stood on an issue, everyone felt they knew him as intimately as he seemed to know them. That's a trick only the greatest broadcasters have and he had it from the night in 1962 when, at the age of 26, he first fronted *The Late Late Show*.[89]

John McHugh, a researcher with *The Late Late Show* from 1983 to 1988 (and credited with introducing the first of the *Late Late Show* music specials), has commented on Byrne's fundamental need as a producer to connect with his audience and to seek out potential researchers who could help him to make this connection to the pulse of Irish life. McHugh had been headhunted to

---

[85] Joan Tuohy, 'It happened on *The Late Late Show*', *Irish Press*, 25 May 1985.

[86] *Ibid.*

[87] 'Behind the scenes: the real Gaybo', *Irish Independent*, 23 September 2005.

[88] This observation does not hold true for Byrne as host on *The Gay Byrne Show*.

[89] John Boland, television critic with the *Irish Independent*, October 2006, quoted in foreword to *Great Biographies* Vol. 10, produced by the *Irish Independent*.

work on *The Late Late Show* after writing an article in *Magill* magazine on homelessness in Dublin. He later went on to work with two other well-known talk-show hosts, Gloria Hunniford and Michael Aspel. McHugh recalls how Ferdia McAnna, another former researcher on the show, got his job, highlighting again Byrne's instincts as producer to cover all his bases: 'Gay asked him what he thought of the show and McKenna answered, "I don't know, I never watched it," and he got the job!'[90]

From his five-year stint on the *Late Late Show* team (along with Mary O'Sullivan, Colman Hutchinson, Bridgid Ruane, Adrian Cronin, Tony Boland and Maura Connolly as Gay's PA), McHugh learned 'the grinding sense of terror'[91] when faced with pitching an idea to Byrne. Like many others who worked closely with Byrne during the early years of the show, there was a huge sense of satisfaction that he had grown and developed as both a producer and presenter. McHugh believes Byrne 'had no real mission' as a producer. He simply wanted to have fun and have a nation talking to itself, and he achieved this by surrounding himself with informed people.[92] All of the *Late Late Show* researchers were required to thoroughly pre-interview guests, providing Byrne with typewritten 6 × 4 index cards with at least ten questions for each of the researcher's guests.[93]

Others who worked with Byrne, in particular during the first two decades of the show, have spoken of his astonishing work ethic and his clarity around which items or not would resonate with his viewers. This enviable work ethic persisted through the final 15 years of his tenure as host of the show, even after he had stepped down as its producer. He always expected his researchers to have a similar work ethic. Mary O'Sullivan, who worked on the programme from 1979–89, recalls the atmosphere of post-programme production meetings as 'scary'. She remembers being constantly 'on the look-out' for potential material

---

[90] John McHugh, in interview with the author, 20 February 2012.

[91] *Ibid.*

[92] McHugh interview, *op. cit.*

[93] 'Behind the scenes: The real Gaybo', *op. cit.*

that had to be of 'interest' and 'entertain' the audience.[94] Byrne's mantra as producer was always 'it's harder to make them laugh than to make them cry,'[95] and all of his researchers were aware of his particular fondness for comedians such as Billy Connolly, Lenny Henry and Hal Roach, a particular favourite.

O'Sullivan confirms that Byrne surrounded himself with people who possessed strong talents in different areas. She, like Byrne, 'loved panel discussions and a good debate, a good row.'[96] Colman Hutchinson, who was responsible for the very emotive specials on alcohol and death, loved entertainment. Brigid Ruane loved political debate, and it was she who devised the divorce debate in 1985, which featured a young Harry Whelan (later to become Attorney General) and Mary La Foy (now a senior counsel), as well as a host of real-life barristers and judges. John McHugh is credited with many of the musical tributes on the show, garnering a Jacobs Award for his special on The Dubliners, while Tony Boland and Ferdia McAnna were always seeking out stories that would 'engage' the audience.[97]

Both O'Sullivan and McHugh strongly believe that Byrne as producer 'did not want to change the world.'[98] His fundamental need was to connect with the audience.[99] Colman Hutchinson agrees that Byrne had 'no crusading agenda'.[100] He admired the fact that Byrne 'never felt he had all the answers. He would go to the heart of the people. He was very trusting.'[101]

It was this trusting nature that allowed Russell Murphy, Byrne's accountant and close friend, to embezzle huge amounts of Byrne's money over a period of 20 years. Former guest on *The Late Late Show* Senator David Norris mentions how impressed he was by Byrne's 'lack of bitterness' after Murphy's betrayal;

---

[94] Mary O'Sullivan, in interview with the author, 17 April 2012.

[95] *Ibid.*

[96] *Ibid.*

[97] Colman Hutchinson, in interview with the author, 21 February 2012.

[98] *Ibid.*

[99] *Ibid.*

[100] *Ibid.*

[101] *Ibid.*

he believed Byrne showed himself to be a 'man of decency' in the aftermath of the traumatic event.[102] In his autobiography, Byrne describes his emotional state at the time:

> The loss of all I had worked for was a shock, the impact of which I will never be fully able to describe. One curious side-effect was for quite a long period I was unable to write by hand. Even to put my signature to a piece of paper was a great effort.[103]

However, Byrne was at heart a showman, and the show must go on. In his role as producer, personal issues were set aside to focus on fine-tuning the programme's content. He was, according to O'Sullivan, very alert to TAM ratings. During post-mortems of the show's episodes, he would ask researchers whose programme items had not worked, 'How did that go wrong?'[104] He was always acutely aware of the limited attention span of audiences:

> Irish television audiences will sit for five minutes to get the taste of a guest and unless you appeal within the next few minutes they are gone. With the way things have changed it is quite a miracle we are still on air.[105]

Challenge and Censure

Throughout the late 1970s and early 1980s Ireland's culture was changing, and audiences were becoming more tolerant. In 1979, for example, Ireland's first test-tube baby, Louise Brown, appeared on the show with her parents, offering a great deal of hope to infertile couples throughout the country. New sections were also added to the show throughout the early 1980s to

---

[102]David Norris, in interview with the author, 23 March 2012.

[103]Byrne and Purcell, *op. cit.*, p. 149.

[104]Mary O'Sullivan, *op. cit.*

[105]*Ibid.*

extend its entertainment brief, including birthday tribute shows for well-known Irish celebrities and the 'one-subject show'.

Nevertheless, since 1978, scrutiny and monitoring of the show from forces within RTÉ had become much more intense. It began when RTÉ's Programme Policy Committee (PPC), which dealt with programme complaints, was renamed the Editorial Committee. One of its first tasks under its new title was to adjudicate on an item on transvestism which had appeared on *The Late Late Show* in February 1979. The Committee agreed that Byrne had handled the issue 'with discretion', but the treatment of the topic of homosexuality generally on RTÉ television was a continuous source of contention within the organisation.[106]

In 1982, Byrne again fell foul of both public opinion and the RTÉ Authority when he embarrassed the esteemed Scottish psychiatrist Dr R.D. Laing during an interview on *The Late Late Show*. During the interview, Byrne questioned Dr Laing's sobriety, telling the eminent guest he was 'under the weather'.[107] Laing had been drinking before the interview, and his slow delivery was far from his usual professional demeanour. Byrne later defended his handling of the incident, asserting that while *The Late Late Show* had certain obligations towards its guests, they too, as paid participants, had obligations to RTÉ, *The Late Late Show* and its viewers.[108] Professor Ivor Browne, a panellist on the show (and friend of Dr Laing), accused Byrne of being 'rude and discourteous', saying that his remark to Dr Laing had been 'out of place'.[109] Tim Pat Coogan, in his column in the *Irish Press*, also disagreed with Byrne's treatment of the eminent psychiatrist:

> In the Laing episode, a man of true calibre was publicly humiliated when it must have been blatantly obvious

---

[106]John Caden, unpublished MA thesis, 'RTÉ's Coverage of the Campaigning on the Eight Amendment to the Constitution on Issues of Objectivity, Impartiality and Fairness' (Dublin City University: Dublin, 2006), p. 67.

[107]'Gay Byrne rude to noted psychiatrist', *Irish Press*, 22 November 1982.

[108]*The Late Late Show*, 2 November 1982.

[109]*Irish Press*, 22 November 1982.

beforehand in the hospitality suite that he should not have been allowed go before the cameras.[110]

Minutes from a subsequent RTÉ Authority meeting note the insistence by Board member Eibhlín Bean Uí Chionnaoith that Byrne make an immediate apology, with the Chairman noting in passing that the Authority had received an anonymous death threat to Gay Byrne, which had been passed to the Gardaí.[111] Bean Uí Chionnaoith also queried whether Byrne had been informed that his contract would be 'reconsidered', highlighting the inconsistency between Byrne's level of authority as producer of *The Late Late Show* and the uncertainty of his tenure within RTÉ. Such barely disguised threats regarding Byrne's continued employment at RTÉ emerged at regular intervals during RTÉ Authority meetings. The pivotal, albeit controversial, role of *The Late Late Show* remained under scrutiny by the RTÉ Authority throughout the 1980s, and Byrne was constantly under the microscope.

Minutes from the meetings of the RTÉ Authority between February and November 1982 are littered with queries and comments regarding Byrne's role as producer of *The Late Late Show*, and later, in 1983, criticism of his adverse influence on public opinion. However, all else paled into insignificance when an RTÉ directive was issued in December 1982 forbidding Byrne and the *Late Late Show* team from airing a planned debate on the proposed 1983 referendum on abortion.

Abortion and *The Late Late Show*

It all began when Cynthia Payne, aka 'Madam Sin', was interviewed on the show in November 1982. She was a retired English 'madam', who had served six months behind bars for

---

[110]Tim Pat Coogan, 'White Wash on the Late Late Show', *Irish Press*, 4 February 1984.

[111]Minutes of the Authority, 11 November 1982.

her role as a brothel keeper,[112] and who had also admitted to having had two abortions. Her candid manner and her stoic defence of her actions shocked many people. However, it was the appearance on the same show of Anna Raeburn, a young, articulate panellist, who wrote for the glamorous women's magazine *Cosmopolitan*, that really precipitated an 'unprecedented adverse reaction … with up to 500 letters of complaint received.'[113] Raeburn admitted to having had an abortion and managed to deliver, unchallenged, the message of the 'woman's right to choose' on Ireland's most popular television show.

As former researcher John Caden points out, this was the first time since the Pro-Life Amendment Campaign (PLAC) began in April 1981 that any woman had said on an RTÉ-produced television show that she had had an abortion.[114] Those in favour of the Pro-Life Amendment must have felt a sense of shock that Anna Raeburn's comments on *The Late Late Show* somehow normalised abortion. The fact that she did not cite any extenuating familial or psychological circumstances to 'excuse' her actions but instead justified her reason for having an abortion as a personal choice born out of the fact that she was 'a single woman' with 'very little money'[115] would have been deemed a political statement in line with the core position of the Irish Woman's Right to Choose Group (IWRCG).

Caden states that Byrne and his team had been aware in advance of Raeburn's life story. She had written in *Cosmopolitan* about her abortion, and the research team knew Byrne would ask her about it, yet the topic was not brought to the attention of the Editorial Committee due to 'an internal breakdown of communication'.[116] The Committee was thus unprepared for the ensuing controversy.

---

[112]'Lunch voucher madame wins cut in jail term', *Guardian*, 16 May 1980.

[113]Minutes of the Editorial Committee, 12 November 1982, quoted in Caden 2006, *op. cit.*

[114]*Ibid.*, p. 105.

[115]*The Late Late Show*, 12 November 1982.

[116]Caden 2006, *op. cit.*, p. 109.

Immediate outrage was expressed from all quarters at both the show and, as Byrne recalls in his autobiography, at him personally:

> Naturally, SPUC (Society for the Protection of the Unborn Child) manned the barricades and organised their campaign against the *Late Late* and RTÉ. The Authority members, used to getting letters at a nice steady trickle, suddenly found themselves buried in the type of avalanche we are used to; and whereas we take that kind of thing in our stride, I understand how difficult it was for members of the Authority suddenly to find themselves as personal targets, in receipt of threats, anger, and perpetual phone calls.[117]

The Anna Raeburn incident, as Caden points out, had much in common with the Bishop and the Nightie affair: a moral issue on *The Late Late Show* had offended a group of Catholics.[118] The displeasure of the Catholic Church at its most senior level was evident when Archbishop Ryan of Dublin intervened to stop a group of Glenstal Abbey monks from appearing on the show to promote an album of Irish Christmas carols.

However, Ireland had changed since the Bishop and Nightie affair, and both RTÉ and *The Late Late Show* reflected this change. Under the Broadcasting Amendment Act, RTÉ was now required to consider the views of a more diverse viewership with conflicting viewpoints.[119] No longer could one powerful lobby hold sway in a country that was slowly straddling the transition from a traditional and conservative society to one that recognised the necessity of accommodating diversity. Yet, mindful of its role as a public broadcaster, RTÉ had attempted to persuade Byrne to make a personal and a corporate apology

---

[117]Byrne and Purcell, *op. cit.*, p. 222.
[118]Caden 2006, *op. cit.*, p. 112.
[119]The Broadcasting Authority (Amendment) Act, 1976: Section 13, which amends Section 17 of the 1960 Broadcasting Act.

on *The Late Late Show* on 13 November 1982. According to Bob Collins, then Deputy Controller of Programmes, 'Gay fudged it – he was opposed to that kind of thing.'[120]

Byrne had indicated on the programme of the Anna Raeburn interview that abortion was a topic to which he would be returning at a later date. However, abortion was the subject of a Constitutional Amendment Referendum at the time, and there was a strong and very vocal anti-abortion lobby. The Director General of RTÉ, George Waters, in agreement with the RTÉ Authority, took the view that the issue of abortion was not to be discussed on either *The Late Late Show, The Gay Byrne Show* or any popular talk programmes in the light entertainment department.[121] Sensitivities surrounding the issue of abortion also led to an unprecedented directive from George Waters to exclude former researcher June Levine from appearing on *The Late Late Show*. Levine, a feminist writer and founder member of the Irish Women's Liberation Group, had just published her autobiography, *Sisters*, in which she told of having had an abortion in 1965.[122] Waters' instructions were unambiguous: 'In view of the nature of the subject matter in the book, could you please take steps to ensure that Ms Levine does not appear on any radio or television programme?'[123]

The media took up the cudgel, with the *Irish Press* vociferous in its denunciation of what it termed in its editorial 'Censorship and RTÉ'. The threat to freedom of speech was raised as an issue of concern:

> Although controversial, the latest ban on a 'Gay Byrne Special' on the constitutional amendment campaign is hardly surprising. Ever since Section 31 of the Broadcasting Act was implemented and RTÉ journalist Kevin O'Kelly was

---

[120]RTÉ Written Archives, Collins 2005, quoted in Caden 2006, *op. cit.*

[121]Caden 2006, *op. cit.*, p. 117.

[122]Levine, *op. cit.*, p. 117.

[123]Letter from the Director General to Director of Television Programmes and Director of Radio Programmes, 29 November 1982, as quoted in Caden 2006, *op. cit.*, p. 118.

jailed, republicans have predicted that the cancer of censorship would eventually pervade all aspects of broadcasting in Ireland.[124]

The issue of censorship was also alluded to by a spokesman for the RTÉ branch of the Federated Workers Union of Ireland, who called for a meeting with RTÉ management to discuss union concerns that the 'normal editorial process was being interfered with' and to discuss the referendum and its coverage by RTÉ.[125] Yet, many letters to the editor of *The Irish Times* were wholly in favour of the ban, believing that 'The RTÉ Authority has not only the right but the constitutional duty to see that justice is done in this regard.'[126] Moreover, another letter writer maintained that Mr Fred O'Donovan, Chairman of the Authority, was 'within his rights, as are the RTÉ Authority, in deciding that public discussion on the Pro-life Amendment Campaign merits exposure on a more serious programme than *The Late Late Show*.'[127]

Mr Tom O'Donnell, Former Fine Gael TD and MEP, congratulated the RTÉ Authority and Mr George Waters, the Director General, for their criticism of *The Late Late Show* and said the Authority would have the support of the 'vast majority' of Irish people, whom he characterised as 'increasingly incensed at the format, content and presentation of *The Late Late Show*.'[128] The Authority issued a statement asserting its wish not to interfere in the editorial process but restricting coverage of the abortion issue to regular news broadcasts and current affairs programmes.[129] Peter Feeney, a producer of *The Late Late Show* from 1980 to 1981, always believed the show had a more diverse remit:

---

[124]'Censorship and RTÉ', *Irish Press*, 14 February 1983.

[125]'Late Late team silenced', *Irish Times*, 4 February 1983.

[126]Letters to the Editor, *Irish Times*, 21 January 1983.

[127]*Ibid.*

[128]'Censure of show praised', *Irish Times*, 20 December 1982.

[129]'RTÉ restricts coverage of abortion issue', *Irish Times*, 31 December 1982.

> *The Late Late Show* has been, and continues to be, a most
> suitable programme for the discussion of serious subjects
> of controversy. To regard *The Late Late Show* merely as a
> 'light entertainment' programme is to misunderstand the
> pivotal role of *The Late Late Show* in RTÉ's output over the
> last two decades.[130]

Very personal comments were also levelled at Byrne from
Authority members. The Chairman stated that, while Byrne had
served RTÉ well for over 20 years, in this instance it did raise a
question mark regarding his capacity as producer.[131] Quick to
defend Byrne was Cork Board member, the impresario Oliver
Barry. He sympathised with Byrne, who he believed had suffered from a 'lack of guidance'[132] from the Variety Department.
At another meeting an Authority member demanded to know
'the expenses paid to Gay Byrne and his guests' on the show,
adding that it was clear that the 'strength of the character' of Mr
Byrne 'was such that there was nobody strong enough in the
RTÉ executive to face up to him … when he erred.'[133]

This particular controversy points very significantly to the
fact that attitudinal changes in Ireland were not uniform. There
were viewers in Ireland in the early 1980s who were not ready
for the challenges issued by Byrne and his guests on *The Late
Late Show*. But for many the incident marked a turning point
in what could be aired on national television. Not long after-
wards, in April 1984, during an entire programme devoted to
the topic of AIDS, Byrne put a condom on his finger, leading
us to reflect on the infamous comment by former Irish politician Oliver J. Flanagan, who claimed there was no sex in Ireland
before the advent of *The Late Late Show*.[134] Indeed, at that time
Ireland's knowledge of AIDS was based on misinformation and

---

[130]Letter from Peter Feeney to Tom Quinn, Secretary to the RTÉ Authority,
12 January 1983, quoted in Caden 2006, *op. cit.*, p. 21.
[131]Minutes of RTÉ Authority Meeting, 26 November 1982.
[132]*Ibid.*
[133]Minutes of RTÉ Authority Meeting, 12 December 1982.
[134]Quoted in 'The chameleon of Montrose', *Irish Times*, 13 February 2010.

ignorance, and its implications were lost on a largely hetero-sexual community who assumed it was a 'gay sickness'. The *Late Late Show* coverage of AIDS was clear and unambivalent. It left no doubt in the minds of viewers that this new plague was a danger to everybody, regardless of sexual preference. The reaction to the programme was measured, and there were no placards outside the Montrose studio. In fact, in its detailed coverage of the issue, *The Late Late Show* not only challenged established beliefs but also went beyond this role to become an informed voice on a significant social issue.

The show continued to deliberately and unapologetically challenge entrenched beliefs. Its readiness to discuss the issue of homosexuality and its support of Senator David Norris and academic Emma Donoghue, both of whom spoke at various times on the show in the 1980s on behalf of the gay and les-bian communities, may well have had a large part to play in the acknowledgement of homosexuality in Irish society. By giving representation to social groups that were outside the national mainstream, *The Late Late Show* challenged the notion of the nuclear family. By introducing and demystifying an issue, sometimes representing it to almost saturation point, the show forced Irish society to consider alternative points of view. An interview with Irish lesbian Joni Sheerin in 1981 reflected these changes.

During the interview, Ms Sheerin spoke of the innumer-able social problems she was forced to overcome because of her sexual orientation. David Norris recalls this interview with Sheerin as a 'very human moment'. He believes one of Byrne's greatest strengths as an interviewer is the fact that he 'doesn't pigeon-hole' people; he treated Norris and others like him as 'an ordinary person with many other interests who happened to be gay.'[135]

Some years later, in the mid-1980s, the Director of *The Late Late Show*, Adrian Cronin, invited former nuns and self-professed lesbians, Americans Nancy Manahan and Rosemary Curb, on

---

[135]David Norris, in interview with the author, 22 March 2012.

the show to discuss their book, *Breaking the Silence*. The story concerned 48 women who had experienced lesbianism as nuns. Rather unusually, it was revealed in the *RTÉ Guide* before the show aired that the nuns would be appearing on the show. In spite of an application by the Director of the Christian Community Centre in Dublin, Thomas Gerald O'Mahony, to ban RTÉ from screening the interview, the interview was broadcast. According to Byrne's biography, the episode received the highest ratings in the history of Irish television at that time.[136]

Before the episode aired, 90 per cent of the calls in relation to it were in opposition to the item being broadcast. After the programme, the balance had swung strongly in the opposite direction.[137] This may have been due to the fact that there was absolutely no sexual content in the interviews with the nuns and, in contrast to the furore over the Bishop and the Nightie affair a decade earlier, the response to the show clearly reflected the changes in public attitudes towards issues of sexuality. A letter writer to the programme congratulated Byrne on his 'excellent handling of a delicately sensitive' topic, adding that the programme would have proved 'instructive and enlightening to many'.[138]

Conclusion

While *The Late Late Show* was still reeling from the aftermath of the abortion issue, *The Gay Byrne Show* was now discovering, under producer John Caden, that politicians and the clergy no longer had sole access to the airwaves. By the early 1980s, Gay Byrne's radio programme had extended access to all, and 'the Establishment' was now being challenged on a daily basis.

Caden reiterates this point when recounting his time working on the *The Gay Byrne Show*:

---

[136]Byrne and Purcell, *op. cit.*, p. 115.
[137]'RTÉ picketed over lesbian nuns interview', *Irish Times*, 14 September 1985.
[138]Courtesy of RTÉ Written Archives, March 1985.

Fortunately it was a time when RTÉ was beginning to see the potential of tabloid radio, with a winning mix of entertainment, public access, iconoclasm and debate. Access by letter, by phone or by studio interview gave ordinary people equal status with government ministers or clergy or anyone else who determined moral and political standards. This levelling of perceived status was in itself revolutionary and contributed hugely to the democratisation of public debate and to opening out the darker secret world of private thought and behaviour.[139]

Writer Colm Tóibín believes the power moved from television to radio sometime in the early 1980s. He believed a number of very memorable radio programmes emerged from what was essentially 'a housewives' choice programme'.[140] These would include the gripping and poignant account of 15-year-old Ann Lovett and the 'silence phenomenon' in Irish life, both of which will be discussed in the next chapter.

[139]John Caden, 'He reigned with a common touch', *Sunday Independent*, 16 August 1998.
[140]Tóibín, *op. cit.*, p. 67.

4

From Silence to Disclosure (1984–1990)

The Gay Byrne Show is credited with airing light-hearted and uplifting segments, but it is perhaps best remembered for its willingness to engage with taboo issues such as teenage pregnancy and the hitherto unarticulated dynamics of Irish family life. Yet, the change in the show's direction towards more serious topics began in an imperceptible fashion, as recounted here by Byrne himself:

> One of the major talking points we came across in the programme, and one which was indicative of the change in our general direction, arose when someone wrote in out of the blue about the phenomenon of 'the Silence'… Our original correspondent had written to say that the mother and the father of the household had not spoken a word to one another for five years but had communicated, even in simple matters like passing the salt at the dinner table, through other members of the family. I read the letter on the air and made some anodyne comment like 'how sad', and assumed that was the end of it. But we were inundated with letters that outlined similar situations that had gone on for fifteen, twenty or even twenty-five years … It was

clearly a perfectly ordinary and accepted phenomenon of Irish life where there was no divorce possible.[1]

Arising out of this original letter, this 'silence phenomenon' was to provide the most riveting hours of broadcast history ever heard on Irish radio to date.[2] It was Byrne's persona that propelled listeners into revealing their innermost thoughts and intimacies live on air. *Irish Times* journalist Fintan O'Toole believes it was this topic of silences that made Gay Byrne what he was in Ireland during his tenure as host of *The Gay Byrne Show*.[3]

The Granard Affair

One of the most famous broadcasts on the show was that concerning the death of 15-year-old schoolgirl Ann Lovett from childbirth in a lonely field in Granard, Co. Longford. The so-called Granard Affair shocked the nation after Byrne covered the story on the radio show in 1984. According to journalist Harry Browne:

> In popular historiography… the moment that is most often cited as decisive came in early 1984. Only four months earlier, conservative Catholics had pushed through a referendum enshrining the right of life of the 'unborn child' in the constitution. In the most extraordinarily awful, symbol-laden rebuke, two children were found dead in a grotto dedicated to the Virgin Mary in Granard, Co. Longford: one was a newborn infant, the other was his 15-year-old mother, Ann Lovett.[4]

---

[1]   Gay Byrne with Deirdre Purcell, *The Time of My Life: An Autobiography* (Gill & Macmillan: Dublin, 1989), p. 216.

[2]   *The Gay Byrne Show*, 24 February 1984.

[3]   Fintan O'Toole, *A Mass for Jesse James: A Journey Through 1980s Ireland* (Raven Arts Press: Dublin, 1990), p. 168.

[4]   Harry Browne, 'Wiles of the Wireless: Radio and Critical Discourse in Ireland', *Irish Review*, 32 (2004).

Even now it is difficult to ascertain whether her parents or friends knew of her pregnancy, so great was the shame of illegitimate birth in rural Ireland in 1984. In their defence, friends of Ann Lovett claimed that while they suspected she was pregnant, she had refused to confirm it. The following is part of a letter written to the *Irish Press* in February 1984:

> Rumours had circulated that Ann was pregnant among some people, but on being asked by close friends quietly, she denied this, saying she wasn't pregnant. Indeed if she had said 'yes', herself and her baby would have been helped in any way.
>
> One may wonder why she said 'no'. From one who knew Ann well, she was very independent and had a mature mind. She had fixed ideas of her own which she was entitled to. She was enthusiastic about school, and keen at sport, especially badminton. She was a very happy and friendly girl.
>
> May she rest in peace.
>
> A Student, Chnoc Mhuire, Convent of Mercy, Granard.[5]

Tragically, Ann had told her best friend, Mary Maguire, of her pregnancy in December 1983. At the Mullingar inquest into Ann's death, Maguire stated that she wanted to tell somebody in the town: 'I wanted to tell Ann's brothers, sisters, but I just thought they'd turn around and say to me that's none of your business.' When asked at the inquest why Ann had not told her she was about to give birth when she stopped by on the day of the tragedy, Maguire said, 'maybe she thought she wouldn't be wanted anymore by her friends or anyone.'[6]

---

[5] *Irish Press*, 23 February 1984.
[6] 'Why I blame myself, by friend of birth tragedy girl Ann Lovett', *Irish Independent*, 23 February 1984.

The fact that 15-year-old Ann went alone to have the child near the grotto in a lonely field prompted the then Minister for Women's Affairs, Nuala Fennell, to describe the tragedy as reminiscent of *The Valley of the Squinting Windows*.[7] These comments were later condemned by Granard town commissioners, who demanded a full public apology from Minister Fennell for her 'cruel and outrageous statement'.[8]

Gay Byrne took up the case on his daily radio talk show, inviting letters from women with parallel experiences – and scores arrived. He devoted two hours of radio time to reading out extracts from these letters. They were read by Byrne and actors in an almost forensic manner. There were poignant tales of 'clandestine childbirth, clumsy self-abortion, brutal husbands or incestuous fathers.'[9]

Producer on the show John Caden recalls how he will never forget the chilling story of a young, 15-year-old girl who had been put into service on a farm by her parents to augment the family income.[10] She became pregnant by the farmer. When about to give birth, she was locked into a room by the farmer's wife, who called for the young girl's father. He arrived with a bucket of water in which he drowned the newborn child. He then wrapped the dead child in a sheet and left with it under his arm. 'It was a relentless onslaught of terrible intimacies' commented *The Irish Times*. 'A sort of secret history of modern Ireland … stories that had been bottled up and swallowed down.'[11]

Twenty years later, former *Sunday Tribune* reporter and current European Ombudsman Emily O'Reilly recalled her thoughts on the Granard tragedy:

---

[7] *The Valley of the Squinting Windows* is a 1918 novel by Brinsley MacNamara which is set in a tiny village in Ireland where everyone is interested in everyone else's affairs and wishes them to fail.

[8] 'Doctor did not know of Ann Lovett's pregnancy', *Irish Independent*, 17 February 1984.

[9] John Ardagh, *Ireland and the Irish: Portrait of a Changing Society* (Penguin Books: London, 1995), p. 179.

[10] John Caden, in interview with the author, 11 March 2007.

[11] *Irish Times*, Editorial, 23 February 1984.

Opponents of the 1983 anti-abortion amendment had a field day. So too did the lobbyists for a more liberal contraception regime, for more sex education in schools, for the loosening of the still tight grip of the Catholic Church on State legislation. A contrary note was struck by one local newspaper editor who said that, rather than dying alone, Ann had in fact died under the loving gaze of the statue of the Virgin Mary. And in the absence of detail of the horror of Ann's story, we got instead on the Gay Byrne radio show the most horrendous details of broadly similar events of just a few decades earlier.[12]

Unlike the media intrusions we have come to expect in twenty-first century Ireland, no photographs were published of Ann Lovett and her baby. Therefore, the images conjured by Gay Byrne on his programme ensured that the grotto in Granard was profoundly imprinted on the national conscience. Singer-songwriter Christy Moore also ensured Ann Lovett's tragic death would not be forgotten when he penned the elegiac song 'Ann Lovett':

It was a sad slow stupid death for them both.
Everybody knew, nobody said,
At a grotto,
In a field,
In the middle of the Island.[13]

Above all, the story of Ann Lovett's death painted a picture of a very different Ireland. Even the fact that the letter was the chosen medium of communication, and not the impersonal distance of an email or text which now make up the bulk of listener access to radio programmes, is a significant reminder of the influence *The Gay Byrne Show* exercised over its listeners.

---

[12] 'Death at the Grotto', *Irish Times*, 31 January 2004.
[13] Christy Moore, 'Ann Lovett' (known also as 'Middle of the Island'), *Voyage*, 1989.

The level of communal intimacy shared with listeners is difficult to imagine now in a society saturated by media excess. On an episode of the RTÉ television programme *Scannal* titled 'Ann Lovett: The story that couldn't remain local,' Byrne commented on the disjuncture between Ireland then and now with regard to the 'Ann Lovett letters radio programme':

> Looking back at those letters now, it seems to me that not only are we living in a different country, not only are we living in a different era, it seems to me like we are living on a different planet.[14]

Caden spoke of 'the huge anger that broke forth' after the airing of the Ann Lovett tragedy. He highlighted the 'extraordinary image of the grotto and the child which had retained so much of our attitude to morality and sexuality and the manner in which our society and the Church had imposed their views.'[15]

In response to the public airing of the Ann Lovett tragedy, both in newspapers and on *The Gay Byrne Show*, the *Irish Independent* in its editorial on 13 February 1984 wrote:

> But no Irish newspaper has blamed or has had cause to blame the people of Granard for the death of the unfortunate girl. Far from it. What happened in Granard could have happened in any town or village up and down the length of Ireland ... and what happened afterwards, when the tragedy was published, must have bought some good because it alerted the whole Irish public to the problem of teenage pregnancies and may well have prevented such tragedies happening again.[16]

---

[14] 'Ann Lovett: The story that couldn't remain local', *Scannal*, RTÉ, 23 February 2004.

[15] John Caden, in interview with Fintan O'Toole on the BBC Radio 4 documentary *A Cup of Tea, A Sticky Bun and an Hour of Gaybo*, 18 January 2003.

[16] 'Granard', *Irish Independent*, 3 February 1984.

The image of a young girl giving birth all alone in a field in Granard has become an iconic image of an Ireland that many would prefer to forget. Yet, these stories would never have come to light without Byrne and his radio show. Colm Tóibín and Fintan O'Toole have both written at various times about Byrne and the emergent ascendancy of his radio programme over its TV counterpart. O'Toole comments on how 'the centre of gravity had moved from television to radio from the dramatic to the confessional, just as the centre of national debate had moved from the public to the private.'[17]

Over the years Byrne had cautiously but relentlessly prised away the layers of Ireland's darkest secrets, and only he could have performed the role of the national confessor. It was, according to O'Toole, 'to our shame that there was no one else to speak to, to our shame that we needed Gay Byrne so much.'[18]

Even in 2008, author Deirdre Purcell, in her book *Days We Remember*, recalled how *The Gay Byrne Show* dealt with the tragedy and the effect it had on Byrne, his staff and his listeners.[19] According to Purcell, reporter Kevin O'Connor, who had previously been commended for his factual reporting on the case of Eileen Flynn (an unmarried teacher who had been dismissed from her job in the south-east of Ireland because she had become pregnant by a married man), was dispatched to cover the story of Granard, where he tried without success to elicit information. However, when he went to the cemetery, there was somebody at Ann Lovett's grave. The information that person divulged became the narrative of *The Gay Byrne Show*, and the informant's identity remained a secret, shared only by O'Connor. To Byrne, 'that was the start of the revelations about what was going on in Ireland. We always knew but we didn't know,' [we always suspected but] 'we didn't suspect'.[20]

[17] 'The Sound of Silence', *Irish Times*, 9 September 1989.
[18] *Ibid.*
[19] Deirdre Purcell, *Days We Remember* (Hachette Books: Dublin, 2008), p. 11.
[20] *Ibid.*

Purcell recounts that sometime after O'Connor appeared on *The Gay Byrne Show* he returned to his home place. There, he met a doctor friend, who, instead of his normal, cordial greeting, looked quizzically at him and commented:

> You'll have to stop doing reports like that. I'm called up into the hills around here every month to deal with the product of incest. I can't report it or the whole place will collapse.[21]

The aftermath of the Granard Affair and its exposure of a censorious Catholic-dominated culture is as worthy of comment as the tragic event itself. The story of Ann Lovett on the programme had burst open a dam of repression and 'liberated, without intending to do so, an almost passionate female voice.'[22] The story had moved from the private to the public sphere. The abortion referendum raged in tandem with the story of Ann Lovett's death. The issue of a constitutional amendment on abortion remained top of the national agenda as the conflict between the older and more conservative Ireland and that of an emerging liberal democracy was being fought. While the Church's successful defence of the constitutional prohibition on abortion temporarily stopped the erosion of its power, by the 1990s the Church's autocracy was severely weakened by a series of abuse allegations that rocked it to its core, many becoming topics for discussion on Byrne's radio and television shows. Back in 1980s Ireland, however, it was stories like that of Ann Lovett which gripped the nation.

A Cup of Tea, a Sticky Bun and an Hour of Gaybo

Many of these stories were encapsulated on the BBC Radio 4 documentary *A Cup of Tea, a Sticky Bun and an Hour of Gaybo*,

---

[21] *Ibid.*

[22] *A Cup of Tea, A Sticky Bun and an Hour of Gaybo*, BBC Radio 4 documentary presented by Fintan O'Toole, 18 January 2003.

presented by Fintan O'Toole.[23] This intimate mood-piece provides a vivid picture of *The Gay Byrne Show* and what it meant to its listeners. Former researcher and producer on the show Julie Parsons revealed in the documentary that *The Gay Byrne Show* was an intrinsic part of Irish society in the 1970s and 80s. To her, it provided a focus for people's dreams, desires, hopes and even fears; 'it literally changed people's lives.'

Also in the documentary, journalist Nell McCafferty makes the point that the 'acceptable face' in Ireland was the priest, a man to be trusted by his congregation. However, soon Gay Byrne was seen as someone who, like the clergy, was trustworthy and reliable. Colm Tóibín nonetheless suggests that many Irish people were in fact fed up with the pretence of Holy Catholic Ireland and that *The Gay Byrne Show* provided a pathway out of the depths of this erroneous image of an Ireland which he felt had been largely constructed by former Archbishop of Dublin John Charles McQuaid.

Controversy on *The Late Late Show*

But it was not just the radio programme casting a forensic light on Irish life and excavating its darker secrets. In one particular instance in February 1984, *The Late Late Show* unearthed a very public and political controversy. The controversy centred on an interview with former Minister for Justice Seán Doherty, a former member of the Garda Síochána. He was invited on the show to discuss his political career to date, and it was suggested that Byrne did not display his customary forensic interviewing style on that occasion. At the time of the interview, newspapers were rife with stories of the 'Dowra Affair',[24] in which it was alleged that a citizen of the North of Ireland, James McGovern, had been arrested by the Special Branch of the RUC[25] to prevent him from giving evidence

---

[23] *Ibid.*

[24] 'Irish Minister at the centre of phone-tapping scandal', *Guardian*, 8 June 2005.

[25] Royal Ulster Constabulary, a British police force in Northern Ireland.

against Garda Thomas Nangle, Seán Doherty's brother-in law. Nangle had been charged with assaulting James McGovern in a public house in December 1981, but the case against Nangle was dismissed due to the non-appearance in court of the principal witness, McGovern.

Also circulating at that time was the arguably more serious issue of the phone-tapping of journalists Bruce Arnold and Geraldine Kennedy by Mr Doherty during the Fianna Fáil administration of 1982. According to Arnold, the involvement of Minister Doherty in both actions indicated 'the spread of a corrupt virus in Irish life,'[26] none of which was queried by Byrne during the Late Late interview. In fact, 'not a word of this emerged',[27] and it was felt that Byrne had 'conducted an item which could only be described as a whitewashing for one of the most controversial figures in Irish politics in the history of this State.'[28] Mavis Arnold, Bruce Arnold's wife, agreed with this analysis, and in a letter to The Irish Times she wrote of her disquiet regarding the Doherty interview:

Sir,

I read in this morning's press that Mr Seán Doherty has 'partially restored his reputation' by his appearance on last Saturday's Late Late Show, unopposed and in front of a totally silent audience ... In 1982 I and my family suffered an unconstitutional intrusion into our privacy ... Responsibility for this was in the hands of the Minister for Justice. Ultimate responsibility, under our Constitution, resides with the Government, which was then led by Mr Charles Haughey ... The Late Late Show was last year considered unsuitable for a debate on abortion when that was a

---

[26] Bruce Arnold, 'This was the period that exposed Haughey at his most dishonest', Irish Independent, 27 December 2013.

[27] 'Rot from the top that ripped the heart out of the Gardaí', Irish Independent, 1 August 2004.

[28] Ibid.

constitutional issue. The tapping of my telephone was also a constitutional issue. If the Seán Doherty appearance is seen purely in the context of his rehabilitation, then, whatever one's reservations about it, *The Late Late Show* would seem a reasonable place for him to stage a come-back. But other people were involved, and in the case of myself and my children, our constitutional rights were infringed. That is why last Saturday's performance was so distasteful.[29]

Letters such as Ms Arnold's accusing Byrne of perceived bias as an interviewer were not uncommon and, at times, were upheld by the Broadcasting Complaints Commission. In 1985 there was a complaint against Byrne of 'clearly aligning himself' with the views of three panel members (Mr Ivor Kenny, Mr Des Peelo and Mr Tom Murphy) on an episode of *The Late Late Show* dealing with 'the state of the nation'.[30] The complaint by Mr Brendan Ryan, an independent member of the Senate, concerned the 'unbalanced' nature of the discussion, during which 'three people with a common point of view were given a full hour to produce an unchallenged analysis of Irish society.'[31]

America Calling!

Yet, by 1985 Byrne began to care little for public disapprobation. America was on his mind, and he had the lucrative US TV market within his grasp. The reason for this proposed move stateside takes us back to the summer of 1984 when Byrne broadcast a number of episodes of *The Late Late Show* from New York. In doing so he attracted the attention of Bill Baker, the boss of the Westinghouse Group, now CBS Broadcasting. He was impressed with Byrne and sent a delegation to Dublin to try to entice him to go to Philadelphia to record two pilot shows.

---

[29] 'Mr Doherty and The Late Late Show', Letters to the Editor, *Irish Times*, 1 February 1984.
[30] 'Complaint against Late Late upheld', *Irish Times*, 18 July 1985.
[31] *Ibid.*

Byrne acquiesced, and conducted what he himself described as 'one of the best interviews of his life.'[32]

When the Westinghouse Group offered him a job as a regional host, Byrne was tempted, saying, 'Given what has happened to me financially in the past year, if an attractive offer comes from the American television company, then I will be very tempted to take it.'[33]

The minutes from the RTÉ Authority Committee meeting of 11 January 1985 record the reaction to Byrne's proposed departure as follows:

> The Chairman said he had had an unprecedented reaction to reports that Gay Byrne was leaving. After some discussion it was agreed that the Chairman would write to Mr Byrne expressing the Authority's regret that he was leaving and indicating that RTÉ was prepared to go to reasonable lengths to retain his services.[34]

But Byrne ultimately decided not to go, citing family commitments and his love of Dublin:

> It is that you feel comfortable in a place and you are among your own. There is nowhere in Dublin that I don't know; I am surrounded by people who know me and like me … from about 12 years of age, I wanted to be what I am now.[35]

No doubt the great professional risk associated with moving to unknown territory in America was also a factor in his decision to stay. While he was certainly a big fish in Ireland, he was unknown to the American public. Close friend and collaborator John McColgan believes that entertainment was in Byrne's

---

[32] Byrne and Purcell, *op. cit.*, p. 206.
[33] Byrne's close friend and accountant, Russell Murphy, embezzled much of Byrne's money: Byrne and Purcell, *op. cit.*, p. 124.
[34] RTÉ Authority Meeting, 20 April 1985.
[35] 'Byrne admits he could be tempted by US offer', *Irish Times*, 4 February 1985.

DNA and that he would have done very well abroad, but he was a 'homebird'.[36] He firmly states that neither Terry Wogan – who at the time was becoming a huge talk-show star in the UK – nor Mike Murphy – a popular Irish TV presenter with his own comedy sketch programme, *The Live Mike* – had what Byrne had: 'a combination of fierce work ethic and creative mind, allied with meticulously high standards.'[37]

Byrne's decision to stay on as host of both *The Late Late Show* and *The Gay Byrne Show* was met with relief from the public. He had become a national treasure, and the prospect of losing him to a country where Johnny Carson, David Letterman and the dollar sign appeared to govern the magic of television was unbearable. In return, Byrne got his wish after 23 years to move *The Late Late Show* from a Saturday to a Friday-night slot.[38] At the time, he not only wanted his weekends free but also believed higher audience figures could be achieved on Friday nights, as there was less competition from other shows.

Tragic Disclosures

So it was that Byrne continued to host *The Late Late Show*, but with its new Friday-night slot. In October of 1985, quite unlike the spectacle involving Seán Doherty, Byrne conducted a sensitive and moving interview with Joanne Hayes, a young Tralee woman accused of killing her infant child. The background to the Hayes story is significant in terms of what it displays of the attitude to women in 1980s Ireland. It is worth reiterating that contraception, divorce and the divisive issue of abortion were all under negotiation by a predominantly male government. In November 1982 Garret FitzGerald's Fine Gael Government did appoint two women to the Government table: Gemma Hussey as Minster for Education and Nuala Fennell as Minister of State for Women's Affairs.

---

[36] John McColgan, in interview with the author, 1 March 2012.
[37] *Ibid.*
[38] 'Late Late Show moves to Friday', *Irish Times*, 19 July 1985.

It was Fennell who had made the 'Valley of the Squinting Windows' comment when referring to local reaction to the Ann Lovett tragedy. Less than two months after that incident, on 14 April 1984, the body of a newborn baby boy was found on White Strand beach at Cahirciveen in Co. Kerry. Joanne Hayes was a 25-year-old local who was known to have been pregnant around that time. She was soon arrested by Gardaí as part of their investigations. It later emerged, through a lengthy tribunal in 1985, that Joanne had given birth to her own baby, but the baby had died shortly after birth and was buried on the Hayes family farm. The Joanne Hayes murder trial, and her interview with Byrne on *The Late Late Show* subsequent to the publication of the tribunal report, raised many questions about the attitudes towards women, family and religion in 1980s Ireland. In her book *A Woman to Blame*, journalist Nell McCafferty looks at the treatment of Joanne Hayes by Gardaí and by the judge who presided over her trial, Mr Justice Lynch:

> A measure of his temperament and attitudes to women in the Kerry babies case is the judicial pronouncement made at the end by Justice Lynch. He asked, 'What have I got to do with the women of Ireland in general? What have the women of Ireland to do with this case?' He presumed to lecture Irish women on what he saw as their misguided support for Hayes in her agony.[39]

By highlighting the Ann Lovett tragedy on *The Gay Byrne Show* and exploring the repercussions of Ireland's attitude towards unmarried mothers with Joanne Hayes on *The Late Late Show*, Byrne provided a conduit for change. As host to the nation, he helped propel into public discourse two very defining moments in Ireland's social history, while simultaneously providing an insight into the changing role of women in Ireland. And change it did. By 1985, the landmark passage of the Family Planning

---

[39] Nell McCafferty, *A Woman To Blame: The Kerry Babies Case* (Attic Press: Dublin, 2010), p. 71.

Amendment Act, which legalised the sale of contraceptives to all those over 18, regardless of their marital status, signified a sharp decrease in the moral authority of Roman Catholicism and loosened the alliance between Church and State.

Ireland's Culture on Display

Consistently and unapologetically, Gay Byrne and the *Late Late Show* research team put all areas of Irish culture on display and under scrutiny. In 1985, an entire programme was devoted to the Traveller community, who made up both the panel and the audience. Television critic Nora Redlich commented that the show's extraordinary success 'was due in no small measure to Mr Byrne's approach, 'which was neither patronising nor facetious' but rather displayed 'a gentleness and kindness which in different situations may be labelled "soft".'[40] In this instance *The Late Late Show* was exploring hitherto unexplored aspects of Ireland's culture and challenging viewers to make their own opinions on the richly diverse Traveller culture. Furthermore, by investigating popular culture through programmes where issues of moral conscience and social change were the norm on an almost weekly basis, *The Late Late Show* provided the mirror through which Irish society was viewed and commented upon.

Humour and Hope on *The Gay Byrne Show*

In a gentler fashion, *The Gay Byrne Show* – amidst the poignant tales of concealed pregnancies and young women forced to separate from their children – aired many anecdotes that evoked a lighter, more humorous response. These included a brave young Dublin woman who proposed, through a self-penned poem, to her embarrassed boyfriend live on air. Moments like this remind us that *The Gay Byrne Show* was primarily about entertainment and not the bleaker moments that tend to

---

[40] Quoted in Robert Savage, *A Loss of Innocence? Television and Irish Society 1960–72* (Manchester University Press: Manchester, 2010), p. 207.

dominate assessments of the show. There were also times when one would expect the show to take a serious tone, but Byrne, in his inimitable way, would inject some humour to keep the listener tuned to the end.

One such instance was his interview with Dr Tiede Herrema in 1985. Herrema, the Dutch Chief Executive of the former Ferenka plant in Limerick, had been kidnapped in 1975 and imprisoned by IRA diehards Eddie Gallagher and Marian Coyle for over 35 days. The kidnappers demanded the release of three IRA prisoners but were eventually traced to a house in Monasterevin in Co. Kildare. Herrema was released, unharmed. Ten years on from his kidnapping, the *Gay Byrne Show* researcher Julie Parsons sent an interview request to Dr Herrema, attaching a press cutting from *The Irish Times* entitled: 'Herrema tells of relationship with captors.'[41] Byrne's subsequent interview with Herrema on 20 February 1985 made for riveting radio. The transcript of the interview is housed in the University of Limerick Library, along with all of Dr Tiede Herrema's papers. The kidnapping was also the topic of a documentary on RTÉ 1 broadcast on 1 December 2005,[42] yet it is the Byrne–Herrema interview that remains most memorable.

During the interview, Dr Herrema recounts to Byrne the almost banal aspects of his kidnapping, including Marion Coyle's use of Oil of Olay and Eddie Gallagher's love of Lucozade. These details had stayed with him since his release from captivity. Byrne listened while Herrema recounted his experiences. Every now and then, in order to bring out the essence of Herrema, Byrne would interject the story with brief, yet probing questions, such as, 'Are you religious?' and 'When you were thirsty did you drink your own urine?', all of which were answered in a forthright manner by Herrema. These were the questions which listeners at home wished to ask but didn't dare

---

[41] University of Limerick Special Collections: *The Dr Tiede Herema Papers*, IE2135 P22, Herrema and the Media, with reference to *The Gay Byrne Show* 1984–85, p. 54.

[42] Rebroadcast on *The Best of The Gay Byrne Show*, RTÉ Radio 1, 6 April 1999.

to.[43] This and other engaging interviews helped to increase the show's popularity throughout the 1980s.

The Gay Byrne Fund

In January 1985, Margaret and Leonard McStay appeared in studio on *The Gay Byrne Show* to ask for Byrne's help. The couple wished to send their son Colin to Pittsburgh for a liver transplant, without which he would die. Byrne allowed the McStays to talk uninterrupted about their son, and many parents listening to the show could not fail to be moved by Margaret McStay's pain and anguish. She was a mother desperate to save the life of her child. Byrne told listeners, 'Let's put this baldly: he is definitely going to die if this operation doesn't happen.'[44] This bold statement from Byrne shocked listeners. Over one million pounds was subsequently raised by the show, and the life of Colin McStay was saved. This heralded the beginnings of the Gay Byrne Fund, which was to remain central to the programme until its demise, raising funds for local and international charitable causes.

Revelations

In 1987, Clare-born Fr Bernard Lynch appeared on *The Late Late Show* to talk about his work with AIDS sufferers in New York's homosexual community.[45] In a pre-interview deal, it was agreed that Byrne would not question Fr Lynch's sexuality, as the priest deemed it to be inappropriate. During the programme, however, Byrne asked Fr Lynch whether he was gay. Fr Lynch felt forced to deny his homosexuality, though he subsequently admitted he was gay at a later stage.[46] At the time,

---

[43] *Ibid.*

[44] *Ibid.*

[45] *Soul Survivor*, a Channel 4 documentary on Fr Bernard Lynch and his involvement in the AIDS pandemic in New York, aired in May 1986. The documentary makes reference to Fr Lynch's appearance on *The Late Late Show* in March 1985.

[46] *Ibid.*

the intimate nature of such a question was severely censured in the Irish media, but Byrne was well aware of the value of shock to maintain viewing figures.

In May of the following year, Fr Lynch was charged, and later fully vindicated, on two counts of first-degree sexual abuse of pupils at Mount Saint Michael Academy, a Marist Brothers' school in the Bronx area of New York.[47] For admirers of Byrne's style, it would appear that the nature of his interviewing technique was unnervingly appropriate. However, his critics questioned his seemingly determined resolve to open up every issue to public scrutiny.

Satellite Competition

By the late 1980s, talk shows were no longer unique, and satellite dishes were providing Irish audiences with a vast array of provocative programming. It had become apparent that the controversies produced by *The Late Late Show* and *The Gay Byrne Show* in the 1960s and 70s were impossible to reproduce in the late 80s and early 90s, simply because people were less shockable. The Gay Byrne phenomenon originated at a time during the 1960s and 70s when Irish people were, to a certain extent, 'stuck' with Byrne on radio and television. People's lives revolved around Gaybo in a way that would be impossible for anyone to achieve now. Byrne created a sense of community which bound Irish people more tightly together.

The fact that Ireland had only one major television talk show should not detract from the achievements of *The Late Late Show* in its latter two decades, when it was both hosted and produced by Gay Byrne. In 1989, for instance, in spite of overwhelming competition from satellite television, 22 of the 37 television programmes with the highest viewing figures on Irish television were episodes of *The Late Late Show*.[48] Since Irish audiences were becoming more sophisticated and less easily shocked in

---

[47] 'Priest in US sex charge here', *Irish Times*, 5 May 1988.
[48] *RTÉ Guide*, 10 January 1989.

the second half of Byrne's reign over *The Late Late Show*, he had to find other ways of engaging people rather than simply stirring up controversy.

Love and Nostalgia on *The Gay Byrne Show*

Meanwhile, on radio, his ability to move fluidly from light to serious issues continued to engage audiences and is evident when one listens to a compilation of the show from the 1980s, *The Best of The Gay Byrne Show*, which was aired over a period of five days from 5–9 April 1999.[49] Highlights from this compilation include reflections on an almost forgotten Ireland. For example, Byrne reminisces on his interview with author Alice Taylor, whose excerpts from her book *To School Through the Fields* really captivated listeners. Byrne's understanding of the necessity to integrate nostalgia with modernity, to blend bleakness with moments of intense light-heartedness, accentuate his deep-rooted comprehension of the Irish psyche. He understood that for many listeners a review of life in a darker, more humble Ireland would serve as a perfect counterpoint to what was becoming an increasingly materialistic and arrogant nation.

Byrne himself recalls in *The Best of The Gay Byrne Show* how the subject of marriage and relationships was an endless source of fascination for his listeners. Perennial questions included how to sustain a marriage over the years, the consequences of falling out of love and how to cope if your husband has an affair. All of these questions emanated from a phone call to the show in 1988. It was from a lady called Mary who was 30 years old and single. She spoke of the difficulties of meeting a man. Many listeners who were separated, widowed or single were inspired by her courage, and they too wrote to the show. The response was overwhelming. All the letter writers had one thing in common: they wished to meet someone without going to dance halls.

---

[49] *The Best of The Gay Byrne Show, op. cit.*, 6 April 1999.

As a result, *The Gay Byrne Show* decided to host a singles night in RTÉ Studio One in Montrose. One hundred single men and women came along, and they danced, sang and talked for hours.[50] The enormous success of this night highlighted the uncanny ability of Byrne and his radio team to measure the heartbeat of the community and effect change in people's lives.

Listening back to people interviewed on that singles night, one is touched by the innocence and sincerity of it all. An interviewee in his mid-forties spoke of his marriage break-up after eight years. He talked candidly of his desire to meet someone and his fear of living alone for the rest of his life. His concerns were highly relevant to Irish people in 1980s Ireland, where divorce was not an option. Throughout the decade there were heated debates regarding the morality of divorce, with many callers accessing *The Gay Byrne Show* to air divergent views on this contentious issue. The engagement of *The Gay Byrne Show* with the issue of relationships encapsulates the uniqueness of its remit.

While for many the moving coverage of the Ann Lovett tragedy in 1984 was a watershed moment in the history of *The Gay Byrne Show*, it could equally be contended that the singles night in 1988 was of equal import in that it highlighted Irish people's desire for recognition of the circumstances of their relationships, whatever they might be.

In 1988, listeners of the show were quite stunned to hear a former nun say she felt that she would like to live with a man first before getting married. This woman perfectly reflected and articulated the changes that were sweeping through Ireland at the time. Another lady who had been married for 25 years before separating from her husband spoke movingly of the need to mourn the loss of her marriage.[51] She highlighted the fact that there was no convention or ritual to mark the end of a marriage, and she shared her turmoil with Gay Byrne.

---

[50] *Ibid.*
[51] *Ibid.*, 7 April 1999.

This diversity of viewpoints, this sharing of raw and very real emotions, was the hallmark of *The Gay Byrne Show*, which reflected diversity in Irish society more accurately than any socio-historical tract. By merely listening to archive broadcasts of *The Gay Byrne Show*, one can readily comprehend the cultural and social transitions experienced by Ireland and its people as they negotiated, together, new moral ground. As Byrne played host to an entire nation, the views and opinions heard on his radio show became central to Irish life.

The Pulse of the Nation[52]

The fact that Byrne was a conservative and a Catholic at heart ensured that *The Gay Byrne Show*, at least until the 1990s, remained within the parameters of acceptable behaviour, albeit at times challenging and controversial. Former researcher Ronan Kelly points to the fact that the programme's time slot, from 9.00 a.m. to 11 a.m., invariably attracted a largely female listenership. However, he asserts that men also tuned in, in particular on issues such as money and religion. Kelly also draws attention to the fact that whilst the show did explore some unfamiliar territory for a radio talk show, such as the issues of abortion and AIDS, it also remained focused on its listeners and never trivialised or undermined the importance of the worries and concerns of the ordinary people of Ireland.[53]

However, due to its oftentimes hard-hitting agenda, *The Gay Byrne Show*, like *The Late Late Show*, was not always popular within RTÉ. By 1988 it was felt by the news and current affairs department that the show was often more hard-hitting than its light-entertainment brief required and that it should be moved. However, according to the show's producer, John Caden, such a move would have drastically altered the appeal of the

---

[52] '*The Gay Byrne Show* prided itself on its ability to half-reflect and half-create the pulse of the nation': Ronan Kelly, in interview with undergraduate student Jennifer Walsh, 12 January 2006.
[53] *Ibid.*

programme. He believed that the format of the show, which allowed the ordinary punter to participate in items, would disappear if the show was to move to news and current affairs.[54]

On its fifteenth anniversary, *The Gay Byrne Show* had over one million listeners, including seven hundred thousand from Ireland, with the remainder listening in on medium wave in England, Scotland and Wales.[55] Callers were ringing the show in their thousands. According to Caden, 'On a perfectly ordinary morning in February 1987 Bord Telecom put a monitor on the show's on-air telephone line; more than 30,000 callers attempted to telephone the programme.'[56]

Caden believes the success of the programme was largely due to Byrne's ability to understand the needs of his listeners and his rigorous professionalism:

> At 8 o'clock each morning when Gay walked into studio, he was handed a file filled with briefs on that day's interviews and issues, listeners' letters, competitions, thought pieces to stimulate debate, jokes, clippings and a music list. But that was only half of the programme: the other half was Gay's performance. What made it such a wonderful programme was his ability to take it off the paper and turn it into a show that would move and enrich the whole country. In doing so he was nobody's patsy. He was not a carrying can for anybody's ideologies or notions. His requirements were simple and honest and forged in the demanding heat of broadcasting as a 'business'. Does it make sense? Does it work? Will it hold an audience? Anything that failed the test was binned.[57]

---

[54] Myles McWeeney, 'Gaybo and the national confessional', *Irish Independent*, 10 February 1988.

[55] *Ibid.*

[56] *Ibid.*

[57] John Caden, 'He reigned with a common touch', *Sunday Independent*, 16 August 1998.

Byrne as Father Confessor

Of course it must be remembered that RTÉ radio was popular primarily because it had a monopolistic hold on the Irish radio market. On certain programmes, such as *The Gay Byrne Show*, it popularised itself by being of and for ordinary listeners, 'a tribune of the people',[58] as it were. Writer John Ardagh believed the material on the radio show, in contrast to that of *The Late Late Show*, was of a more private nature. Byrne's use of a more soothing, intimate style transformed him into 'a kind of national agony aunt', who talked gently to his predominantly female listeners, who phoned in with intimate personal details they might normally tell no one.[59]

The troubled caller could speak without seeing Byrne's face, and it was far more comfortable than kneeling near the anonymous grid of the confessional. Byrne did not prescribe penances or offer opiates. He simply listened, and that was most of the cure. His ordinariness was also reassuring for his legion of female listeners. He often referred to his lack of a third-level education, but this enhanced rather than obstructed his bond with listeners, who admired his working-class lack of pretension.

Yet, access to the programme, and to RTÉ radio generally, was highly mediated in that its popularity did not mean that RTÉ was in some way democratic in its treatment of issues. It simply meant that in the absence of any real competition, in particular up to the late 1980s when local radio had still not come on-stream, RTÉ and its then flagship radio programme, *The Gay Byrne Show*, was in a position to challenge and impose its views on Irish society.

Journalist Medb Ruane believed Byrne 'spliced compassion into showmanship and created a new genre.'[60] The radio show had become a strange, restless hybrid, somewhere between a

---

[58] *Ibid.*
[59] Ardagh 1995, *op. cit.*, p. 179.
[60] Medb Ruane, 'Gaybo's Ireland', *Irish Times*, 15 August 1998.

hustler's stall and a confessional booth. The sheer ebullience of the rising New Ireland jostled uncomfortably alongside testimonies of misery and abuse. Byrne had his own virtual community, with its own belief system, one where values of honour, decency and forgiveness combined with a compassion never before extended on so public a scale. If institutions were not yet listening to the pain inflicted in the name of Old Ireland, then Gay and his audience were.[61]

This ability to get people to talk is clearly one of Byrne's greatest assets. In an interview with former researcher on *The Late Late Show* Oliver Donohue, Byrne commented:

> I think I am a very good listener. And I think a lot of people in the business are not good listeners. And that is one of the secrets.[62]

Byrne also admitted to preferring the medium of radio to that of television:

> Radio is much more accessible and easier ... It is much more accessible in so far as you can talk to people on the telephone and they will talk to you in a different way from the way they would in a television studio. They simply forget that they are talking to you on the air.[63]

In her article 'Intimacy from a media lay priest',[64] journalist Katherine O'Brien comments on Byrne's ability to somehow make it right to talk about emotions or sex or child abuse. She wonders why so many isolated and usually reticent people have confided their most intimate secrets to Gay, while half the country listened in. O'Brien maintains it is due partly to his

---

[61] *Ibid.*

[62] Oliver Donohue, *Interviewers Interviewed* (Marino Books: Dublin, 1996), p. 31.

[63] *Ibid.*, p. 47.

[64] Katherine O'Brien, 'Intimacy from a media lay priest', *Irish Independent*, 10 February 1996.

manner which is 'firm and friendly' and partly due to 'his lack of flirtatiousness'. Certainly there is also the fact that Byrne is always gallant but never familiar, with an ability to talk about sex without needing to be funny or crude. The easy magazine format of the show, the songs, the silly stories, balanced by more serious subjects, gave it an unexpectedness that kept listeners alert and engaged.

In January 1988 a distraught woman rang Gay because it was her fortieth birthday, and she couldn't face being 40. She felt it was the end of her life. Gay sympathised with her and sent her a bunch of flowers, to the fury of a group of self-righteous matrons who wrote in to say that Mrs 40 should get a grip. Byrne, however, was dismissive of begrudgers. In response to a different group of ladies who wrote in to complain when on another occasion he sympathised with a lady who had broken an expensive bottle of perfume, he retorted in complacent tones, 'Have you never ever done anything foolish?'[65]

Byrne's strength on radio lay in his distant intimacy. He was neither a brother figure nor a husband figure. He was certainly not a lover figure or even a father figure. Rather, he was a priest-like figure, as pointed out by O'Brien, who refers to Byrne as 'a media lay priest who specialised in a secular kind of liberal theology.'[66]

Majella Breen, in her MA Thesis, 'The Representation of Women in Irish Radio Talk Shows', cites examples of what she terms 'women's issues' taken from *The Gay Byrne Show* in 1986 and 1996.[67] These include items on male hygiene, unhappy marriages, male infidelity, lack of financial independence for women, and birth mothers and adoption. Byrne also hosted in-depth interviews with author and feminist Nuala O'Faolain and rally driver Rosemary Smith. O'Faoláin talked intimately about

---

[65] *Ibid.*

[66] *Ibid.*

[67] Majella Breen, 'The Representation of Women in Irish Radio Talk Shows: Taking Sample Periods 1986 and 1996' (MA in Communication and Cultural Studies, Dublin City University, 1997).

her troubled childhood, her experience of boarding school in the 1950s and her involvement in the women's movement.[68] For her part, Rosemary Smith spoke candidly about being a deserted wife and the importance of introducing divorce legislation in order to allow her to marry the man with whom she was living.[69]

Most of the letters to the show which Breen cites in her thesis are from 1986. The producers of the programme at that time were Colin Morrison, Nuala O'Connor, Philip Kampf and Frank Murphy, with John Caden as senior producer. The following extract reflects a time when divorce was still illegal, and many women felt trapped within a loveless marriage:

> Gay reads out a letter regarding a dirty husband and an unhappy marriage. He reads out a letter from a woman in Templeogue who says that most Irish men are no good in bed and adds that all she asks for is love and affection. Another letter is from a woman who writes about bad husbands. She wants divorce legalised and signs herself 'another victim'. Another letter on the programme is from a married woman who says women should not tolerate infidelity from their husbands.[70]

The Ideology of *The Gay Byrne Show*

The above excerpt from Breen's thesis highlights the diversity of viewpoints on women's issues on *The Gay Byrne Show*. However, central to any view of Gay Byrne and his overall impact on listeners is the argument of how he used his power as a radio host. People have been critical of his propensity to jeer, oftentimes under the guise of his 'funny voices' persona, which he used to great effect (particularly in the 1980s) to ridicule the Government and its running of the country or to question foreign influence in Ireland, or indeed change itself. Byrne sometimes

---

[68] Nuala O'Faolain on *The Gay Byrne Show*, 14 April 1986.
[69] Rosemary Smith on *The Gay Byrne Show*, 18 April 1986.
[70] Majella Breen, 1997, *op. cit.*

used the common touch, such as his 'decent Dub' persona, as a weapon to ridicule minority points of view.

Commenting in 1988, former editor of *The Irish Times* Geraldine Kennedy said she believed Byrne had bought about more change in social attitudes than anyone else, yet she felt he had also contributed to the 'denigration of politicians', who, in effect, had 'allowed Gay to create a climate here which is hostile to them.' She felt Byrne took 'a rather glib attitude towards them which they don't entirely deserve.'[71]

Of Byrne's radio persona, the now-deceased politician Tony Gregory, while acknowledging Byrne's enormous contribution to social change, was also critical of his 'excessive arrogance' and his reluctance to ever admit that he's in the wrong.[72]

Journalists Mary Leyland and Nell McCafferty spoke of Byrne's differing personas. Leyland felt that Byrne had 'liberated a passionate female voice'.[73] In contrast, McCafferty saw Byrne as patronising and condescending. She humorously recalled how her mother was just dying for a call from Byrne so that if he greeted her with his traditional 'How are ya, missus?' she would have great pleasure in telling him to 'F-off' while slamming the phone down.[74] O'Toole does concur that Byrne, as radio host, could be patronising, but 'his professionalism elevated trivial chit-chat into a form of entertainment.'[75]

Former Tánaiste Mary Harney had the following to say about Byrne and his radio show:

I admire the courage he's shown in standing up to the Provos [the provincial IRA]. He has one failing though, and although he is not sexist in his attitude to women, he does have an annoying habit of invariably asking married

---

[71] Geraldine Kennedy, in interview with Eddie Holt in 'The Mammie's Boy', *Independent Weekender*, 17 September 1988.

[72] *Ibid.*

[73] Mary Leyland, in interview with Fintan O'Toole on *A Cup of Tea, A Sticky Bun and an Hour of Gaybo*, BBC Radio 4, 18 January 2003.

[74] Nell McCafferty, in interview with Fintan O'Toole, *ibid.*

[75] *Ibid.*

women what their husbands do. He doesn't treat married women as individuals in their own right.[76]

As for men, particularly in the early years of the show, they tended to dislike Byrne, and wrote letters to newspapers levelling a wide range of accusations against him. He was 'a leading anglophile' who had the temerity to 'jibe at our national anthem for its warlike words.'[77] Or the rather back-handed compliment from the radio critic of *The Irish Times*, who said:

As a broadcaster in the pretty broad field of light entertainment Mr Byrne has few peers anywhere, despite his occasional descent to the level of cutesy-poo and his habit of mimicking the distinctive regional accents of some of his telephoning guests.[78]

Byrne was well aware of the simmering antipathy of the Irish male:

I don't blame them really. I know that if I came home each evening to listen to my Kathleen quoting what Byrne said on his radio programme that morning, I would hate me too.[79]

Forever the pragmatist, Byrne and *The Gay Byrne Show* tapped into the pulse of the nation. Like a tiny microscope that enlarges everything within its sight, *The Gay Byrne Show* highlighted hitherto hidden areas of Irish life. There were, according to former researcher and producer Julie Parsons, lots of letters from people who were looking after elderly parents.[80] These were poignant tales of men and women who had never married

---

[76] 'Return of the great guru', *Irish Independent*, 1 September 1990.

[77] 'Cultural goals', *Irish Press*, 19 March 1980.

[78] 'Jockeying the Discs', *Irish Times*, 6 August 1973.

[79] 'Byrne's own history', *Irish Press*, 30 May 1981.

[80] Julie Parsons, in interview with Fintan O'Toole in *A Cup of Tea, a Sticky Bun and an Hour of Gaybo, op. cit.*

and felt that they had lost out on life. From its origins as a programme that appeared to lack an overt political ideology, it
soon carried more muscle and bite as it tackled more difficult
subjects, often with Caden as executive producer.

Pioneering Ideas and Listener Reaction

According to Byrne, Caden was 'the best producer' he ever
had, with Alex White as a 'close second'.[81] To Byrne, a producer
had to be a very good manager. For him, the halcyon days of
the show included those with Caden, Ann Walsh and Philip
Kampf, with Brigid Ruane being 'a real find'.[82] June Levine had
'a huge effect'[83] on Byrne as part of his dream-team, alongside
Julie Parsons and Lorellei Harris, with Alice O'Sullivan and her
own brand of original research coming later.

   According to Caden, when the show began to tackle moral
areas, Irish society had moved on from a situation whereby
programme makers would have been obliged to have a priest
present to participate in the discussions. Now it was paedophile priests going to jail who were being discussed.[84] As noted
earlier, Caden recalled that when *The Gay Byrne Show* began in
the 1970s, radio access was for the elite only, as telephone technology had not yet reached the masses. A decade later *The Gay
Byrne Show* and radio in general were challenging these elites.
The three main pillars of Irish society – the Catholic Church,
the Government and the Gardaí – came under intense scrutiny
from both the print and broadcast media.[85]

   Philip Kampf, as a researcher on the show during the early
1980s, remembers the environment of *The Gay Byrne Show* as
being 'highly competitive'.[86] He recalls heavy pressure bearing
down on the production team not to cover certain controversial

---

[81] Gay Byrne, in interview with the author, 2 September 2011.
[82] *Ibid.*
[83] *Ibid.*
[84] John Caden, in interview with the author, 11 March 2007.
[85] *Ibid.*
[86] Philip Kampf, in interview with the author, 1 September 2011.

areas, most notably the subject of the Artane Boys and institutional abuse – an issue that would emerge over a decade later.[87] Because the show 'came off the back' of the *Morning Ireland* show, it was, according to Kampf, 'incumbent on you to be original', with Caden constantly asking, 'What's the story? Is it logical? Does it add up? Is it genuine and real?'[88]

Kampf notes that the fact that Caden was 'left of centre' and Byrne 'right of centre' was how 'the magic happened'.[89] Caden knew there was more to Byrne: he could not only entertain but also enlighten. Kampf believes Caden had a 'vision rather than an agenda' and that *The Gay Byrne Show* had 'the potential to be significant' over the course of its two hours on air.[90]

Alex White, who would go on to produce the programme in the 1990s, disagrees, and believes Byrne's anti-IRA outbursts on the programme during the 1980s were 'fuelled and influenced' by Caden's Workers' Party ideology on the North.[91] White believed the calibre of debate on the issue of Northern Ireland on the programme was 'abysmal', and he wished to stop all that when he became producer.

White was not the only dissenter regarding Byrne's views on Northern Ireland. Letters to the *Irish Press* reveal an intolerance with Byrne's 'anti-Republican opinions'.[92] One letter writer queries why 'no one else is allowed to argue an alternative point of view rationally' and states that RTÉ should do something

---

[87] St Joseph's Industrial School, Artane, was an industrial school run by the Christian Brothers in Artane, Dublin, from 1870 to 1969. As a result of complaints over a period of decades, the Commission to Inquire into Child Abuse, more commonly known in Ireland as the Ryan Report, was published on 20 May 2009. The Report proclaimed through oral testimony it could state beyond a doubt that the treatment of children in industrial schools was akin to the kind meted out to prison inmates rather than people with legal rights, and that some religious officials encouraged ritual beatings, shielded by their order amid a culture of self-serving secrecy.

[88] Kampf interview 2011, *op. cit.*

[89] *Ibid.*

[90] *Ibid.*

[91] Alex White, in interview with the author, 30 November 2011.

[92] 'Gaybo's Views', letter to the *Irish Press*, 28 March 1989.

about 'this abuse of the license fee.'[93] A journalist with the *Irish Press* also refers to Byrne's 'incessant attacks on republicans on his radio programme' and wonders why Byrne and RTÉ have ignored the ruling of the Broadcasting Complaints Commission when it declared that 'RTÉ must ensure that Gay Byrne state that these are his own and not RTÉ's opinions.'[94]

Deaglán de Brédun, a critic at *The Irish Times*, while acknowledging that Byrne was a 'superb broadcaster', was tired of his oftentimes 'cranky and crotchety' manner on the radio show. He observed that this frequently occurred when Byrne was 'beating that law-and-order drum which he keeps in the studio, underneath the file of newspaper clippings from irate mothers of ten.'[95]

Yet, from a show that was in the light entertainment department in the 1970s, *The Gay Byrne Show* had, by the 1980s, become one of the most important sources of information for listeners. A team of twelve ran the show, with Byrne scanning the *Irish Times, Daily Mail* and *Daily Telegraph* newspapers for items. The content of the show was 99 per cent chosen by the producer, though at the centre of things, in front of the microphone every morning, was Gay Byrne. According to White, Byrne had a personality that could 'engage people and force active involvement. He can cross a huge range of emotions during one programme.'[96]

Topics of the Day from 1986

The wide-ranging content of the show is evident from a programme selection from 1986. A dip into some of the programme content of *The Gay Byrne Show* for that year, catalogued by the RTÉ tapes library, reveals an extraordinary range of in-depth social commentary, intermixed with pure unadulterated fun

---

[93] *Ibid.*

[94] 'Gay Byrne on the North', *Irish Press*, 20 March 1989.

[95] *Irish Times*, 21 September 1982.

[96] Quoted in 'Gay Byrne ushers in twentieth year of RTÉ's most successful radio show', *Irish Times*, 7 September 1992.

and humour. A glance through the calendar months reveals how *The Gay Byrne Show* shaped and reflected popular culture at that time, as Byrne listened to a nation talk. The early months of 1986 were taken up with the issue of unemployment and the thorny subject of working mothers versus stay-at-home mothers. Other items of interest include a light-hearted section on how to catch and marry a wealthy man,[97] a daring section on sex and the elderly,[98] and Byrne's interview with John, a homosexual married man with two children.[99] This latter piece provoked both caller controversy and empathy throughout March of 1986.

In April, programme items on marriage and divorce, calls for the closure of the nuclear plant at Sellafield, and the price of a pint kept the nation talking. The issue of single mothers dominated the programme's agenda in early May,[100] along with the notion of the package holiday and the virtues of the microwave, items that were introduced for the first time on the show.[101] A poignant letter from a woman with two adopted children who said she will 'never forget the pain of wanting a baby'[102] set the nation talking, as did Byrne's interview in October of that year with Jimmy and Gillian Bremner from the BBC studios in Edinburgh, who were involved in the clinical testing for a new contraceptive pill. On that same programme disquiet regarding the health system began to percolate when a woman called Kay told of her twice-cancelled operation, and further controversy arose when journalist John Cummins from the *Irish Press* suggested, tongue-in-cheek, that golf clubs were no place for a woman.[103]

This random programme selection from 1986 provides us with important socio-documentation on public discourse at that time. In fact, listening back to many of the show's broadcasts,

---

[97] *The Gay Byrne Show*, 11 February 1986.

[98] *Ibid.*, 13 February 1986.

[99] *Ibid.*, 10 March 1986.

[100] *Ibid.*, 6/7 May 1986.

[101] *Ibid.*, 13 May 1986.

[102] *Ibid.*, 21 May 1986.

[103] *Ibid.*, 20 November 1986.

a hugely eclectic mixture of content is evident. The apparent random nature of the show contributed to its huge appeal. Most days the show had a listeners' quiz, a mystery sound, and some form of poetry or writing competition. Added to these were book reviews, a resident film reviewer in the form of Maura Clarke, and regular segments where various experts were in studio to take calls from listeners or to answer letter queries, including Colm Rapple on taxation, Noel O'Sullivan on social welfare entitlements, Dr Austin Darragh on medical matters, and Professor Maureen Gaffney on relationships.[104]

Complaining and Congratulating

Throughout the 1980s, certain segments on the radio show provoked controversy. One such item reached the airwaves via letters from scores of mothers who claimed their children's education was being adversely affected by large numbers of teachers absent on maternity leave. The Irish National Teachers Organisation (INTO) was outraged. Its general secretary Gerry Quigley claimed teachers 'were incensed by the one-sided presentation of the issue' on *The Gay Byrne Show*,[105] while Mrs Sylvia Meehan, Chairwoman of the Employment Equality Agency, denounced the attacks on teachers taking maternity leave as 'a blatant contradiction of the pro-life message … in effect they are ordering women to terminate their pregnancies if they wish to continue working.'[106]

Years later, issues concerning childbirth and pregnancy were to emerge even more vocally when the show addressed the Constitutional Amendment on Abortion in 1985. According to Journalist Fintan O'Toole there was 'a civil war' on the issue,[107] yet Byrne never shied away from a challenge.

More controversy raged after a 'technical breach' of Section 31, a law introduced from 1968–94 prohibiting RTÉ from

---

[104] *The Best of The Gay Byrne Show, op. cit.*, 7 April 1999.
[105] 'Gay Byrne Show angers INTO on maternity issue', *Irish Times*, 14 October 1982.
[106] *Ibid.*
[107] *A Cup of Tea, a Sticky Bun and an Hour of Gaybo, op. cit.*

interviewing any spokesperson for Sinn Féin or the IRA. This occurred when a senior Sinn Féin officer, Lydia Comiskey, was interviewed live on the show on an item on emigration, albeit in a personal manner and not as a spokesperson for the organisation.[108] An RTÉ spokeswoman maintained that 'if Sinn Féin chose to mislead production researchers, it is very difficult for RTÉ to prevent it.' She further added that RTÉ 'is not in the business of interrogating people, it is not a security organisation,'[109] in response to accusations that *The Gay Byrne Show* was aware of Ms Comiskey's role within Sinn Féin.

Like *The Late Late Show*, *The Gay Byrne Show* was never far from controversy. On a programme in 1985, Byrne was accused of being biased against the legal profession. According to the *Irish Press*:

Some who listen [to Gay Byrne's radio show] are acutely aware of his power to sway people. From a lesser being a mere adverse opinion on an august institution will draw no response, from Gay Byrne it shakes foundations.[110]

Byrne's unbridled comments were in evidence again in 1986, when *The Gay Byrne Show* linked up with BBC Radio 4. In conversation with Irish broadcaster Tom McGurk, who was hosting the BBC programme, Byrne did not hold back on his views on unemployment, the national debt, 'the Provos and Gerry Adams', ending with the statement: 'Ireland has been cursed with generations of politicians telling us how great we were. Basically we are a rather indolent people.'[111] Byrne also admitted that he would have been better off in Britain, but quipped in typical Gaybo style that he 'would have been run over by a bus.'[112]

It was the persistently pioneering nature of *The Gay Byrne Show* that provides us with a glimpse into Byrne's modus

---

[108] *The Gay Byrne Show*, 23 March 1988.
[109] 'Gay Byrne hosts senior SF officer', *Irish Times*, 24 March 1988.
[110] 'Situation is hopeless says Gay Byrne', *Irish Press*, 2 September 1986.
[111] Gay Byrne, in an interview with Tom McGurk, BBC Radio 4, 8 February 1986.
[112] *Ibid.*

operandi. His refusal at times to back down from issues and to articulate exactly what he felt augments his complex nature; at other times he could appear to have no set opinions or agenda. Byrne's more opinionated side was manifested in 1988 when the issue of legalising pirate radio stations was mooted. Byrne, and RTÉ, feared the loss of jobs and revenue, and he took every opportunity to say so on his radio programme. Fine Gael TD Gay Mitchell was once again incensed by Byrne's interference: 'Gay Byrne has a virtual monopoly, with all his prejudices and all of his points of view, he has media influence in this country… he can be infuriating.'[113] Nevertheless, Byrne continued to talk on issues that even by today's standards would be considered risqué. For example, he spoke with a woman who was married to a gay man, in an interview that was moving and intimate.[114]

The show was equally unequivocal when it came to the thorny subject of consumer rights, continuing on from its pioneering days in the 1970s. In 1986, two researchers from *The Gay Byrne Show* revealed they had obtained, with ease, 'potentially dangerous antibiotics and growth-promoting drugs,'[115] for which they should have had a veterinary prescription. Following these revelations on the show, the Department of Agriculture launched a full investigation into the alleged breaches.

The show also seared through bogus claims of advertisers and marketers. In the 1980s, a decade characterised by mass emigration and high unemployment levels, *The Gay Byrne Show* reflected the country's expectation of value for money. In 1988 it took on board a listener's suggestion to look at cheap airfares by allowing four reporters to travel to London on different airlines on the same day. The reporters all had the same ultimate destination – Trafalgar Square. The results revealed no major time difference between any of the routes, despite high-pressure advertising to the contrary by the various airlines.[116]

---

[113]'RTÉ fears some casualties', *Irish Press*, 6 January 1988.
[114]*The Best of The Gay Byrne Show*, 6 April 1999.
[115]'Drug code breaches to be probed', *Irish Times*, 4 March 1986.
[116]'The Great London air race', *Irish Times*, 29 March 1988.

At other times, the show provided relevant consumer information regarding issues as diverse as playground safety,[117] underage drinking,[118] and the perennial issue of how parents should deal with sexual questions. Agony columnist Angela MacNamara, who was often on hand to provide insights into teenage sexuality, reminded listeners that 'when it came to sex education, boys were far more neglected than girls, as embarrassed fathers adopted a "they can't get pregnant so what the heck" attitude.'[119]

Byrne's bottom line for a story was always, 'Is it going to entertain people? Is it something the woman in Ballyfermot and the woman in Ballyhooley will listen to?'[120] This is reflected in his radio show's humorous consumer report on the length and depth of Sunday sermons.[121] Twenty minutes, Gaybo observed, was far too long to hear one voice and, thus, the script-writing skills of priests were put under public scrutiny. One caller recalled how a local priest who had just delivered a lengthy monologue was quizzed outside the church regarding the piece of newspaper stuck to his chin:

'Well, wasn't I concentrating on my sermon when I cut myself shaving,' the priest explained to the parishioner, who in turn explained to the priest, 'In future, Father, concentrate on the shaving and cut your sermons!'[122]

Homeliness and Hopelessness

The Gay Byrne Show uniquely highlighted the inherent innocence and quaint provincialism that existed in Ireland before the Celtic Tiger and the mobile phone culture it spawned. On 6 December 1988, Marjorie O'Brady from Galway faced a

---

[117]'Playgrounds unsafe, says survey', *Irish Times*, 6 April 1988.
[118]'Vintners share concern over under-age drinking!', *Irish Times*, 14 October 1988.
[119]*The Gay Byrne Show*, 24 January 1989.
[120]Gay Byrne, in interview with the author, 2 September 2011.
[121]*The Gay Byrne Show*, 5 December 1988.
[122]*Ibid.*

communication quandary. Her young son, who had emigrated to London, had been offered a job interview in his home town. He had no phone in London, so Marjorie rang his flatmate Fintan's mother to pass on the message that he must come home immediately for the job interview. However, Fintan had already phoned home earlier that night and wasn't due to ring again until the following week. Fintan's mother did, however, know the number of the public phone box that Fintan had used to call her. Marjorie tried getting through to this phone box 'for ages and ages' until finally a complete stranger answered:

> Could you ever get a message to my son? Yes, I know it's a public phone box and you don't know me from Adam, but he lives around the corner, and could you tell him to phone home? Where's home? Don't worry, he knows where his home is.[123]

It was a very funny, colloquial and warm story. Marjorie's son did ring home half an hour later. Within two days he was back in Galway and had the job.[124]

From the warm provincialism of the Galway mammy to the poignant tale told some weeks later by a woman whose love affair had ended. Here, Gay Byrne was at his best. The woman, who was unmarried, had been seeing a married man. He had two children, 18 and 13 years old, and his wife was five months pregnant. However, the woman knew none of this when he first asked her out. The end of the affair came slowly and painfully: 'He had been working up the courage for such a long time to tell me about this that when he finally did, well, initially I was nonplussed. I was staggered,' said the caller. She even had a 'vague sympathy' for him and for the baby.[125] But Byrne was

---

[123] *Ibid.*, 6 December 1988.
[124] 'Emigrant blues', *Irish Times*, 6 December 1982.
[125] *The Gay Byrne Show*, 28 March 1988.

having none of it. The man was 'a schmuck'[126] said Byrne, and so said all of his female listeners!

Celebrating a Nation

Byrne challenged and cajoled his listeners, all the while explaining and making more palatable the massive changes that had taken place in Ireland over the years. Former producer Alex White maintains that Byrne grew out of a more homogenous Ireland and grew in popularity throughout the decades. He believes Byrne changed with the programme and with society, but still managed to keep a traditional audience. In ways, Byrne was a 'gentle introduction to a changing Ireland for many people.'[127]

However, you cannot affect change without being affected by it, and along with many other RTÉ programmes, *The Gay Byrne Show* began to experience audience erosion due to the emergence of local radio stations. There was something ironic in this, as since the early 1970s Byrne had inadvertently given audiences a prototype for local radio, a way in which people could use radio to talk to each other. Now people around Ireland no longer needed *The Gay Byrne Show* to talk to each other; they had their local radio station. Nonetheless, the real energy that drove *The Gay Byrne Show* was the power of revelation. Byrne gave the nation an outlet to reveal its deepest secrets, and according to journalist Liam Collins:

> People were listening. They were able to pin-point the people in these stories, or if they didn't they knew of someone who did beat their wife, or cheat on their husband or did send their daughter on the boat to England for an abortion. He brought it all out in the open. But he didn't

---

[126] *Ibid.*
[127] *Ibid.*

do it for any great political or intellectual reasons. He did
it because it was riveting radio.[128]

Byrne charted social change on a daily basis, and the show
was very dogged in its pursuit of certain issues. Throughout
the 1980s, the topic of emigration was a recurrent one. There
were the happier stories, such as the success story of journalist
Olivia O'Leary who returned from a career in London to work
with RTÉ, and the more tragic tales of illegal emigrants in the
USA.[129] Yet, times were rapidly changing, and some listeners
wanted more than Byrne's perceived familiarity and wholesome homeliness.

Changing Audiences

In the mid-1980s, Byrne was complimented on the altruistic
nature of his show, with one letter writer to the *Irish Press* prais-
ing and thanking him for 'the good work he is doing'.[130] Another
letter writer commented on his 'great charm and conviviality'
on *The Gay Byrne Show*. In her view, Byrne was 'a real power
in this land – far above any Taoiseach, Tánaiste or President,
because he can talk to anyone and shows interest in people and
that is what it is all about, isn't it?'[131]

By 1988, the honey-voiced host had been going strong on
the radio for 15 years, with producer John Caden confidently
asserting, 'People never tire of Gay. Shows may come and go
but Gay goes on forever.'[132]

But nothing lasts forever. That autumn Julie Parsons took
over as senior producer, and the programme was about to
change direction again. Parsons believed there was too much
talk on radio and felt it was important that *The Gay Byrne Show*

---

[128]'He lifted the lid with Gay abandon', *Sunday Independent*, 8 September 2004.
[129]*Ibid.*
[130]'A helping hand', letter to the *Irish Press*, 7 March 1985.
[131]'Please don't go, Gay', letter to the *Irish Press*, 27 March 1985.
[132]'Radio show anniversary', *Irish Press*, 6 February 1988.

provide entertainment. Her mission was 'to bring a smile to the lips of the nation … after *Morning Ireland* and the *News*,' as the audience deserved 'a bit of light relief'.[133]

For his part, Byrne was unhappy with the 'rotten' radio scheduling, suggesting *The Gay Byrne Show* should be followed by 'a light music programme', instead of more talk with *The Pat Kenny Show*.[134] And so, little by little, *The Gay Byrne Show* audience began to slowly implode, as listeners sought more provocative themes.

On 16 September 1988, as Byrne was discussing anorexia, the tracing of a father, education and allergies, Gerry Ryan on RTÉ 2 was proffering an improbable mix of Jack the Ripper stories and experiments on condoms. JNLR[135] figures from 1988 show that Byrne had 670,000 listeners, three out of four of whom were over 35, while Ryan had 125,000 regular listeners, four out of five of whom were under 35. On age profile alone, Ryan's younger-based audience had the most potential to expand. By the late 1980s, the notion of the taciturn father and martyred mother upon which Byrne had built his radio listenership was beginning to sound trite and tiresome. Although it would be another decade before Byrne would bid a final adieu to his radio show, he was mindful, as always, of the dangers of overestimating one's importance:

> There is always a danger, I notice it in some of the younger fellows coming in. Within a few weeks they start believing their own publicity. That is the most dangerous thing that can happen to anybody in our business. Once you start believing the bullshit, you're in grave danger.[136]

Contrasts between *The Gay Byrne Show* and *The Gerry Ryan Show* centred on the vastly differing broadcasting styles of both

[133]'"Rotten" radio scheduling, says Gay Byrne', *Irish Times*, 8 September 1988.
[134]*Ibid.*
[135]Joint National Listenership Ratings.
[136]'Gaybo – He's back and he's still the king of broadcasting', interview with Gay Byrne in *RSVP* magazine, February 2012.

presenters, as outlined here by Gavin Duffy, founder of the award-winning local radio station LMFM:

> Gay Byrne could read a script so fluently he sounded like he was ad-libbing. Gerry Ryan could ad-lib so fluently he could have been reading a script.[137]

Ryan's radio show was becoming increasingly relevant for a younger, altogether more demanding modern nation. The Ireland that had tuned into *The Gay Byrne Show* in its early years was an insular place, a country full of secrets. By the end of the 1980s, the show was no longer needed, as all the nation's secrets came tumbling out anyway. Byrne no longer fitted the bill of the cheeky choirboy, the thirty-something upstart with the sixties sideburns. He was now the grey-haired, middle-aged 'Uncle Gaybo'. The grand era of monolithic broadcasting – an age which Byrne so clearly symbolised – was over. *The Gay Byrne Show* was swamped by competing stations, and some listeners tired of the five days each week of Byrne's 'consoling, advising, chastising and reminiscing,'[138] with others wondering why the listening public was 'so obsessed by the man'. RTÉ was urged to face the reality that 'Gaybo is not immortal' and that 'someone will have to take over his mantle.'[139]

But finding a successor for Byrne, for both his radio and television shows, was still almost a decade off. Both shows endured throughout the 1990s, and the issue of inheriting Byrne's 'mantle' was not resolved without a measure of controversy and public debate. More importantly, would both *The Gay Byrne Show* and *The Late Late Show* remain significant barometers of Irish life, without their host, the ever-challenging Gay Byrne? Changes to *The Gay Byrne Show* in particular showed that its remit as 'the pulse of the nation' was gradually losing sway in

---

[137]'How King Gerry beat local radio pretenders', *Sunday Independent*, 9 February 2010.
[138]'Time for Gay to go?', *Irish Press*, 31 August 1989.
[139]*Ibid.*

an increasingly multicultural and rapidly changing Ireland. The next chapter will look at the gradual demise of *The Gay Byrne Show* as its host prepared to exit mainstream radio, but not Irish life, forever.

5

Hosting the Nation: The Final Years of *The Gay Byrne Show* (1990–1998)

By the 1990s, despite competition from newer and more modern radio shows, *The Gay Byrne Show*, which did not broadcast throughout the summer months, was still hugely popular, as evidenced by the many letters sent to Irish newspapers whenever its popularity was queried. On one occasion accusations of 'shameless voyeurism', 'odious narcissism', 'arrogant self-righteousness' and 'sensationalism' were levelled against the show.[1] Listeners swiftly rushed to the show's defence in the letters pages of *The Irish Times*. These included the following samples:

> Sir,
>
> Mr Conroy queries the popularity of the Gay Byrne radio show. The answer is both simple and obvious. A dedicated team, attention to detail and the consummate professional Gay Byrne. Next question![2]

---

[1] Letters to the Editor, *Irish Times*, 22 March 1993.
[2] *Ibid.*, 27 March 1993.

Sir,

The answer to Mr Conroy's question as to why the Gay Byrne radio programme remains so popular is because he has allowed people to raise issues and describe harrowing experiences, which those who do not wish to know about would like to dismiss as 'auld blather'. Without his programme, there are issues that would still be safely out of sight and out of mind, and many people would have continued to suffer in silence.[3]

Gaybo versus the Ryan Line

Added to these laudatory comments, a JNLR survey in June 1990 revealed *The Gay Byrne Show* was the second most listened to programme on RTÉ radio (after *Morning Ireland*), with 48 per cent of housewives tuning in.[4] This was in contrast to the 14 per cent listening to Gerry Ryan, the 32-year-old former rock DJ with a ponytail, whose radio show was launched in March 1988. Nevertheless, *The Gerry Ryan Show* (aka the 'Ryan Line') was beginning to compete more aggressively with *The Gay Byrne Show*.

Ryan had from the very start become master of the intimate conversation and was beginning to worry Byrne, who was aware of his rival's appeal. The veteran broadcaster complained in an *Irish Times* interview in September 1988 that both radio presenters were 'dipping into the same bucket.'[5] Byrne seemed rattled by Ryan. The latter's three-hour programme, which ran until his untimely death in April 2010, enjoyed huge listenership figures, largely due to his off-beat fascinations and sexual innuendos.

Ryan, who liked to think of radio as 'eavesdropping on dirty talk'[6] was Gay Byrne for those under 35. By the late 1980s he

---

3   *Ibid.*
4   'RTÉ scores strongly in major survey on listenership', *Irish Times*, 29 June 1990.
5   'A brilliant character who earned our trust', *Irish Times*, 4 May 2010.
6   *Ibid.*

had seized a market where consumers wanted their talk sexier, brasher and more emotionally intense. It was based on the US style of radio known as Zoo Radio – a vibrant, irreverent and unpredictable style of on-air presentation.[7] Ryan proved to be more liberal, more urban and more colloquial in style than Byrne, and this added to his appeal for younger audiences. Ryan was fascinated by the unpredictability of radio and the rush to the airwaves by listeners wanting their voices to be heard, an observation which still rings true in twenty-first century Ireland:

> It's that magical mixture of debating sensitive issues like health cuts or adoption one minute, then suddenly you find yourself in some mad discussion about battery chickens. And it's also democratic radio from the point of view that people are given a platform to air their views. Irish people don't complain to their TDs or to the relevant service or authority, yet they will come on air because the radio is there and say: damn it, all I have to do is lift the phone and tell Gerry Ryan about it.[8]

Ryan's candid telephone techniques in the early years of his show landed him in hot water. On a programme in October 1989 he phoned the Department of the Environment live on air, seeking advice on how to dispose of his fridge without damaging the ozone layer. The questionable ethics of putting an official live on air unbeknownst to him was the stuff of Ryan's tabloid radio style – a style quite contrary to Byrne's almost avuncular and traditional approach.

By 1990, Ryan had defeated Byrne in catching the 16–34 age group in the Dublin area.[9] The show had taken on the quality

---

[7] The name comes from Morning Zoo. This is the format of morning radio shows common in English-language radio broadcasting. The name is derived from the 'wackiness and zaniness' of the activities and overall personalities of the show and its hosts.

[8] Gerry Ryan, *Would the Real Gerry Ryan Please Stand Up* (Penguin Ireland: Dublin, 2008), p. 66.

[9] 'JNLR figures released', *Irish Times*, 17 April 1990.

of an addictive soap opera, with its regular contributors such as Terence the agony uncle, the three barflies who talked in tangents, and dietician Denise Sweeney, who would drop in for daft competitions such as a 'smell-the-cheese' phone-in.[10] In contrast, Byrne would read out twenty letters per programme, in a dry, safe way, interspersed with funny voices. Ryan rarely used letters, instead allowing the steady stream of phone calls to shape and mould the show, a much riskier style of broadcasting that would yield huge dividends for the outspoken presenter.

Like Byrne, Ryan brought in huge audience figures, in spite of the stiff competition from local radio stations. Unlike Byrne, he could calculatedly admit or feign ignorance on any subject before becoming an instant expert. Although both presenters were facing the serious challenge posed by the advent of local radio, Ryan met the challenge head-on, as outlined here by former director of local radio station LMFM[11] Gavin Duffy. He recalls how Paul Claffey of Midwest Radio began to make a breakthrough by opening his talk-radio show with death notices. Soon all local radio stations began broadcasting death notices from 9.00 a.m. to compete with Ryan and Byrne. In early 1993, irked by the loss of listeners from the first half of his programme, Ryan decided to devote an entire programme to death notices and death and asked callers to ring in with their dream funeral arrangements. Duffy recounts the response to this particular programme:

> Along with those wishing to have their ashes cast over the Cliffs of Moher, or to be buried under the goalposts at Croke Park, was a gem – a caller infamously declared his dream internment would be to be buried up to his bollocks in Bibi Baskin.[12] Long before Twitter or the net, the entire nation was abuzz that day, everyone asking 'did you hear

---

[10] Ryan, *op. cit.*, p. 37.

[11] LMFM is a local radio station in the midlands of Ireland.

[12] Bibi Baskin is a former RTÉ presenter who hosted her own Saturday-night talk show, *The Bibi Baskin Show*, in the early 1990s on RTÉ television.

the guy on *The Gerry Ryan Show*?' King Gerry had wrestled back his crown from the local radio pretenders.[13]

However, the gradual demise of *The Gay Byrne Show* was never simply due to the challenge posed by Ryan's antics on the Ryan Line or the rise in popularity of local radio. There was also the issue of the housewives of Ireland entering the workforce at a rapid pace. Figures compiled by the Central Statistics Office for the period 1992–5 indicate that approximately seventy thousand women returned to work. Many of these women had listened to *The Gay Byrne Show* every morning. Alongside the loss of this core audience, by the 1990s broadcasters had acquired 'the right of entry into the bedroom of the nation.'[14] Secret fantasies and desires, which once lay too deep for utterance, were now being shared with the world. Radio critic Tom O'Dea believed that Byrne got his message across by a mixture of subtlety and innuendo, while Gerry Ryan had a 'rough mouth'.[15]

When a woman rang Byrne in 1990 to say that her daughter was on the pill and had a boyfriend, he asked, using the old-fashioned language of nudge and wink, 'Do you think they're up to something?' His language went to the heart of the question, but it left the worried and confused mother with the shreds of her dignity still about her. In O'Dea's view, 'If Gay Byrne's greatest contribution as a broadcaster has been to sweep aside the taboos that kept certain matters from being discussed on air, it is equally arguable that Gerry Ryan's most noticeable effect has been to coarsen the very language and content of broadcasting itself.'[16]

Byrne's on-air language may well have been more dignified than that of Ryan's – a fact that is hardly surprising given their very different ages and backgrounds – however, like Ryan, Byrne himself never veered from controversy. In January 1990,

---

[13] 'Why Irish life will be poorer without Gerry', *Evening Herald*, 5 May 2010.
[14] 'Sex is in the air', *Irish Independent*, 28 April 1990.
[15] *Ibid.*
[16] *Ibid.*

Byrne spent a whole week tapping into the pulse of the nation and finding out their views on homosexuality. Civil liberties campaigner David Norris (now a senator)[17] spoke eloquently about the phobias and untruths regarding gay people. He had become increasingly agitated by remarks and letters to the show regarding the 'homosexual act'. 'There is,' explained Norris, 'no such thing as a homosexual act. I think this is a rather low argument – it's an attempt to embarrass people by particularising physical intimacies between them.'[18] On Thursday, 18 January 1990, the show ran a day-long telephone poll. Of the ten thousand respondents, 66 per cent were in favour of legalising gay sex.[19] Byrne recognised it was not a highly scientific method. However, it did place the debate regarding the rights of gay males near the top of the political agenda for many months after.

These types of challenging programmes helped keep listenership figures of *The Gay Byrne Show* high in the 1990s. Nonetheless, it was the addition to the show's team in September 1990 of a working-class young man from Ballyfermot in Dublin's north side that would help steer *The Gay Byrne Show* in a more exciting and dynamic direction.

Joe Duffy, the Only Male Producer on *The Gay Byrne Show*

The arrival of Joe Duffy, who left his role as a producer on *The Pat Kenny Show*[20] to join *The Gay Byrne Show* as its only male producer, vastly improved the show's appeal. The move to *The Gay Byrne Show* was, according to Duffy, 'more dangerous than scaling the Berlin Wall.' He was seen as a 'big girl's blouse' for defecting to the women's programme.[21] For 'Huffy Duffy, the roving reporter with the motor-mouth Dublin wit,'[22] this decision

---

[17] Norris lectured in Trinity College Dublin in the 1980s and was a tireless campaigner for civil liberties for homosexuals.

[18] *The Gay Byrne Show*, 16 January 1990.

[19] *Ibid.*

[20] A morning radio show presented by Pat Kenny.

[21] Joe Duffy, *Just Joe: My Autobiography* (Transworld Ireland: Dublin, 2011), p. 248.

[22] 'Radio review: The Me Decade', *Irish Times*, 12 December 1989.

to become part of the *Gay Byrne Show* team would make him a household name.[23] When attempting to get into RTÉ, Duffy had highlighted his different background, his experience as a social worker, even emphasising his 'lack of journalistic or broadcasting experience as a positive.'[24] However, his real motivation was to work with Gay Byrne, whose work ethic, determination and focus he found inspiring. Indeed Byrne's daily routine was truly impressive, outlined here by Duffy:

> After having already opened his mail and attended to his duties as producer of the *The Late Late Show*, Byrne would arrive into the radio centre at the exact same time every morning, 8.11 am, and after heading down to Studio 6 at 8.20 to prepare his show, apart from a good morning, even if you won the lotto, you did not converse.[25]

Many innovations were introduced during Duffy's tenure as roving reporter on *The Gay Byrne Show*. These included the daily use of a mobile phone to link up with Gay in the studio, as well as the outside broadcasts and 'workers' playtime', a concept Duffy borrowed from the UK and introduced into Irish broadcasting. It began in canteens throughout Britain in 1941 and was a 'mixture of morale-boosting comedy and music' presented by the employees of a firm from their workplace and broadcast nationally.[26]

During his time on the show, Duffy received a Jacobs Award[27] and also got to see the world. Highlights included Sydney with Irish emigrants at Christmas, Moscow for St Patrick's Day, and an Irish walk along the Great Wall of China, not forgetting New York for the 1994 World Cup! However, it was at home where the real magic happened, as Duffy gained access to public

---

[23] Duffy, *op. cit.*, p. 252.
[24] *Ibid.*
[25] *Ibid.*, p. 253.
[26] *Ibid.*, p. 259.
[27] Duffy's piece on Bertha, the oldest cow in Ireland, won him a Jacobs Award in 1993.

institutions and illuminated hitherto unseen areas of Irish life and culture. He conducted interviews from inside the walls of Arbour Hill and Mountjoy prisons in Dublin; he visited the Poor Clares' convent in County Clare, an enclosed order of nuns; he broadcast the incredibly illuminating interview with Professor Anthony Clare from inside St Patrick's Psychiatric Hospital in Dublin; and one of his most memorable and harrowing interviews was with convicted paedophile priest Father Brendan Smyth.[28] All of these are testament to Duffy's ingenuity and expertise as an interviewer, but more significant is the fact that they allow an insight into the measure of his mentor. Byrne understood the heartbeat of the nation and was, according to Duffy, 'fearless' in his approach to excellence in broadcasting, welcoming provocative topics.[29]

Revelations and Relationships

By the early 1990s the show was covering issues as diverse as the Maastricht Treaty to sexual problems and consumer complaints. It was also administering The Gay Byrne Fund, which could hold as much as IR£100,000 at a time.

But a sad reminder of the bleaker side of Ireland's social history came in 1992, when 37-year-old Christine Buckley spoke to Byrne about the years of abuse she had suffered at the hands of the Sisters of Mercy congregation at St Vincent's Industrial School within the Goldenbridge Convent at Inchicore in Dublin. The interview evoked a torrent of responses from others who had suffered similar treatment. Reaction to Christine Buckley's interview on *The Gay Byrne Show* was articulated in the 2009 publication of the report of the Commission to Inquire into Child Abuse (CICA), commonly referred to as the Ryan Report, over 17 years after the

---

[28] No recording devices were allowed in Magilligan Prison in Derry where Smyth was imprisoned on child abuse charges: Joe Duffy, in interview with the author, 11 November 2011.

[29] Joe Duffy, in interview with the author, 11 February 2012.

issue was first highlighted on *The Gay Byrne Show*.[30] Louis Lentin's documentary film *Dear Daughter* was also an important by-product of Buckley's interview. According to Lentin, *Dear Daughter* 'has enabled hundreds to break silence and reveal their brutalised childhoods in orphanages throughout the country.'[31]

By 1992, the show was a little over twenty years old. From a one-hour show of music, phone-ins and greetings, it had evolved into a two-hour information programme. Byrne was hosting wide-ranging discussions on myriad forms of relationships on the show, and these provided a fascinating socio-cultural insight into Ireland at that time. Interviews included those with former Ireland rugby coach Mick Doyle, who spoke about his marriage break-up. However, it was Byrne's daring interview with 'Stephen', a practising paedophile who admitted to having had over 150 'relationships' and to 'picking up' boys aged between 13 and 17 in public toilets, that provoked a huge public reaction.[32] The *Kerryman* newspaper accused Byrne of 'going overboard in the licence he gave his guest … who was allowed time to justify his perversion in a most persuasive and sickening way.'[33] The programme was accused of stooping to sensationalist and irresponsible journalism by the Chief Executive of the Irish Society for the Prevention of Cruelty to Children, Mr Cian O'Tighearnaigh:

> There would appear to be an emerging view in live media that a journalistic balance is about giving a platform to anybody you see fit and balancing it with a counterviewpoint. Viewpoints which incite to violence, criminal activity or abuse are not acceptable in the media.[34]

---

[30] *The Gay Byrne Show*, 8 February 1992.

[31] 'Doubting the orphanage victims' truthfulness only betrays them again', *Irish Times*, 5 April 1996.

[32] *The Gay Byrne Show*, 22 November 1994.

[33] 'New low for Gay Byrne Show', *Kerryman*, 4 December 1994.

[34] 'Garda stop man after radio admission of paedophilia', *Irish Times*, 26 November 1994.

In contrast, the *Irish Times* Social Affairs Correspondent Padraig O'Morain wrote that Byrne was providing an important public service in broadcasting the interview and believed that Byrne has been criticised for being too 'soft' on the man, but 'to this listener's ear, Gay Byrne radiated disapproval throughout this interview.'[35] The interview also caused much debate within RTÉ at the time, with Deputy General Mr Bobby Gahan opposed to its being broadcast. Nevertheless, it was approved by Director of Radio Mr Kevin Healy.[36]

Less than a year later, in May 1995, Joe Duffy broadcast live from a transvestites' club in Dublin and spoke with two married, heterosexual men who went there regularly in women's clothes to 'talk like women' for an hour or two. While Duffy asked rather tentative and anodyne questions, Byrne back in the studio raised more awkward issues regarding sexual arousal and the reaction of their wives, questions which listeners at home were eager to ask.[37] The programme was thought-provoking and informative, without a hint of prurience, due no doubt to the rigorous and sensitive research of the *Gay Byrne Show* team and Byrne's own instincts as a broadcaster. In contrast, Duffy's attempt in 1995 to interview Pia and Linda, a pair of business-minded prostitutes, was not well-received by an *Irish Times* critic who claimed it contributed little to our understanding of the complexities of prostitution but did dispel the cliché of 'whore with a heart of gold' in favour of 'madam with an MBA!'[38]

Of course, Byrne did not always get it right. In 1994, the media went into a frenzy with the revelations that Fr Michael Cleary, a very popular and media-savvy Catholic priest, had fathered a child some twenty years previously. The *Irish Press* was critical of Byrne's interest in the scandal 'and the man barely cold in his grave.'[39] Byrne, who accused the media of 'muck-raking'

---

[35] 'Paedophile interview informed the public', *Irish Times*, 28 November 1994.

[36] 'RTÉ's director general approved interview', *Irish Times*, 3 December 1994.

[37] *The Gay Byrne Show,* 10 October 1994.

[38] 'Trotting out the oldest profession', *Irish Times*, 23 May 1995.

[39] 'Can Gaybo have it both ways?', *Irish Press*, 14 January 1994.

by publishing stories by unnamed sources, was in turn attacked for having double standards, with the newspaper querying why 'the item was the first one on the show.'[40]

That same year *The Gay Byrne Show* made a 'slithereen of Irish radio history'[41] when it broadcast on a weekend for the first time for its annual Christmas extravaganza from Dublin's Grafton Street, a permanent event on the Irish national calendar.

In effect, *The Gay Byrne Show* was becoming increasingly eclectic, with items as diverse as recipes to public confessionals, all attempting to maintain its listenership. Byrne even made his singing debut on air in 1995 with a rendition of George Formby's famous tune 'Leaning on a Lampost',[42] as part of a gala concert going out live on *The Gay Byrne Show*. The audience loved what appeared to be the ad hoc nature of the show, and listeners were eager for its return after each summer off the air.

Revamp of *The Gay Byrne Show*

By 1994, the show was gradually descending into a marked decline, primarily because Byrne, due to health reasons, had announced that he wished to cut down on his workload. Names of would-be presenters were bandied about, but a senior producer in RTÉ (rather prophetically) made the following statement to the *Irish Press* in March of that year:

> There is no way that you could have the kind of programme the 'Gay Byrne Show' without Gay himself. It's not just about being a morning chat show. The audience that it holds is largely as a result of Gay's own personality, and I don't think that anyone else could keep the same number of people tuning in, morning after morning.[43]

---

[40] *Ibid.*

[41] 'The GB Show on a Saturday?', *Irish Times*, 24 December 1994.

[42] 'Gaybo's singing debut', *Irish Times*, 5 January 1992.

[43] 'To whom it concerns', *Irish Press*, 5 March 1994.

It was eventually decided that from September 1994, Byrne would present the show on Wednesdays, Thursdays and Fridays only, with Duffy taking over as host on Mondays and Tuesdays. Duffy was replaced in 1996 by former 2fm DJ Gareth O'Callaghan. RTÉ had tried to revamp the show in June 1996. The most obvious manifestation of the revamp was the swapping of the Gay Byrne and Pat Kenny slots. Less obvious was the decision not to allow Byrne to cover more weighty material. Kenny, on *Today with Pat Kenny*, was now given first shot at the heavier, potentially controversial stories. Byrne resisted pressure to do a more music-driven show. Nevertheless, by 1996 the ethos of the show had changed utterly, and the production team was made up of showbiz rather than current affairs people.

According to RTÉ presenter Ronan Kelly, this contrasted audibly with the golden age of producer John Caden:

> When he had John Caden as his producer – someone with a serious commitment to public service broadcasting – the radio show had huge scope and range. All human life was there.[44]

By 1998 Byrne had signalled his decision to depart *The Gay Byrne Show* by December of that year. This allowed the then Head of Radio Helen Shaw[45] to make radical schedule changes. According to Shaw, by 1997 '*The Gay Byrne Show* was already in sharp decline' and had 'changed dramatically'.[46] She believed it needed to be reconfigured, but the job-sharing with Gareth O'Callaghan 'was too radical', and the show was 'dying on its feet as a phenomenon.' Gareth and Gay 'were the wrong match', and Shaw believed there was no integration between their separate parts of the show. She felt she had 'a duty of care' to Byrne's faithful radio audience, and by commissioning highlights of past shows, called *The Best of The Gay Byrne Show*, she

---

[44] Ronan Kelly, in interview with the author, 1 September 2011.
[45] Helen Shaw was Head of Radio at RTÉ 1, 1997–2004.
[46] Helen Shaw, in interview with the author, 14 March 2012.

believed the show could go back to one hour a week and go out 'with a bang'. Her remit essentially was to bring 'Gaybo back into people's lives' and 'show how special the show was, to define it, to celebrate it.'

Shaw had come from a news background, having served time as Director of Current Affairs on RTÉ radio's flagship programmes *Today at 5* and *Saturday Review*. She was aware that no one in the show's production team wished to confront the issue of its decline, but she was adamant that she did not want the show 'to fade away'. Her whole concern was to make the show as strong as possible. She did not want it to 'become less' before Byrne's retirement. To this end, she restructured the production team, putting in staff such as Ronan O'Donohue, who had just come from his role as Editor of *The Pat Kenny Show*. Shaw knew Byrne wanted to retire, so having him return to a five-day week or even moving the show to a weekend slot would not work for him. According to Shaw, Byrne wished to go out 'on a high'. For her part, she wanted to ensure that he would go back to 'being relevant', once more hosting 'the conversations of the day'.[47]

Former researcher Alice O'Sullivan was commissioned to put together *The Best of The Gay Byrne Show*. Her task was to bring on board top producers and researchers as part of Shaw's plan to 'bring Gaybo back into people's lives'.

Speaking on *Liveline* with Joe Duffy in 1998, Byrne said:

> What I've agreed with Helen Shaw and the DG [Director General] is that I'll do the radio programme until Christmas, and then I think it'll be a good time to call it a day, and I've also agreed to do *The Late Late Show* for one more season and call it a day on that as well.[48]

When Duffy asked Byrne what his formula was, after spending 26 years at the top of his game, Byrne replied: 'I haven't

---

[47] *Ibid.*

[48] Gay Byrne speaking to Joe Duffy on *Liveline*, 7 April 1998.

the faintest idea.'[49] He said *The Gay Byrne Show* had taken off from the word go. At one point it had 860,000 listeners, and it was 'like a huge village getting together every morning. But we couldn't keep up in the new circumstances. People will always find local radio, in certain respects, more congenial.'[50]

The Demise of *The Gay Byrne Show*

It was not just local radio that was to prove challenging to *The Gay Byrne Show*, however. By 1998 Radio Ireland had been re-launched under the new name Today FM, and with popular presenters such as Ian Dempsey and Ray D'Arcy, the station was providing an alternative national voice to RTÉ radio. *The Gay Byrne Show* was also facing competition from the raucous exhibitionism of Gerry Ryan, as well as the less flamboyant style of public confessional on the *Liveline* phone-in show, now presented by Byrne's former co-host and protégé, Joe Duffy. Now-deceased journalist Jonathan Philbin Bowman wrote:

> Who is the most powerful man in the country … Bertie Ahern? Wrong. The new centre of power in our now whingocracy is in RTE's Radio building, from where Joe Duffy dispenses justice, favours and distils demands each weekday from 1.45.[51]

There was also the sense that Irish life was changing rapidly by the close of the 1990s. Journalist Fintan O'Toole has written about the sense of loss of community in Ireland. It would be too ambitious to assume the end of *The Gay Byrne Show* in 1998 contributed to this 'separatist society' that O'Toole refers to.[52] However, while the show remained on air, it reminded people

---

[49] *Ibid.*

[50] Christine Newman, 'Byrne leaving *The Late Late Show* at end of season', *Irish Times*, 11 September 1998.

[51] 'Talking to Joe', *Sunday Independent*, 12 December 1999.

[52] Fintan O'Toole, ed., *The Irish Times Book of the Century: 1990–1999* (Newleaf: NY, 1999).

of the importance of community and of openness. It was this distinctive quality – that of absorbing popular culture and re-playing it back to its listeners in its own unique manner – that made *The Gay Byrne Show* such essential listening.

The show remained popular right into the 1990s, and its ultimate demise was not attributed to a decline in listenership[53] but rather, according to former *Gay Byrne Show* producers Parsons and Kelly, the fact that 'Gay was not interested in it anymore.'[54] Byrne still presented *The Late Late Show*, and the workload was taking a toll on his health. Therefore, it seemed wise to scale back his hours.

It could also be contended that by the 1990s, the format of *The Gerry Ryan Show* was more suited to the changing social climate. More people now listened to the radio in their cars rather than at home. This notion of 'people on the move' heralded a new era of Irish broadcasting. It was no longer necessary to fill those empty mornings for mothers who were at home caring for their children. Ireland was embracing change and moving rapidly towards the era of the Celtic Tiger. Scandal and sound bites were, it seemed, all listeners had time for.

For many, the show had lost its relevance. At the beginning of the 1980s the programme was bold and pioneering in its style and intent, and it responded to many of the social and political events of that time. The emergence of cases such as that of Eileen Flynn[55] and Ann Lovett provoked a huge public response, and *The Gay Byrne Show* used these events to begin a debate on issues such as unmarried mothers, relationships and

---

[53] Ronan Kelly and Julie Parsons, in interview with University College Cork undergraduate student Jennifer Walsh on 12 January 2006 for her undergraduate dissertation on the *The Gay Byrne Show*.

[54] *Ibid.*

[55] In 1982, Eileen Flynn, a teacher at the Holy Faith Convent in New Ross, Co. Wexford, was dismissed from her job for being pregnant while unmarried. She was living with her partner, Richie Roche, the father of the child, who was separated from his wife. Divorce was illegal at that time. Ms Flynn, who died in September 2008, took unfair dismissal cases to the Employment Appeal Tribunal, the Circuit Court and the High Court, but she lost all cases. Her dismissal became a cause célèbre in the 1980s in Ireland.

sexual practices in Ireland. However, despite the show's ability to mediate and, at times, serve as a catalyst for change in Irish life, by the time of its departure from the airwaves in 1998, Ireland had become a 'post-modern' society.[56]

Commentators have noted Byrne's inability to move with that fast-paced society that embraced Ireland in the 1990s. Nonetheless, in contrast to *The Gerry Ryan Show*, Byrne's radio programme has contributed more overtly and more significantly to much debate and discussion in the public sphere, especially in its earlier years where it remained unchallenged by other indigenous radio talk shows.[57]

It has been argued that Byrne was in some respects the architect of his own demise, especially with the decision to opt for the split-shift format on his radio show. Others felt that when he swapped slots with Pat Kenny, he didn't bring his listeners with him. It has been claimed that in the final incarnation of *The Gay Byrne Show,* Byrne was surprisingly and admirably devoted to older listeners. It was as if Byrne and his team recognised the new pluralism of the country, and of the radio market, and selected as listeners the people who had been with him all along.

There were also rumours at the time of his departure from RTÉ radio that Byrne could have clinched a deal with Rupert Murdoch and gone digital with Sky Television. Radio producer Seamus Hosey once commented on Byrne's utter lack of ego on radio, in contrast to many other broadcasters. Hosey was particularly impressed with the ability Byrne had 'to literally disappear, so that he would not appear to be bigger than his subject.'[58]

In 1998, former senator Brendan Ryan, while paying tribute to Byrne's obvious technical and broadcasting abilities,

---

[56] Richard Kearney, *Post-Nationalist Ireland: Politics, Culture and Philosophy* (Routledge: London, 1996), p. 151.

[57] Sara O'Sullivan, 'Understanding Irish Talk Radio: A Quantitative and Qualitative Case Study of the Gerry Ryan Show', University College Dublin, 2000 (unpublished thesis).

[58] 'The return of radio's pioneering maiden aunt', *Irish Times*, 13 June 2002.

nonetheless felt Byrne never really tackled the real issues on his radio programme. Ryan observed:

> Byrne was convinced that we were being completely overburdened with tax. And if you tried to counter that argument with figures, he'd dismiss it as boring. He was safe dealing with the issues that annoyed him, not the issues that annoyed Irish society.[59]

Ryan also criticises Byrne's handling of the crime issue, an aspect of Irish life that was hugely controversial in 1990s Ireland:

> I don't believe he ever did a programme that tackled white-collar crime, or crime in business. You had all this evidence on corruption. And nothing was ever done about it.[60]

As for Byrne's celebrated jousts with the Catholic Church, Ryan makes the following point:

> Byrne was safe in his liberal constituency. He was in a liberal compound in Montrose ... And he was always wrong about the North. He believed that if only the IRA went away, the problem would be solved ... Once people like Albert Reynolds, with help from Haughey, began to think like that the problem began to be resolved. But it was done in the teeth of opposition from the liberal establishment of which Gay Byrne was a leading member.[61]

With the exception of Joe Duffy's controversial interview with paedophile priest Brendan Smyth in 1994 and Bono's call to the programme on 27 March 1990 in which he professed an urge 'to moon all over LA' – such was his delight following Brenda Fricker and Daniel Day-Lewis's Oscar awards for the Irish film

---

[59] 'Going, Going, Going', *Magill*, 10 December 1998.
[60] *Ibid.*
[61] *Ibid.*

My Left Foot – a glance through the programme content from 1994 through to 1998 reveals a less innovative and challenging show, leaving behind rather dull programme transcripts, such as the following:

> An Post will send 100 cassettes to America for free as a promotion for *The Gay Byrne Show*. People can record a set of sounds from home for loved ones in America.

> Mrs O'Reilly is to be cremated after she dies; she says you have to buy the coffin you are cremated in. She wants to know if you can rent one anywhere. A listener is annoyed that Mary Robinson is set to reduce her staff. The listener urges all politicians to take action and let the planes refuel in Shannon.[62]

Moreover, the eclectic mixture of light and dark had disappeared from the latter years of *The Gay Byrne Show*, with Byrne's interest in politics becoming more evident through the type of newspaper headlines that caught his eye in the 'In the Papers' section of the programme. However, it was his interview with former British Prime Minister Margaret Thatcher that highlighted the flagging energies of the host. The interview proved controversial not due to its content but as a result of the apparent obsequiousness of Byrne's interviewing style, as indicated here from the letters page of *The Irish Times*:

> Sir,

> Gay Byrne's recent radio interview with Lady Margaret Thatcher was remarkable for the gentle manner in which Mr Byrne treated his august guest. His voice was hushed and reverential, and at times scarcely audible. His attitude bordered on the servile and was a source of embarrassment to many listeners, even to those who are ardent

---

[62] RTÉ Tapes Library.

admirers of the former British Prime Minister. His handling of the Thatcher interview was in marked contrast with his conduct of the Annie Murphy interview on the 'Late Late Show' last year, when his truculence raised a storm of protest from fair-minded people from all walks of life. Perhaps Mr Byrne learned from these protests and has decided to project a more gentle image. Or could it be that he sets out to condemn and antagonise only in situations where he feels confident that he can dominate without fear of retaliation?

Yours, etc.[63]

The *Irish Press* also took issue with Byrne's interviewing style:

Gaybo will be only fooling himself if he looks back on this as one of his better interviews. His style has always been more inquisitive than interrogatory, anyway, but as Thatcher was allowed to blow lengthy trumpet solos with but the mildest of interruptions, one could only yearn for the toughness of an Olivia O'Leary or the incredulity of a Jeremy Paxman.[64]

Goodbye Gaybo

When the final episode of *The Gay Byrne Show* was broadcast on Christmas Eve 1998, it was moved from its traditional Christmas Eve location at Bewley's on Grafton Street to Stephen's Green, in order to accommodate the enormous crowd of listeners who turned out to bid farewell to Uncle Gaybo. This was the honey-toned usher who heralded us into the strange new Ireland,[65] and he was departing the airwaves, albeit temporarily, but forever

---

[63] 'Letters to the Editor', *Irish Times*, 5 March 1993.

[64] 'Gaybo gets the Maggie treatment', *Irish Press*, 27 October 1993.

[65] Harry Browne, 'The honeyed tones of burning ambition', *Irish Times*, 11 August 2001.

from *The Gay Byrne Show*. At the end of 1998 he was named Ireland's Entertainment Personality of the Year.

The sheer diversity of topics, the subtle counterpoising of witty and humorous letters with painful and raw ones, the quizzes, the mystery sounds, the book and film reviews, the reading aloud of serious and humorous newspaper snippets, all disappeared with the departure of *The Gay Byrne Show*.

Despite accusations to the contrary,[66] Byrne and his team had never stooped to sensationalism. They didn't have to. In fact, in spite of its popularising of social issues and its mission to explore what were then unchartered areas of Irish culture, it was essentially the quirky items which reflected the true tenor of the show. It was the unashamedly Irish humour – and what is more important, Byrne's understanding of that humour – that made the show so durable and endurable. He could seek out quirky issues and comments and know the nation would appreciate the humour.

A typical example of this style of humour is Byrne reading aloud a survey conducted in the US regarding the status of the Contras in Nicaragua.[67] The results indicated that 15 per cent of those asked believed 'the Contras' was either a heavy metal rock band or a tooth-cleaning agent. Snippets such as this, quirky and eccentric, epitomised vintage Byrne.

The Gay Byrne Show came to an end in December 1998, with a surprise tribute to Byrne live on air, hosted by his former RTÉ colleague Mike Murphy. Family, friends and a host of musicians and celebrities all listened in as Ireland's president, Mary McAleese, paid tribute to Byrne, saying she believed the most important aspect of *The Gay Byrne Show* was 'Gay Byrne himself' and the way he could 'mix humour and fun with the serious issues.'[68] Former Taoiseach Bertie Ahern commented that 'in the 26 years of the programme it has been very much part of our

---

[66] For example, with regard to Byrne's interview with paedophile Stephen on *The Gay Byrne Show*, 27 November 1994.

[67] *The Gay Byrne Show*, 18 May 1988.

[68] 'Fans tune in to hear Byrne fade out', *Irish Times*, 17 December 1998.

lives,' adding that 'nobody could ever ignore the programme; it had a huge influence on how things happened in this country.'[69] Another former Taoiseach, Charles Haughey, gave his views on the success of *The Gay Byrne Show*:

> I think possibly one reason why Gay and the show stayed up there for so long unassailably was that there were never any ordinary people as far as *The Gay Byrne Show* was concerned. They were all special.[70]

Byrne himself quipped that if he had known he was half as popular, 'Not only would I have stayed, but I would have asked for more money.'[71] For Byrne, the greatest achievement of his radio career was conducting the first radio interview in Ireland in the early 1960s from Henry Street in Dublin, for his programme *Music on the Move*. Byrne also took great pride in the fact that the Gay Byrne Fund had, by 1998, raised over IR£2 million for charitable causes.

Historian Terence Brown once commented that 'it wasn't just what Gay Byrne talked about; it was that we talked about him and what he said.'[72] Journalist Fintan O'Toole shares this view of Byrne, saying that 'there was a collective discourse that probably will never be again and he was the arbiter of that.'[73] In contrast, journalist John Waters believes too much is credited to Gay Byrne and claims that 'we imply that we could not make a cup of tea before *The Gay Byrne Show*.'[74]

While bearing in mind that restraint is required when assessing the contribution of Gay Byrne and *The Gay Byrne Show*, it nevertheless cannot be ignored that in 1980s Ireland the show

---

[69] *Ibid.*

[70] *Ibid.*

[71] *Ibid.*

[72] Terence Brown, *Ireland: A Social and Cultural History 1922–2002* (Harper Perennial: London, 2004), p. 70.

[73] Fintan O'Toole, *The Ex-isle of Erin: Images of a Global Ireland* (New Island Books: Ireland, 1997), p. 29.

[74] John Waters, *Irish Times*, 9 December 1999.

was particularly revolutionary, albeit for the most part unintentionally. For that it must be acknowledged. Like its television counterpart, *The Gay Byrne Show* massaged and manipulated the radio talk-show genre to suit its Irish audience. It identified the issues of the time, and in dealing with them, it provided 'a national service'.[75]

Byrne would continue to host *The Late Late Show* for one more year after his departure from *The Gay Byrne Show*. His role as conduit to a nation talking to itself provided the essential ingredient of success for both programmes. Through these talk shows, Byrne facilitated change – something that could not have occurred without the interdependence of each part. For Byrne, like Hamlet, 'the show is the thing', and the show(s), in turn, were nothing without their protagonist, Gay Byrne.

Unlike the radio show, which gradually exited Irish life as Byrne gently removed himself from its helm, *The Late Late Show* went out with a bang, with Byrne remaining pivotal to its final years of controversy and debate. It is to these final years of *The Late Late Show* that we now turn, as Byrne – the consummate ringmaster – ensured, through increasingly controversial and moving interviews, that the show remained relevant to Irish life.

---

[75] 'Byrne's radio show identified the issues of the time. And then it dealt with them', *Irish Times*, 12 August 1998.

6

On Your Bike: The Final Years
of *The Late Late Show*

Posturing and Politics on the *Late Late* Platform

By 1990, *The Late Late Show* was still the most popular forum
for debate on Irish television. In October of that year, the Irish
electorate watched at home as a discussion on the suitability of
Ireland's three prospective presidential candidates, Brian Lenihan, Mary Robinson and Austin Curry, was played out on live
television.[1]

For the most part, Byrne was never publicly accused of
overtly pushing a social agenda. He usually appeared on both
his radio and television show as 'Uncle Gaybo', benefactor
of 'one for everybody in the audience' and devil's advocate.
Moreover, by the beginning of the 1990s, *The Late Late Show* still
held consistently high audience ratings and continued to set
the agenda for public debate. The *Sunday Independent*'s television critic commented on the significance of the show and the
centrality of Byrne in popular culture. He noted how impossible it was to think of any major issue of public concern that had
not been thrashed out on the *Late Late* platform. He saw Gay

---

[1] *The Late Late Show*, 2 October 1990.

Byrne 'woven into the very fabric of Irish life' in a way that is unique.[2]

Yet, the show began to grow quite dull in the 1990s. Perhaps it was the fact that people were less shockable and there was a lack of new material coming to the surface. Irish people were now ready to embrace change, even to initiate it, without having to look to *The Late Late Show* to define appropriate social parameters. To many critics, the dullness of the programmes seemed due to the fact that Byrne himself was aging and his opinions becoming more transparent and more unpopular. Examples cited include his veneration of presidential candidate Brian Lenihan on a programme ostensibly to celebrate the former Minister's birthday.[3] Byrne's additional role as Executive Producer of *The Late Late Show* is an important factor in his perceived unbalanced interviewing style on the show at that time.

The interview was supposed to centre around the publication of Lenihan's book *To Mayo and Back*, recounting his recent illness and liver transplant. However, there was much criticism, from both opposition political parties and the public in general, of what was termed 'a stage-managed Fianna Fáil love-fest.'[4] Lenihan was portrayed in a roguish light, telling anecdotes of Ministers pub-crawling and deals being done with a wink and a nod, revelations that would have been deemed inappropriate on other programmes. But *The Late Late Show* was different. This aspect of the show – its ability to get away with things by being under the banner of 'light entertainment' – was a constant source of irritation to those in the news and current affairs division, where such revelations would not be permitted.

This particular episode, however, demonstrated something very significant about Ireland's political culture at that time, a point best articulated by journalist Fintan O'Toole, who claimed that it was not unreasonable to present Brian Lenihan as the epitome of Irishness, because we, as Irish people, are amused at

---

[2] 'The Late Late Show', *Sunday Independent*, 7 February 1993.
[3] *The Late Late Show*, 30 March 1990.
[4] 'Counting the legitimate bed-nights', *Irish Times*, 6 April 1990.

our own follies. Back then, at least, we saw ourselves as a nation of nodders and winkers:

> When you're winking, you have one eye open and one closed, and we haven't yet decided whether we want to look at the country with both eyes open. Until we do, the wink will remain our most eloquent political gesture.[5]

This perceived abuse of the show's public service broadcasting remit in allowing viewers more public access to Brian Lenihan than to the other two presidential candidates raised the question of who was shaping whom. Were the issues pertinent at that time to Irish society reflected in *The Late Late Show* or did the show, on occasions such as the Brian Lenihan interview, reflect the personal views of its presenter/producer Gay Byrne specifically and of the viewing public generally? It would be remiss to ignore that on an occasion such as this the show has harnessed and shaped, rather than reflected and challenged, the views of the public.

Media coverage of *The Late Late Show* throughout the 1990s is in itself an interesting topic of study. Since 1962, the show became a popular media outlet, but its relationship with the press was fraught with mutual hostilities. Even now, commentary on *The Late Late Show* is to a large extent mediated through the letters pages of newspapers or through articles written by journalists and television critics. The concern here is the way in which journalists assess those episodes of *The Late Late Show*, and how the public responded to their comments while negotiating their own interpretations of the show. If journalistic reports can be deemed to have significant similarities to accounts of research in the social sciences, then hermeneutic analysis may be legitimately used to highlight the issues involved in distinguishing between objective and subjective accounts of the show. In contemporary terms, hermeneutics is the term used to denote a specific system or method of interpreting texts. Put

---

[5] 'In the land of wink and nod', *Irish Times*, 5 April 1990.

simply, it is feasible to argue that much of the criticism levelled at *The Late Late Show* was, and to a certain degree still is, media-managed. Take for instance the letters page of *The Irish Times*, which was full to overflowing with criticisms of Byrne and his abuse of public service broadcasting to promote Brian Lenihan in a wholly uncritical light. Comments included the following sample:

Sir,

What a nauseating display of gushing rhetoric we had to endure on *The Late Late Show* on March 30th. Gay Byrne's fawning to Brian Lenihan and the invited audience exceeded even his usual syrupy exertions.[6]

Many such letters presented Byrne in an unfavourable light. While it is feasible to expect people to feel this way about him and his interviewing style, it is also plausible to assume that there were many others who enjoyed the Brian Lenihan interview, yet the media chose to ignore this angle as it was not 'newsworthy'. The point to note here is that while much criticism of *The Late Late Show* has been motivated entirely by viewers' dislike of Byrne or of the show, there has also been much criticism that has been media-manipulated. In other words, editors decide to 'gate keep'; they decide what the public need to know and they channel their information accordingly.

Media bias was also evident in 1991 when newspapers were rife with articles regarding the importance of the emigrant vote. *The Late Late Show*, acknowledging the timeliness of this issue, had as its guest the then Taoiseach Albert Reynolds. To many viewers the interview proceeded without controversy. However, in subsequent newspaper reports it was alleged that members of the Irish Emigrant Vote Campaign were much aggrieved by the 'negative tones of the interview' and that emigrant vote organisations in Britain deemed Byrne to be 'at his

---

[6] *Ibid.*

worst in attempting to stir up controversy.'[7] The programme, it was reported, was 'particularly insulting to emigrants in Britain.'[8]

The Peter Brooke Interview

In 1992, controversy of an even more serious kind raged when Northern Ireland Secretary Peter Brooke made one of the biggest gaffes of his political career. He sang 'My Darling Clementine' on *The Late Late Show* just hours after news broke of the Teebane bombing in which eight Protestant workmen carrying out building work for the RUC were killed by an IRA landmine.[9] After the singing blunder, Brooke offered to resign. An *Irish Times* headline, 'Brooke song on *Late Late* causes anger,'[10] referred to calls by DUP politicians for his resignation and criticism of the programme makers at RTÉ for allowing such a blunder to happen. The *Daily Telegraph* described Byrne as a 'sophisticated, two-faced, scheming Irish TV viewer.'[11] The *Kerryman* had the following to say on the controversy:

> Of course the real culprit in all this was Gay Byrne himself, although he is not man enough to admit it. Byrne manipulated Brooke a lot more skilfully than Brooke had managed to manipulate the Northern parties. Byrne walked Brooke into the quagmire and then left him to sink or swim.[12]

At the time, the most cynical interpretation of Brooke's gaffe was that Byrne, because of his loathing of politicians (more evident on his radio programme), intentionally plotted to embarrass Peter Brooke. This would concur with the argument that media commentary complicates the resolution of political

---

7   'Reynolds criticised by emigrants over votes', *Irish Times*, 6 March 1992.
8   *Ibid.*
9   *The Late Late Show*, 17 January 1992.
10 'Brooke song on Late Late causes anger', *Irish Times*, 2 January 1992.
11 'British Press', quoted from the *Daily Telegraph* in the *Irish Press*, 22 January 1992.
12 'Gay Byrne was the real culprit in the Brooke affair', *Kerryman*, 24 January 1992.

controversies because the media 'modify the rules of the game, forcing politicians to justify themselves to an ever large public.'[13]

However, to someone familiar with Byrne's style, a more plausible explanation of the gaffe was that he loved to surprise his guests. Nevertheless, RTÉ admitted that, given the tragic circumstances, it was an error to have had Mr Brooke sing on television.[14] Letters to the press, such as the following, expressed outrage at Byrne's treatment of Mr Brooke:

Sir,

Honourable men apologise when they realise they have done something wrong. Secretaries of State, such as Mr Peter Brooke, tender their resignation after singing a song during a time of mourning. Chat-show hosts, such as Mr Byrne, whose egos have long since consumed their moral scruples, never apologise.[15]

In a later statement, Byrne apologised for any offence caused by Mr Brooke's appearance on the show, but he insisted that the rumpus caused by the programme had only served to deflect from the appalling atrocity that had given rise to it.[16] In the same statement Brooke accused Byrne of 'laying traps for people, particularly politicians.'[17] Byrne, in an angry response to Brooke's accusation said, 'This is a man who has been a politician for 30 years ... and he was afraid of Gay Byrne.'[18]

Byrne also claimed that Brooke knew of the massacre in Teebane and should have said he did not think it was a night for singing. Instead, Byrne commented:

[13] G.E. Lang and K. Lang, *The Battle for Public Opinion: The President, the Press and the Polls during Watergate* (Columbia University: New York, 1983), p. 85.

[14] 'RTÉ apology over Brooke on the Late Late', *Irish Times*, 21 January 1992.

[15] Letters to the Editor, *Irish Times*, 29 January 1992.

[16] 'Brooke blames himself for singing gaffe', *Sunday Independent*, 22 January 1993.

[17] *Ibid.*

[18] *Ibid.*

He fancied himself as a singer and he wanted to sing and that was that. It wasn't as if he was taken by the hand and forced into doing something he didn't want to do by this ogre Gay Byrne.[19]

If after this debacle Peter Brooke had resigned (in April of that year, in a cabinet reshuffle by Prime Minister John Major, he was replaced by Sir Patrick Mayhew), it would have been very bad publicity for *The Late Late Show*, perhaps the worst ever. But Byrne was not to be scapegoated. Teetering on the brink of a tightrope was what gave *The Late Late Show* its unique frisson. Byrne's picture was in the paper, and the show's ratings soared over the following weeks,[20] as viewers waited expectantly for more of the unexpected.

Byrne survived to host some of the most controversial live television in Ireland's broadcasting history, most notably his interview with the former lover of Bishop Eamon Casey.

The Annie Murphy Interview

In May 1992, Eamon Casey resigned his role as Roman Catholic Bishop of Galway, when *The Irish Times* revealed that he had fathered a son, Peter, in 1974 with American divorcee Annie Murphy, with whom he had had a six-month love affair. In 1993, Annie Murphy published a book on the affair, *Forbidden Fruit: The True Story of My Secret Love for the Bishop of Galway*, which would provide the focus of her interview with Gay Byrne on *The Late Late Show* on 4 April 1993. However, it is significant that in February 1992, when *The Irish Times* was first contacted by Arthur Pennell – stepfather to Peter Murphy – regarding the affair, it conducted a thorough investigation of Pennell's revelations before going to print with the story. It sent its Washington correspondent, Conor O'Clery, to visit Annie Murphy to

---

[19] *Ibid.*

[20] Gay Byrne with Deirdre Purcell, *The Time of My Life: An Autobiography* (Gill & Macmillan: Dublin, 1989), p. 83.

clarify both the affair and allegations of abuse of diocesan funds by Bishop Casey.[21] Mindful of its long history of a Protestant tradition, *The Irish Times* was not comfortable with the role of whistle-blower against the Catholic Church, whose representative – according to *Irish Times* Religious Affairs correspondent Patsy McGarry – warned the paper prior to its publication of the story in February 1992, that if the story was untrue, it would spell its death-knell.[22]

When Murphy appeared on *The Late Late Show* in 1993 to discuss her book, she became the subject of scorn and accusations.[23] *The Late Late Show* was perceived by many critics as instrumental in her humiliation. The Bishop's secretary and his close personal friends, who were all in the audience, called her a liar and a fallen woman. To those who felt sorry for Murphy, Byrne presented himself on the side of the Bishop, who was 'in retreat' and not present to face the charges against him.

From the point of view of the studio audience, some of whom spoke disparagingly about Murphy, Byrne's interviewing style seemed to be appropriately interrogatory. It is worth noting that Casey was a regular guest on *The Late Late Show* and someone Byrne had openly admired. To audiences at home, opinions were divided. Depending on where their sympathies lay, Byrne was alternately perceived as the aggressive interrogator, hell-bent on protecting the integrity of the Bishop, or as the usual 'no-holds-barred' interviewer that he had always been.

Journalist Nell McCafferty believes that Byrne's treatment of Annie Murphy was 'typical Gay' and that his 'mask was removed', displaying his latent condescension towards women.[24] Former Ireland rugby coach Mick Doyle, a regular guest on *The Late Late Show*, wrote of Byrne's 'pinched,

---

[21] Within days of the *Irish Times* allegations, the Bishop repaid the funds in full. The money was sent by the Bishop to Annie Murphy for the upkeep and education of their child, Peter, in the US.

[22] Journalist Patsy McGarry on TV3 series *Print and Be Damned*, 8 August 2013.

[23] *The Late Late Show*, 2 April 1993.

[24] Nell McCafferty, in interview with the author, 7 February 2012.

censorious mien' and believed Byrne 'set himself up as Annie Murphy's judge with Eamon Casey's supporters as jury.'[25]

Because of the controversial nature of the interview, close analysis is called for. Examples of hostility to Murphy could be garnered from Byrne's reference to her 'coquettish' behaviour.[26] Her denial of Casey's seduction elicited the following response from Byrne: 'What woman doesn't pursue a man?'[27]

Journalist Mary Kenny interpreted this comment as follows:

> I think his gender attitudes emerged in his interview with Annie Murphy; he did a professional job as he always did, but fundamentally, I think he regarded her as a femme fatale who had very easily seduced Eamon Casey and many an older woman around Ireland would have thought, and Gay's mammy would have thought, the same thing.[28]

Throughout the interview, Byrne also made intimations regarding Murphy's unsuitability as a mother, and accusations of untruths were levelled at her by relatives and friends of Casey. Concluding the interview, Byrne asked Murphy to accept that her son Peter would not 'be doing too badly' if he turned out to be half the man his father was. She retorted, 'I'm not so bad myself, Mr Byrne,' and left the interview as the cameras were still running.

Historian Diarmaid Ferriter believed the interview with Murphy was Byrne's 'most disgraceful interview as host of *The Late Late Show*' and claimed Byrne 'blamed Annie Murphy for the downfall of Bishop Eamon Casey after she gave birth to their son Peter.'[29]

---

[25] 'Gay Byrne's friend simply ran away', *Sunday Independent*, 4 April 1993.
[26] *The Late Late Show*, 4 April 1993.
[27] *Ibid.*
[28] Mary Kenny, in interview with the author, 5 January 2012.
[29] Diarmaid Ferriter, *Occasions of Sin: Sex and Society in Modern Ireland* (Profile Books: London, 2009), p. 531.

Although Byrne never professed any regret over the interview, he did attempt to clarify his controversial parting comment to Murphy:

> That was unfortunate and may have been misinterpreted. What I was thinking of quite frankly and with my hand on my heart was that she started the interview by telling me what she loved about Eamon Casey, which was his ebullience, his extrovert nature, his generosity, his expansiveness, his way with people and so on and that was in my mind at the end of the interview about the young fellow ... I'm sorry it was misunderstood but I know why I said it.[30]

Regarding Byrne's comment to Murphy, Maura Connolly, special programming assistant and researcher on *The Late Late Show*, claimed Murphy had been aware of the questions she was to be asked in advance and was also told who was to be present in the audience.[31] In line with US talk shows, it was claimed, Murphy walked off the set as soon as the interview was concluded. In a statement to the press later that day, Murphy denied that she had walked out of the show, stating that she had been exasperated by the studio audience, whom she felt were against her, and was blinded by the bright lights and confused by the length of the show.[32]

Byrne, both on the show and on many subsequent occasions, referred to Casey as 'the champion of the Irish in London' who was a 'visionary' in the work he initiated in Camden Town for many of the homeless Irish. Byrne believed that 'under the Broadcasting Act' he had a 'responsibility to represent' Casey's views and that Murphy did not walk off 'because I was antagonistic towards her' but rather due to 'the antagonism towards

---

[30] 'Why greying Gay won't be there for the fans on Monday morning', *Irish Times*, 17 September 1994.

[31] Maura Connolly, in interview with the author, 16 May 1996.

[32] This remark, according to Maura Connolly, was made by Annie Murphy to journalists later that day but was never printed.

her from the studio audience.'[33] He adds that Murphy was a 'most attractive and intelligent woman' and claims that she thanked him for 'the best interview she had ever done.'

This approach was typical of Byrne. He would always probe. He would always ask the awkward question. And if he so desired, he would comment in the forthright manner that made him both the *bête noire* and Uncle Gaybo of the viewing public.

Byrne's interview with Annie Murphy is of socio-historical significance in that the Catholic Church, a revered and respected institution in Irish society, was humanised by a woman telling a tale of her personal involvement with a bishop. Viewers could make their own assessment of the situation. Moreover, much media criticism of this and subsequently controversial interviews focused on the techniques and tactics of the television medium rather than on the nature of the interview itself. Again, it must be noted that commentators in the media in general, replete with their own personal bias and individual agendas, tend towards polemical rather than consensual opinions in order to whet the appetite of their readers and increase newspaper sales.

The newsworthiness of the Annie Murphy interview, with its attendant issue of priestly celibacy, proved too much of a field day for newspaper editors and journalists desperate to show that it was now the turn of the Fourth Estate to lecture on public morality. Though there may have been viewers who agreed with Byrne's stance in the Annie Murphy interview, none of these viewers, for whatever reason, felt it necessary to articulate their support in print. Was it a fear of censure – of being out of kilter with what appeared to be overwhelming support for Annie Murphy – that prevented those with contrary views from printing their opinions? This was in marked contrast to the relentless flow of letters to *The Irish Times*, all seemingly at one in their defence of Annie Murphy and their condemnation of Byrne. Samples include the following:

---

[33] Gay Byrne, in interview with the author, 2 September 2011.

Sir,

May God protect Annie and Peter Murphy from those not humble enough to accept that an Irish bishop may sin. We were most disheartened to see that little alternative to the prevailing uncharitable and unchristian attitude was given air-time. It was distressing to see someone who remained dignified, as did Annie Murphy, treated in such a rude, insensitive and chauvinistic manner.[34]

Sir,

Gay Byrne's interview with Annie Murphy was biased, rude, unfair and unprofessional. Undoubtedly, when the Bishop writes his version of the story there will be a copy for everybody in the audience of what Mr Byrne undoubtedly will view as being the definitive version of the good book.[35]

Further letters in defence of Annie Murphy were published in the *Irish Press*:

'I hope your son turns out to be half as good a man as Bishop Casey.' In putting this to Ms Annie Murphy on *The Late Late Show* does Gay Byrne mean if Peter Murphy fathers a child he will deny him for nine or ten years?[36]

Letters ceased, the print media took the moral high ground, and journalists seemed all at once unanimous in their support of Annie Murphy and in their condemnation of Byrne's interviewing techniques. He was considered 'conservative', which to their minds was regressive and dull. He was censured because

---

[34] Letters to the Editor, *Irish Times*, 5 April 1993.

[35] *Ibid.*, 6 April 1993.

[36] Letters to the Editor, *Irish Press*, 14 April 1993.

his view was no longer one they wished to hear. It did not fit with their modern world view.

The media, who have themselves been accused of promoting a liberal agenda, i.e. an 'anything is acceptable philosophy once it is trendy and modern',[37] viewed the Annie Murphy interview as a denigration of Irish women and as an attack on mother-hood itself.

Nonetheless, what is culturally significant about the Annie Murphy affair is not, as the media claimed at that time, the scan-dal of a fallen bishop, but the disturbing Irish phenomenon of absolute trust in the clergy. Journalist Mary Cummins referred to the whole affair as the 'alternative Kerry Babies Tribunal' and went on to say that attitudes displayed on *The Late Late Show* and by some members of the press the following morning at a press conference were 'the usual typically Irish attempts to reduce the woman, to cast her in the role of the calculating and evil seductress who catches the poor fool of a man who, inno-cent and unworldly, hardly knows what he's doing.'[38]

Journalist Dick Walsh of *The Irish Times* felt that people who trusted *The Late Late Show* had been let down. He felt that what people got from Byrne was a performance that drew on the pre-judices of the 1950s, where women still had an unequal place in Irish society.[39] This type of media comment can be perceived in itself as biased. So, too, can comments from representatives of single-issue organisations who felt they had to defend their cause. Chairwoman of the Council of the Status of Women, Ms Anne Taylor, accused Byrne of allowing his personal rela-tionship with Eamon Casey to blur his professionalism:

I feel the he [Mr Byrne] handled it very badly. From the professional presenter he normally is, he shifted right into his own personal viewpoint. I think he lost it. As a

---

[37] S. Robert Lichter, Stanley Rothman and Linda Lichter, *The Media Elite* (Adler and Adler: Minessota, 1986), p. 111.

[38] 'Very Irish Questions at Annie Roadshow', *Irish Times*, 5 April 1993.

[39] 'Late Late tries to turn back the clock', *Irish Times*, 10 April 1993.

professional dealing with it, his attitude left a lot to be desired.[40]

It can be argued that many of these commentators had their own personal reasons for taking issue with Byrne's treatment of Annie Murphy. However, media condemnation of Byrne's interviewing style appeared to this author to be totally at odds with what was evidenced on the television screen. To viewers at home, manifest by the hostile questioning of Murphy by both Byrne and members of the studio audience, there appeared to be unanimity in their disapproval of Murphy.[41] In fact, the studio audience seemed not at all offended by Byrne's treatment of his guest and seemed at one with his cultural values. Therefore, if it is acknowledged that bias and at times, condescension, pervaded this interview, what was sociologically significant about this exchange on *The Late Late Show* was the emergence of a strong wave of support for Byrne on the night of the interview, in contrast to the media's hostility in the aftermath of the event.

Moreover, the picture painted in the media – that of a woman 'pillorised' by Byrne and a 'select audience' – seemed to this author to be inaccurate. Apart from a handful of invited guests relevant to the programme, journalists are aware that tickets to *The Late Late Show*, even now, are a prized commodity. This author has attended the show on three occasions, and it would appear that audiences are, in the main, from all corners of Ireland and from all walks of life. During the Gay Byrne era, the majority of audience members would have waited up to two years to be present as part of the studio audience. For the media at that time to dismiss the studio audience as a select group of 'Bible thumpers' and 'die-hard Catholics'[42] seems grossly inaccurate. This misrepresentation of the facts could perhaps highlight more about the inability of the press or the Fourth

---

[40] 'Byrne's attitude on Late Show draws criticism', *Irish Times*, 5 April 1993.

[41] *The Late Late Show*, 4 April 1993.

[42] Terms in use pejoratively in the media throughout the 1990s, in reference to very committed and conservative Catholics.

Estate to acknowledge dissenting viewpoints on an issue of controversy in Irish society at that time.

Another notable aspect of the Annie Murphy interview was the age profile of the studio audience on that particular night. Upon a reviewing of the show it was clear that the audience tended towards people in the 40-plus age group. It can be argued that the viewing audience for *The Late Late Show* in the 1990s began to age with the programme, and thus shared a similar world view to Byrne. To younger audiences at that time, Byrne may have appeared as the benign Uncle Gaybo, utterly confused and shaken by the morals and mores of women in modern society. To many of his peers, however, he was considered crusading and open-minded, particularly on women's issues.

This view was endorsed in 1991 by Pan Collins, a former researcher on the show, who, unlike Mary Kenny and Nell McCafferty, believed:

> Gay Byrne has done more than any other Irish male to promote the liberation of women from the entrenched chauvinism of men ... Gay likes women. He always lends a sympathetic ear to women's problems and, back in 1970, he devoted a whole *Late Late Show* to the emerging Women's Liberation Movement. And his favourite guest of all time was a woman – Mother Teresa of Calcutta.[43]

This polarisation of attitudes to Byrne and to *The Late Late Show* reflected the oppositions that existed within Irish society. Ireland in the 1990s was undergoing a rapid period of change. Modernity and tradition clashed in Ireland's simultaneous status as a Celtic Tiger economy and a country where Sunday Mass and traditional Catholic teachings were still generally revered, in spite of a spate of Church scandals. It was inevitable, therefore, that confrontations between traditional and modern ideals, as evidenced by the Annie Murphy interview, were bound to provoke controversy.

---

[43] Pan Collins, 'Whatever will be, will be', *RTÉ Guide*, 6 September 1991.

From Adams to Keane: Affairs of the State to Secret Affairs

Throughout the late 1990s, criticism of Byrne and *The Late Late Show* began to outweigh the laudatory remarks. The interview with Annie Murphy was just one of the incidents that raised the hackles in many viewers. Television critics at that time argued that Byrne had become more dominant in discussion, more critically motivated and was in danger of losing his sense of balance. For many, these characteristics were on display in his interviews with Sinn Féin leader Gerry Adams and with Terry Keane, the mistress of former Taoiseach Charles Haughey.

In the case of the Gerry Adams interview, controversy and comment of a different nature was to occur with the appearance of the Sinn Féin leader on the show in 1994. In his autobiography, Byrne commented that his ambition as an interviewer would be fully realised if he could interview Gerry Adams on *The Late Late Show*. He wished to 'travel the labyrinthine canals of his mind to try to find out what makes him tick.'[44] At that time, it was out of the question to speak to Gerry Adams on *The Late Late Show* due to restrictions imposed by Section 31 of the Broadcasting Act that disallowed interviews with members of a paramilitary group and even those suspected of being a member of such an organisation. The fact that Adams could not be heard on either television or radio made the prospect of interviewing him a most challenging one for Byrne. With the implementation of Section 31, RTÉ and certain elements within the Irish political arena had created a mystique around Adams. Of course, it can be argued that RTÉ's implementation of its restrictive policy was not entirely balanced. RTÉ prohibited a voice to extremist Republican mouthpieces, while at the same time allowing the prominent Unionist figure Reverend Ian Paisley to appear as a guest on *The Late Late Show* in the early 1990s.

However, in light of the IRA ceasefire in 1994 and the optimism surrounding the future of Ulster, the ban on Gerry Adams was lifted. In October of that year, on an otherwise normal

---

[44] Byrne and Purcell, *op. cit.*, p. 154.

edition of *The Late Late Show*, Adams appeared. It was a coup for Byrne to finally have Adams on the show. The fact that *The Late Late Show* provided the forum for Adams's first post-ban Irish television interview was of itself significant in Ireland's broadcast history.

Introduced by Byrne as 'the most controversial and the most hated man in Ireland,'[45] it was presumed Adams would be portrayed as an extremist, eliciting a negative audience response. However, the fact that Byrne did not shake hands with Adams, as was customary on the show,[46] and in the face of critical comments from Byrne and his panel, meant that Adams chose his words carefully. He thus emerged as a much put-upon ordinary man, confused by the hostility of the panel, but calm under pressure. The manner adapted by Adams for this interview militated against Byrne, who many viewers believed displayed a conscious bias.

It could be argued that Byrne felt an obligation to the Irish public to probe deeply and to ask the questions the audience at home wished to pose. Equally, those familiar with Byrne's style and his penchant for the theatrical, could point to the fact that this was just another role for Byrne, a form of courtroom drama, with Byrne as judge, the panellists the prosecutors, and Adams the defendant. Byrne was, after all, an actor. Chameleon-like, he could change persona from Mr Nice to Mr Nasty. It was not meant to be personal, just a change of role.

The Adams interview was also a defining moment for all Irish people, as the nation came face to face with its violent past. The interview bought the 'Troubles' once again into the national arena and bluntly reminded people that it was their war too. This point was made even more poignantly with the appearance on a later episode of *The Late Late Show* of the parents

---

[45] *The Late Late Show*, 8 October 1994.

[46] Gay Byrne, in an interview with the author on 2 September 2011, stated that RTÉ management instructed him not to shake hands with Gerry Adams. Byrne felt this was not the right action to take and subsequently was vindicated in that belief based on the negativity it provoked.

of a child who was killed by an IRA bomb in Warrington, Cheshire in 1993.[47]

It was not, however, the historical significance of Adams's appearance on the show that evoked comment, but rather the manner in which he was treated. The latter provoked an unprecedented level of negative responses from Irish television audiences, and more cynical comments from journalists in both the British and Irish print media. Byrne and the very lexicon of *The Late Late Show* were under siege.

Tom Humphries of *The Irish Times* commented:

> What made last night's programme compulsory viewing was the reaction of the audience, the reaction of a random slice of middle Ireland to seeing the great *bête noire* of Northern politics in the flesh. Gerry Adams, like it or not, has a grasp of the new vocabulary. Most of the applause wrung from last night's TV audience flowed towards Adams. Gay Byrne bungled his way through the old lexicon, the ancient gestures. Pointedly he avoided shaking Adams' hand; theatrically he stood yards away from Adams as he un-reeled his questions. His need to give a demonstration of his personal distaste for Adams was self-serving and in the end self-defeating.[48]

It was reported in all of the daily newspapers that Joe Duffy, at that time the occasional presenter of *The Gay Byrne Show*, had received over two hundred calls on the Monday morning after Adams's appearance on *The Late Late Show*. It was estimated that 80 per cent of those who managed to get through felt the Sinn Féin President had been harshly treated by Gay Byrne and a panel that included Austin Currie (Fine Gael), Michael McDowell (Progressive Democrats), Dermot Aherne (Fianna Fáil) and playwright Hugh Leonard (whose comments to Gerry Adams

---

[47] *The Late Late Show*, 6 May 1995.
[48] 'Old language fails in a changed scenario', *Irish Times*, 29 October 1994.

included: 'You are a liar and a hypocrite. If you lie down with dogs, you're going to get up with fleas.'[49]).

In the Letters to the Editor section of the Skibbereen-based *Southern Star* newspaper, Councillor Cionnaith O'Suilleabháin made the following points:

> The gurus in RTÉ who attempted to set up the character assassination of Mr Gerry Adams in front of over one million viewers on *The Late Late Show* indeed exposed themselves and their policy with disastrous results ... I predict that it will be many a long day before Gay Byrne attempts an exercise like this again, given the overwhelming critical comment by the public in the aftermath.[50]

The letters page of *The Irish Times* included the following comments:

> Sir,
>
> I would like to protest at the way Mr Adams was treated on *The Late Late Show*. It seemed to me that Gay Byrne had prepared his strategy in such a way that Mr Adams and all he stood for was totally responsible for the horror of the last 25 years. Gay's narrow vision made for a very one-sided debate which was helped by a well-chosen panel. Mr Adams may have been better treated by a Loyalist panel.[51]
>
> Sir,
>
> As a humble Irish person, I am writing to express my deep disquiet and sadness at the treatment received by Gerry Adams on *The Late Late Show*. My outrage extends to the producer, presenter, the other panellists on that item, and the

---

[49] *The Late Late Show*, 28 October 1994.
[50] Letters to the Editor, *Southern Star*, 10 October 1994.
[51] Letters to the Editor: 'Adams on the *Late Late*', *Irish Times*, 9 November 1994.

vast majority of the audience. It is the manner in which Mr Adams was pilloried, demonised, alienated, which to borrow John Major's quote 'made my stomach turn'. Programmes such as these are only a hindrance to the peace process, to which all fair-minded people are deeply committed.[52]

Most of the other letters published in *The Irish Times* echoed similar sentiments. Conversely, people working within media settings were somewhat more critical of the Adams interview. Many journalists and media experts acknowledged that the interview highlighted the potency of television as a manipulative medium at its most effective. Journalist Eddie Holt made the following comments:

> *The Late Late Show* went for the steamroller approach. Inevitably, the more the presenter and the panel steamed, the more the sympathy rolled toward Gerry Adams. The studio audience did not like the pillorying on view ... The show was out of its time, and in attempting the steamrolling of Gerry Adams, it was quite simply out of its mind.[53]

Others, such as journalist Sam Smyth, felt that Byrne and his panel did not go hard enough on Adams, adding that:

> Unfortunately for Byrne, the panel forgot that people watch TV, they don't listen to it. All people will remember is the gentle demeanour of a TV guest ... And Gerry Adams has mastered the TV medium.[54]

Social Studies lecturer Harry Ferguson made a similar point:

> What we got on *The Late Late Show* was a highly stylized performance by Adams, who skilfully managed a particular

---

[52] *Ibid.*, 5 November 1994.
[53] 'Gaybo's own goal', *Independent Weekender*, 5 November 1994.
[54] 'Call me Mr Reasonable', *Sunday Independent*, 30 October 1994.

kind of public display of being (new) man which can serve to separate him in the minds of many from the institutional power and accountability he has for violence.[55]

Media commentator Eoghan Harris thought the explanation for the overwhelming public support for Adams was due to a 'leaky national consensus'. He stated:

> Consensus is a contradiction. We do hate violence, but the hatred can be suspended while we are watching a television programme. That is because television is theatre. For the duration of the programme we agree to suspend disbelief, to forget what we know about the person in the chair, and to take it on its merits. Consensus sets up a Stockholm syndrome in a television studio: from whom panellists who loathe each other form a common front against the threatening technology of cameras and lights.[56]

The solution, according to Harris, to ensure that public sympathy was not aroused by Adams, was to treat Adams like everybody else:

> Put one person on the panel against him. A victim to counter his victimhood. Make sure the audience accurately reflects the majority who support the Dowling Street Declaration. Sit back and let Gay Byrne do the work.[57]

Even within the ranks of RTÉ the repercussions of the Adams interview were reverberating. The then RTÉ Deputy General, Bobby Gahan, confirmed to the *Evening Echo* that the format of that particular interview would be reviewed by senior executives.[58] But the controversy stopped there, and there was no

---

[55] 'Late Late puts Adams in good light', *Irish Times*, 3 November 1994.

[56] 'A legitimate target if ever there was one', *Sunday Times*, 6 November 1994.

[57] 'Call me Mr Reasonable', *op. cit.*

[58] 'Adams on the Late Late', *Evening Echo*, 31 October 1994.

review, only a comment from Byrne that he had no regrets about the programme, which he thought had turned out very well. In an interview with the author in relation to the event, Gerry Adams has commented on the 'abusive panel' and on Byrne as an 'ungracious host'.[59] Adams recalls how he had been advised by his press officer, Richard McCauley, that the *Late Late Show* interview would be 'an ambush in waiting', and that he (Adams) would be treated 'as a hostile witness' who would be 'savaged by the panel'.

However, Adams does believe that in this instance *The Late Late Show* provided 'an important service': it allowed a large part of Ireland to hear a Sinn Féin member, something that had theretofore not been possible due to Section 31. Adams felt that he 'received an acknowledgement' that he knew more about the RUC than Austin Curry and believed his view 'that the RUC was not an acceptable police force in Northern Ireland was accepted and understood by the audience.'[60] Adams, in retrospect, despite his initial post-interview criticism, is quite gracious in his comments on Byrne and his role as a talk-show host:

> I like what Byrne does as a broadcaster. He has never disguised his abhorrence for people like me. I have watched the show for years and years. I generally like chat shows, but I always felt *The Late Late Show* was unique – ordinary folk having craic, lively music, social commentary and debate.[61]

Indeed, Byrne's abhorrence for Republican violence was more manifest on his radio programme and seemed oddly inappropriate here. Moreover, in this instance, the orchestration of the panel, the unexpected media sophistication and Adams's understanding of the television medium mitigated against Byrne, whose interviewing style and increasing personal bias were once more under scrutiny.

---

[59] Gerry Adams, in interview with the author, 12 October 2012.

[60] *Ibid.*

[61] *Ibid.*

Byrne and Bias?

The style of the programme was again under attack in 1995. It featured European Parliament candidates for Dublin Orla Guerin and Bernie Malone. Columnist Mary Cummins took issue with the way in which *The Late Late Show* presented people within a media-manipulated sexist setting:

> Here, again, the viewers were shown two of their Euro-candidates for Dublin in the most unattractive, combative light. Again, women in politics were slapped into the entertainment slot – to thrill the nation. It is a vivid insight into the huge difference in media handling of women and men who run for public office.[62]

The female candidates were urged by Byrne to give personal accounts of their suitability as a European candidate, with Byrne showing particular interest in Guerin's time as RTÉ's Eastern Europe correspondent, with very few challenges directed at both candidates regarding their individual policies and aspirations for the European post.

Further criticism levelled at the show focused on the limits of what was acceptable public behaviour. It was argued that with the rapid pace of change in 1990s Ireland, the show had lost touch with contemporary social issues and was pandering to an older audience. Amidst all the criticism of the show's format and of Byrne's personal style, the following question was relentlessly posed: For how long more would the popularity of the show and Byrne survive?

By September 1994, after 23 years of rising at 6.15 a.m. to present a live morning radio show and 33 years of producing and presenting his mould-breaking live television show, the energies of this 'media vampire' were beginning to flag. Yet, Byrne was still not ready to retire. At 60, he chose to simply do a bit less, ceding the title of *Late Late* producer, and in effect

---

[62] 'As usual it's the President who has the answer', *Irish Times*, 10 March 1995.

the show's direction and content, to experienced RTÉ producer John Masterson. According to Byrne it was 'time to bring in a new mind, and a new vigour and a new enthusiasm.'[63] He did not, however, cede full control and continued to hold the title of executive producer, giving him a powerful veto over individual items put forward for the show.

Nonetheless, Masterson was aware of the enormity of sustaining audience interest for a four-part live talk show, a situation unique to any television station. He had garnered a long list of credentials for his work on the RTÉ current affairs programme *Today Tonight*, and would now mark the beginning of a new and final phase of the show with lots of groundbreaking discussions on issues as diverse as Scientology, foxhunting, drink-driving legislation and topical political discussions and debates.

In 1995, he was responsible for a programme special on the Catholic Church in Ireland, where his only proviso was that 'everyone in the audience was a committed Catholic.'[64] Here *The Late Late Show* provided the forum for an open debate on the series of scandals inflicted on the Church from within its own ranks. The audience was made up of clergy. The panel itself featured the Head of the Catholic Church in Ireland, Dr Cathal Daly, who during the programme had a lively exchange with Fr Brian D'Arcy on the lack of communication between clergy and lay people.

The show was the first of its kind to provide a forum for constructive and healthy debate on the state of the Catholic Church in Ireland. Critics could argue that it was little more than a public relations exercise and, to a large extent, that view would be justifiable. The very fact, however, that a Church crisis would be publicly debated by a select group of Irish clergy on a talk show that was previously denounced by its members as crude and immoral[65] points to a significant change in attitude to the show by the clergy. That such a distinguished turnout from its ranks

---

[63] 'Why greying Gay won't be there for the fans on Monday morning', *op. cit.*

[64] John Masterson, in interview with the author, 19 September 2011.

[65] See the 'Bishop and Nightie' incident in Chapter 3 for details.

appeared on the programme signalled an acknowledgement by the Catholic Church in Ireland of the wide-ranging significance and influence of *The Late Late Show* in Irish life. This awareness of the quintessential role played by *The Late Late Show* in challenging all areas of Irish life took over 35 years to acknowledge.

From a programme that had survived the Bishop and the Nightie affair, and from the attacks made by the Catholic Church at that time, it was ironically fitting that *The Late Late Show* was instrumental in its attempts to popularise and humanise the Church, which had, for many people, become a faceless institution with outmoded and outdated conventions and methods. For Byrne, the positive response of the clergy and the audience to this programme served as a kind of vindication for him and his team and for what *The Late Late Show* stood for.

Making the Ordinary Extraordinary

Nevertheless, the question remained whether a new producer with some pioneering ideas would be enough to save the integrity of *The Late Late Show*. By the mid-1990s, many television critics maintained that Byrne had become unpredictable and self-opinionated. Journalist John Cooney believed this trait would have been tolerated when the public was more diffident and passive. However, in a more critical age, 'people are less awed by the media and the egos of mega-stars.'[66]

Accusations of imbalance and bias continued to be levelled at Byrne. It can of course be argued that Byrne had always been dominant in discussion and that accusations of imbalance came into play only when members of the media did not happen to agree with this bias. Byrne was also accused of sounding increasingly jaded and bored. Equally, there was an acknowledgement that he was still capable of conducting interviews of exceptional sensitivity.

To less harsh critics, Byrne was inimitable in his unique ability to make an extraordinary guest speak the language of the

---

[66] 'Rollercoaster on the Late Late Show', *Irish Independent*, 4 February 1994.

people. His wish to safeguard certain truths and values drew criticism from certain quarters. Yet, these traits could be said to mirror those of his own generation. Until the end, his show accommodated all shades of opinion, no matter how diverse.

On 31 March 1995, Byrne introduced the anti-fascist band Pop Will Eat Itself to a shocked audience who refused to clap after a performance that included the band thrashing a drum kit live on stage.[67] After the show the band were escorted off the premises by RTÉ security. According to producer John Masterson:

> They were obviously in some sort of altered mental state. When they finished their performance they burned up some of the sound gear in the studio.[68]

In that same year, TD for County Louth Brendan McGahon was a guest on the programme, celebrating his retirement from politics. In response to a question on how to deal with spiralling crime rates, he explained he would shoot all drug-pushers and bring back hanging and flogging. He went on to say he had nothing but contempt for 'bleeding heart liberalism' and he thought that gays were 'psychologically twisted.'[69] Certain sectors of Irish society did not, and do not, agree with these views but, on the other hand, they cannot be dismissed as outmoded and outdated. After all, 6,672 voters in the Louth area gave Mr McGahon their first preference vote in the 1995 general election. In spite of frequent accusations of bias, the ethos of *The Late Late Show* has remained unchanged since its inception in 1962 – the exposition of Ireland's culture in all of its inglorious diversity.

The Late Late Show continued to challenge and shape political and social issues in Irish society almost as simultaneously as they occurred. Ideologies and personal philosophies were heard on a regular basis on the show. In an end-of-season programme in 1996, writer Joe O'Connor was asked whether he

---

[67] *The Late Late Show*, 11 October 1995.
[68] John Masterson, in interview with the author, *op. cit.*
[69] *The Late Late Show*, 11 October 1995.

was a non-believer or an agnostic.[70] He replied that he believed in the fictional Fr Ted, to loud applause from the audience. In the same show, the late comedian Dermot Morgan, alias the fictional Fr Ted, ridiculed the formidable former Archbishop of Dublin John Charles McQuaid. Furthermore, Galway politician Máire Geoghegan-Quinn talked of becoming the first female Taoiseach and leader of the Fianna Fáil party.[71] In 2009 she was appointed Ireland's first female EU Commissioner.

Between 1996 and 1998, the show limped rather than vaulted towards its final finishing line in May 1999. There were some intermittent minor controversies, some a little absurd. Take, for instance, the embarrassment to Byrne and the show caused by the infamous 'chairgate' incident. This involved Donegal woman Siobhan Maloney, who claimed to have restored a ruined Regency period library armchair into a prize-winning antique as part of an antiques special of *The Late Late Show* broadcast on 10 May 1997. Over a million viewers saw her walk away with the top prize of IR£1,000 worth of Paul Costello glassware before it emerged that a Dublin-based upholsterer had been commissioned to restore the chair. There was further intrigue when a Galway bookbinder insisted that it was he who had carried out '98% of the work on the antique book' that Ms Moloney also claimed to have restored.[72] Byrne made numerous attempts to contact Ms Maloney through his radio programme, but he finally resigned himself to the fact that she had 'gone to ground.'[73] RTÉ was left with a defamation action to contend with.[74]

It is worth noting that the earlier controversies evoked by the Brooke, Murphy and Adams interviews failed to be mentioned in the minutes of the RTÉ Authority meetings or the Editorial Committee meetings. This omission perhaps reflects a less intrusive monitoring of the show and an awareness by

---

[70] *The Late Late Show*, 30 May 1996.

[71] *Ibid.*

[72] 'It's time for bed', *Ireland on Sunday*, 16 May 1999.

[73] *Ibid.*

[74] 'Real restorer vindicated by humble apology', *Irish Independent*, 9 February 2000.

the RTÉ Authority in particular that Irish television audiences were increasingly more liberal in outlook and less scandalised by hitherto condemnable exchanges.

A far more serious and tragic societal issue was addressed on the show in 1998. This was the Omagh Special in November of that year. The Omagh tragedy was the result of a car bomb attack carried out by the Real Irish Republican Army (RIRA), a splinter group of the IRA. The attack in Omagh, Co. Tyrone, in Northern Ireland left 29 people dead and more than 20 injured, some of whom were present on this very moving episode of *The Late Late Show*. Many of the show's researchers recounted how they spent the weekend in tears as they organised the show.[75]

In the audience was Clare Gallagher, who lost her sight in the bombing. The tragedy of the event was also captured by Mick Grimes who lost his wife, Mary, his daughter Avril Monaghan (who had been pregnant with twins) and his granddaughter, Maura. The potency of television was palpable, as Byrne masterfully interwove their separate tragedies to create a very memorable show.

Old-Fashioned or Just Old?

Nonetheless, like its radio counterpart, it was the fun-filled episodes of *The Late Late Show* that proved perennially popular, and none more so than the annual Toy Show – 'known to RTÉ Sales Division as The Longest Running TV Commercial in the World.'[76] It began in 1971, the brainchild of Pan Collins, and was the only show that Byrne ever announced in advance. Each year, for almost 30 years, Byrne would abandon his customary shirt and tie for a yuletide woolly jumper. Christmas was never the same without the Toy Show, and it is a tradition that still continues to this day.

---

[75] Gay Byrne, in interview with the author, 2 September 2011.

[76] Pan Collins, *It Started on the Late Late Show* (Ward River Press: Dublin, 1981), p. 105.

Yet, towards the end of the 1990s, Byrne began to sound like the establishment to some viewers. The late Brian Lenihan's unchallenged tale about an unfortunate Garda who was offered a drink or a transfer when he found certain politicians drinking after pub closing time reminded viewers how embedded Byrne was in the old Ireland. This, along with his perceived rudeness when interviewing Annie Murphy, began to grate on viewers. Once the age of tribunals began in earnest, Byrne's studio-staged debates started to feel old-fashioned and trite. Irish society had created a new means of self-interrogation and Byrne's state-of-the nation set pieces were no longer relevant. Byrne himself saw no problems with being a member of the liberal establishment. Not long after his interview with Annie Murphy, he recalled how one journalist at a Sunday paper had been given a directive to 'have a go at Gay Byrne':

> When I look back at this piece in the Sunday paper and this fellow's conclusion, his final conclusion – now this is the Gay Byrne who was the anti-Christ for so long and paid directly from Moscow and a Leninist-Trotskyite, pornographer, everything – and this man opined that 'the trouble with Gay Byrne is that he's a right-wing conservative, old-fashioned Irish Catholic,' and I thought, Jaysus, I've come right around full circle now.[77]

The Remit of *The Late Late Show*

For some critics, the perception of the show as a barometer of social change was inaccurate as it did not deal effectively with issues such as institutional abuse and the links between big business and politics. In response to these criticisms, former researcher June Levine (whom Byrne claimed 'had a huge effect' on his way of thinking[78]) maintains that in the early years of the show, 'We

---

[77] Gay Byrne, in interview with Kathy Sheridan, *Irish Times*, 17 September 1994.
[78] Gay Byrne, in interview with the author, 2 September 2011.

didn't know about those issues.'[79] Adrian Cronin, who directed *The Late Late Show* from 1963–88, says of the early days:

> I don't think there was any subject we didn't touch that was of interest to the public. We covered the whole spectrum. And in doing that certain toes were stood on but generally speaking I think we handled them in a manner that was useful to society.[80]

By May 1999, Byrne still had his loyal production team around him. Cillian Fennell was the only fledgling, and he had become producer of the show in 1996, replacing John Masterson. Other than Fennell, and a perfectly balanced research team made up of Will Hanafin and Padraig O'Driscoll from Cork, and Yvonne Nolan and Paulette O'Connor from Dublin, all the main production team had been with Byrne for quite some time. Maura Connolly, Byrne's personal assistant, had been with the show for 30 years. Senior programme researcher Brigid Ruane had worked with the show since 1980. Colette Farmer, of 'Roll it there, Colette' fame and show director since 1991, had started with *The Late Late Show* as a research assistant in 1964. The late Pan Collins, who worked on the show for 21 years and introduced the concept of the now legendary Toy Show, epitomised this notable allegiance to Byrne. On the prospect of his retirement, she commented:

> If he were to give it up, a big chunk of my life would go with it. Although I retired eight years ago, Friday nights are still sacred, and I do not answer either the telephone or the doorbell when *The Late Late* is on air.[81]

---

[79] June Levine, in interview with Diarmaid Ferriter on the RTÉ Radio 1 series *What If?*, Autumn 2003.

[80] 'Goodbye Gaybo', *RTÉ Guide*, 14 May 1999.

[81] *Ibid.*

But Collins need not have fretted. Byrne would ultimately retire in May 1999, with a swathe of new controversies and media outrage in his wake.

Entrapment: Byrne v Flynn

This time, the controversy centred on Pádraig Flynn, Ireland's EU Commissioner at that time, and his boast about his three houses in Dublin, Castlebar and Brussels. To contextualise Flynn's comments, it must be noted that the cost of a new home in late 1990s Ireland had spiralled by 16.5 per cent nationally and by 17 per cent for second-hand homes over a five-year period. Irish people were really struggling to come to terms with the downside of the Celtic Tiger. Following a gentle coaxing by Gay Byrne, Flynn managed to bring his political career to a sudden end, 'without even noticing.'[82]

Pádraig Flynn also made comments about property developer Tom Gilmartin and his wife being unwell, comments that prompted Gilmartin to reconsider his decision not to give evidence to the Flood Tribunal that was investigating planning irregularities in Ireland in the 1990s. Byrne gives this account of his interview with 'Pee' Flynn:

> During the interview I knew he was in trouble when he dismissed Tom Gilmartin as being unwell – that could mean anything ... And his remark about running three houses was crass and condescending in the extreme ... But I have a secret theory that at that time, he'd completely lost touch with reality ... and that's the effect Brussels has on people.[83]

When he received the message that Mr Gilmartin was watching in Luton and he wished to make it clear that he was not sick, and had never felt better, Byrne realised:

---

[82] 'ME & PEE', *Life, Sunday Independent*, 21 September 2004.
[83] *Ibid.*

that Pee had put his foot in it. And I knew that with our studio audience, at least, he was not flavour of the month. And as always, the studio audience was merely a microcosm of the rest of the land.[84]

Byrne would later also claim he was genuinely sorry for Flynn's subsequent downfall and that of his family. He insisted, however, that whereas *The Late Late Show* may have hastened it a little, it was not the cause. The seeds of the downfall had been sown a long time before.[85]

John McColgan, a close friend of Byrne's and a former RTÉ producer, notes that the Flynn interview was quintessential of Byrne in that he would 'lead people to the point where they would expose themselves.'[86] David Norris notes that 'the naughty side' of Byrne came to the fore in this much-cited interview.[87] The television critic of the *Connacht Sentinel* did not quite appreciate the subtlety of Byrne's interviewing and could take no more of it:

> If there was a prize for the most obnoxious interview of the year Gay Byrne would win it hands down for what was easily one of the worst interviews of his career. Had I a sledgehammer in my hands I would certainly have driven it with venom through the television screen directly at Padraig Flynn's block for what was the ultimate in cringe viewing. He is affectionately known as Pee – a perfect description of everything he had to say on the programme.[88]

As a result of his appearance on *The Late Late Show*, Pádraig Flynn, a man who by his own reckoning had had 'a charmed political existence' and a 'wonderful political career',[89] was

---

[84] *Ibid.*

[85] *Ibid.*

[86] John McColgan, in interview with the author, 1 March 2012.

[87] David Norris, in interview with the author, 22 March 2012.

[88] 'Pee's posturing drives me round the bend', *Connacht Sentinel*, 19 January 1999.

[89] Former EU commissioner Pádraig Flynn, in interview with Gay Byrne on *The Late Late Show*, January 1991.

thrown into the heart of the Flood Tribunal's investigations into payments to politicians. Together with his daughter Beverley's unsuccessful libel action against RTÉ, this brought to public attention affairs which the Flynns would rather have kept secret, involving tax evasion and personal enrichment from a huge political donation.[90] While *The Late Late Show* was not the sole catalyst in the downfall of Pádraig Flynn, the potency of the show and its continued relevance as a conduit of change is evident in its willingness to challenge in equal measure complacency and corruption.

Kiss and Tell!

More controversy came on Byrne's penultimate episode of *The Late Late Show*, broadcast on 14 May 1999, when he interviewed the gossip columnist Terry Keane, who controversially revealed her 27-year affair with former Taoiseach Charles J. Haughey. Though the affair was a well-kept secret in media and political circles, the revelation that the 'sweetie' who appeared in Keane's gossip column in the *Sunday Independent* was in fact Haughey led to a media frenzy and an attack on an Irish newspaper industry that had blatantly applied self-censorship for over a quarter of a century on one of Ireland's most controversial political figures and his lengthy extra-marital affair. The audience was palpably hostile to Keane as she claimed that Haughey had 'shaped and moulded her',[91] not entirely evidenced through her portrayal in the RTÉ mini-series *Charlie*, broadcast in January 2015.

Keane, who was paid for the 'kiss-and-tell' articles which were published in *The Sunday Times*, returned to *The Late Late Show* in 2006 and claimed that 'Going on *The Late Late* [in 1999 and revealing her affair] was not a spiteful gesture, but it was the most selfish thing I've ever done.'[92]

---

[90] 'Flynnasty', *Scannal*, RTÉ, 24 January 2007.
[91] *The Late Late Show*, 3 May 1999.
[92] *The Late Late Show*, 6 February 2006.

Once again, Byrne's interviewing style was called into question. Due to his personal friendship with former bishop Eamon Casey, he had been accused of bias in his interview with Annie Murphy. Here again his allegiance to his friend Charles Haughey made for a very soft-focused interview. The television critic at the *Connacht Sentinel* had this to say:

> There are many reasons why Gay Byrne should call it a day and last Friday night's farce with Terry Keane was one of them. The manner in which she was allowed to make unchallenged claims about her extra-marital affair with Charlie Haughey purely for financial gain was nothing short of disgraceful.[93]

Media expert Colum Kenny voiced his objection to the sheer lack of good taste in having Terry Keane (and singer Sinéad O'Connor) reveal all on *The Late Late Show* when he said:

> Sinéad O'Connor and Terry Keane recently rushed onto *The Late Late Show* and into print, risking contempt and ridicule as they shared their personal emotions and private lives with all of Ireland. Right to the very end Gay Byrne knew what people liked, and never mind the gurus of good taste.[94]

Television critic Eddie Holt disagreed:

> Keane's performance was, by any standards, a compelling one, in a very 1990s genre, gossip as personal confession … watching Terry Keane recount her love for a rogue former Taoiseach – and all on a variety show – was certainly compelling.[95]

---

[93] 'Blunt edge of Gaybo's line of questioning', *Connacht Sentinel*, 18 May 1999.

[94] 'Of surrogate listeners and vicarious thrills', *Sunday Independent*, 23 May 1999.

[95] 'The other Keane', *Irish Times*, 22 May 1999.

Despite a personal friendship between Haughey and Byrne, at the end of the day the showman in Uncle Gaybo, the applause and the ratings all took precedence on this penultimate episode of *The Late Late Show.*

On Your Bike: The Final Show

Byrne presented his final instalment of *The Late Late Show* on Friday, 21 May 1999. His decision to leave was prompted by health concerns. He felt on the verge of a nervous breakdown and 'could no longer cope with the demands that people were making on him.'[96] He was, he admitted, 'living in a prison of my own making, which was a six-and-a-half-day week.'[97]

Byrne's final *Late Late Show* began at 9.30 p.m. and ran for a marathon four hours, twice as long as a normal episode. The guests on the final programme were a veritable who's who of Ireland's celebrity and political culture. Music was provided by The Corrs, Sarah Brightman and Christy Moore, with some vintage comedy from comedienne and singer Rosaleen Linehan, a long-time favourite on *The Late Late Show.* President Mary McAleese and former Taoiseach Bertie Ahern acknowledged the role of Gay Byrne in the pantheon of the talk-show genre and, much to Byrne's disbelief, U2 band members Larry Mullen and Bono presented him with a Harley-Davidson, a 'rock-and-roll'[98] symbol of gratitude for his decades of support for the band.

Tributes poured in for Byrne from all quarters of Irish life, including from comedian Billy Connolly, sports broadcaster Des Cahill, veteran DJ Larry Gogan, friend and broadcast colleague Mike Murphy, broadcaster Marian Finucane, and many more celebrities and friends. Historian and journalist Ryle Dwyer said of Byrne on his impending retirement from *The Late Late Show:*

---

[96] 'The Edge of Keane', *Sunday Independent*, 20 September 1998.

[97] *Ibid.*

[98] Bono made this comment as he and Larry Mullen presented Byrne with a Harley-Davidson on his final episode of *The Late Late Show* in May 1999.

Gay Byrne probably deserves more credit than any politician. His *Late Late Show* raised a whole variety of issues … He prodded, stimulated and led public opinion in an imaginative and constructive way. In the process he did more for tolerance in this part of the country than anyone, and thereby probably influenced more changes in Ireland than any politician.[99]

In May 1999, having presented the show for over 37 years (and producing it for 33 of those 37 years), along with presenting his five-day radio show for over 26 years, Gay Byrne stepped down from full-time broadcasting.

His departure caused quite a stir. The veteran broadcaster seemed rather bemused by the whole fuss, as former *Late Late Show* researcher Will Hanafin asserts:

To the end, Gay remained an individual. He treated U2's parting gift of a Harley-Davidson with complete bemusement, secure in himself not to rattle off some one-liner which showed he was hip to the whole motorcycling trip. All his *Late Late* shows strung together had the complexity and depth of the great novel which has never been written about contemporary Ireland.[100]

Byrne's retirement was to have massive repercussions for RTÉ. *The Late Late Show* had been the flagship programme of the station for almost four decades; without it, RTÉ risked losing its Friday-night dominance. Terrestrial viewers not only had the UK's BBC One and Two, ITV, Channel 4 and a plethora of satellite channels to choose from, but also TV3 and TG4. There were intense arguments regarding the future of *The Late Late Show*. Media commentators reckoned that the talk-show phenomenon was over, and it was time for a change in scheduling. It was also

---

[99] 'This is the man who shaped a nation', *Examiner*, 17 April 1999.
[100] *Life*, *Sunday Independent*, 3 February 2008.

argued that Byrne was too synonymous with the show for it to be a success without him.

But RTÉ disagreed and, with Byrne's support, decided to keep the show, arguing that it was too valuable a franchise to lose. The media endlessly speculated about Byrne's successor. Patrick Kielty and Graham Norton were both touted as possible successors. Sources close to Byrne believed his protégé Joe Duffy was ripe for the role. However, the show was offered to Byrne's main talk-show rival, Pat Kenny, who at the time hosted his own Saturday-night show. Thus it was that *The Late Late Show* continued without Byrne, but how would the talk show in general, on both radio and TV, survive without the iconic Mr Byrne at the helm? The following chapter looks at how the notion of the television talk show in Ireland essentially started with Byrne, and his influence is acknowledged by legions of talk-show hosts both in Ireland and internationally.

RTÉ broadcaster Gay Byrne in a 1964 publicity still for RTÉ Television's *A World of Film*, which Byrne presented throughout 1964 while commuting between Dublin and Granada TV in Manchester.

Broadcaster Eamonn Andrews (right) chats with Gay Byrne and Kathleen Watkins on their wedding day on 1 June 1964.

Gay Byrne with playwright and Trinity College student Brian Trevaskis on *The Late Late Show*, 22 February 1969, three years after his controversial appearance on the show on 22 March 1966 when he called the Bishop of Galway a 'moron'.

The *Late Late Show* research team in their office in May 1969. From left to right: visitor Barbara Sinclair from ATV, Joan Tuohy (behind the typewriter), Myles McWeeney, Pan Collins and Maighread Durcan.

Gay Byrne in a publicity shot for his new radio programme *The Gay Byrne Hour*, taken on 1 January 1973. *The Gay Byrne Hour* was a precursor of *The Gay Byrne Show*, which began in February 1973.

Gay Byrne at the microphone in RTÉ's recently acquired mobile studio in June 1974. *The Gay Byrne Hour* was broadcast from different locations around Ireland during the week, beginning 1 July 1974.

RTÉ agony aunt Frankie Byrne in February 1981.

Gay Byrne cuts a cake during celebrations marking the 20th anniversary of *The Gay Byrne Show* on 5 February 1983. Broadcast assistant Mary Martin is standing beside Byrne, helping him to cut the 'wireless' cake. Presenter Joe Duffy is standing next to Mary Martin and producer Alex White is holding a glass in celebration.

RTÉ broadcaster Doireann Ní Bhriain and Marian Finucane in a publicity shot for the RTÉ television programme *The Women's Programme* in October 1983. The programme ran from 1983 to 1986 and was produced by Clare Duignan and Nuala O'Faolain.

:ulptor P.J. Herity of the National Wax Museum in Dublin, at work on a model of Gay Byrne in February 1984.

Former Fianna Fáil Taoiseach Charles Haughey greeting party colleague Brian Lenihan during an episode of *The Late Late Show* dedicated to Lenihan, 30 March 1990.

Annie Murphy, the woman with whom Bishop Eamon Casey had a child, during her interview with Gay Byrne on *The Late Late Show* on 2 April 1993.

Gay Byrne joins Christy Moore and guests on an episode of *The Late Late Show* devoted to Moore, 31 October 1994.

The Late Late Show production team in 1996. From top row, from left to right: Mary, Cillian,

Joe Duffy and Gay Byrne in January 1996, posing for an article in the *RTÉ Guide* about their co-hosting of *The Gay Byrne Show*.

Gay Byrne interviewing Sinn Féin leader Gerry Adams on *The Late Late Show* on 29 November 1996, two years after his first interview on the show in 1994.

Gay Byrne with Welsh singer Charlotte Church on the annual *Late Late Toy Show* on 4 December 1998.

Gay Byrne surrounded by a crowd on Dublin's Grafton Street during the broadcast of the final edition of *The Gay Byrne Show* on Christmas Eve 1998.

RTÉ presenters Gerry Ryan (left) and Joe Duffy chatting together at a public affairs online meeting on 22 March 1999.

Gay Byrne with fellow Irish broadcasters Graham Norton and Terry Wogan on the set of *The Late Late Show* on 30 April 1999.

Gay Byrne with Bono (middle) and Larry Mullen of U2, on Byrne's last night as host of *The Late Late Show* on 21 May 1999, where Byrne was presented with a Harley-Davidson.

Postal stamp of Gay Byrne.

7

It Started with *The Late Late Show*:
The Evolution of the Television Talk Show

The eighteenth century marked a turning point in the history of public conversation. Members of the emerging middle class debated the more controversial issues of that time in taverns, coffee houses and at private dinner parties. These conversations were subsequently converted into print by journalists and publicly disseminated. This commodification of the talk worlds of the eighteenth century prefigured the television talk world of today. Essentially, the television talk show takes a very old form of communication and transforms it into a low-cost, highly popular form of information and entertainment. The television talk show developed from the antecedent talk traditions of radio. However, television talk is in itself a genre of television, anchored or framed by an announcer or host. In the US in particular it is a highly ritualised event, shaped and stage-managed by a team of producers and technical crews.

In Ireland, there is no actual history of the Irish television talk show, as *The Late Late Show* has dominated the domain since 1962. Moreover, Gay Byrne has largely dictated its format. Few programmes could match the attraction of this home-grown talk show. Even in the 1970s, when the show was pitted against the BBC's *Parkinson*,[1] viewing figures remained high. Byrne reached an even bigger viewing audience when in 1984 Channel 4 began to broadcast a one-hour version of the previous week's show to British audiences.

However, in the late 1970s, as well as *Parkinson* there was also competition from the popular, candid-camera style comedy chat show, *The Live Mike*,[2] hosted by the very personable Mike Murphy. In a hilarious sequence filmed at Trinity College Dublin in January 1982, Murphy managed to get the better of Byrne when he interrupted a piece his rival was filming. He disguised himself as an intrusive Frenchman who kept getting into Byrne's shot as he was trying to shoot a piece to camera. Watching the suave Byrne become increasingly irritated and eventually uttering a minor expletive provided great entertainment for those who had never seen Byrne appear so flappable.[3]

Byrne's personality was central to the success of *The Late Late Show*. The significance of his style of broadcasting has been singled out by journalist Mary Kenny, who refers to Byrne as 'probably the greatest broadcasting genius of our generation – in any country.'[4] She comments upon Byrne's understanding of the art of entertainment:

> Gay knows that this is about entertainment (which includes creating a sensation). Serious issues have been taken up, and he has taken them up with great skill; but fundamentally it's entertainment, and the Gay Byrne personality that works best for *The Late Late Show* is the showman, the entertainer, the Great Barnum.[5]

---

[1] *Parkinson* was a BBC TV talk show hosted by Michael Parkinson. It ran from 1982–2007 and won a British Academy of Film and Television Arts (BAFTA) Award for best entertainment programme in 1999. Michael Parkinson (Parky) has cited Byrne as one of his all-time favourite talk-show hosts and his idol.

[2] *The Live Mike*, RTÉ 1 Television, 1979–82.

[3] 'Gay Byrne Framed', RTÉ Archives, 8 January 1982.

[4] Mary Kenny, 'The Great Television Turn-off, *The Sunday Independent Weekender*, 24 July 1993.

[5] *Ibid.*

Australian talk-show host Mike Walsh, who emigrated from Ireland in 1967, attributes the success of his eponymous talk show 'down under' to *The Late Late Show* and the 'easy skill of its presenter.'[6] From the very outset of his career in Australian television, Walsh made it known that he was modelling his style on Byrne and ran his show along the same lines as *The Late Late Show*. Furthermore, Irish-born Graham Norton, now the BBC's premier talk-show host, also cites Byrne's *Late Late* as the template for his own talk show:

> In Ireland we had *The Late Late Show*, hosted by Gay Byrne who will probably be horrified to hear that he inspired my show in any way, but he did. It was an endless show – it lasted about three hours – and was very free-form and brilliant.[7]

Yet, in spite of Byrne's obvious skills as a television host, falling ratings in the 1990s suggested it was time for him to go. The television critic for the *Longford Leader* believed the days when issues were very black and white and when Ireland was a grey and grim place were over. Audiences now watched in full technicolour, as Ireland crept out of its past into a brighter era. The ending of the show in May 1999 marked what he believed was a rite of passage for this nation.[8]

In 1996 television critic Eddie Holt argued that talk shows were dead and had been replaced by 'quasi-freak' shows that relied heavily on embarrassing gimmickry. He lamented the demise of the traditional talk show, which was, as he saw it, replaced by 'PR engineered hype and controversy.'[9] Byrne had made clear his intentions to leave the show before his Television Audience Measurement (TAM) ratings plummeted[10] and

---

[6] 'Gay is flattered by Down Under show imitation', *Irish Press*, 1 October 1987.

[7] 'Graham Norton on biting his nails, getting older and how telly's gone tame', *Radio Times*, 19 October 2012.

[8] 'Too Much Talk?', *Longford Leader*, 5 May 1999.

[9] 'Talk Television', *Irish Times*, 10 April 1996.

[10] Gay Byrne, in interview with the author, 1 January 1996.

once commented that he could not see himself continuing as presenter of *The Late Late Show* beyond 1992: '[Thirty] years of the same show would be enough for anyone; and even if RTÉ decides to continue the show I may take myself off it at that point – maybe!'[11]

Byrne's ultimate departure from *The Late Late Show* in 1999, and the previous year from *The Gay Byrne Show*, marked the advent of a fourth national television channel, TV3 – Ireland's first commercial television broadcaster. In March 1997, Radio Ireland (now Today FM) was launched, leading to a further fragmentation of television and radio audiences. RTÉ was also haemorrhaging money, as it incurred half the running costs of the all-Irish television channel, Teilifís na Gaeilge (now TG4). By 1999, Irish audiences were changing rapidly, and RTÉ was confronted with the harsh commercial fact that they had nurtured very little new talent and were over-reliant on the old. The State broadcaster had grown complacently dependent on Byrne and *The Late Late Show* and had done little to stem the exodus of disillusioned viewers who wanted more from the licence fee than a weekly talk show.

Kenny at the Helm

In September 1999, Pat Kenny became the new host of *The Late Late Show* and immediately set about putting his own personal stamp on the show. He dispensed with its title music, introduced a new opening theme in 2003 and, gradually, all that remained of the old show was the Toy Show at Christmas. Even the element of suspense was done away with, as Kenny revealed his guests in advance of the show. The television critic from the *Connacht Sentinel* believed *The Late Late Show* should have retired with Gay Byrne:

---

[11] Gay Byrne with Deirdre Purcell, *The Time of My Life: An Autobiography* (Gill & Macmillan: Dublin, 1989), p. 237.

When Gay Byrne retires, *The Late Late* should retire with him … Pat Kenny is very hard to swallow on a Saturday night and the last thing we need is any further misery in our weekends.[12]

Many critics were also unhappy with the continued use of the *Late Late Show* name with Kenny as host. In 1999, journalist Eamon Sweeney expressed his disquiet with the talk-show genre and also questioned the continued use of the *Late Late Show* brand, which he felt should have been retired with Byrne. He claimed RTÉ was still 'poncing' off the reputation of the show that Gay built:

The *Late Late Show* is the world's longest-running talk show, they proudly boast in Monstrose. Really? The Mousetrap is the world's longest-running play, and it's dire. And anyway, it's not *The Late Late Show*, it's *Kenny Live* in disguise.[13]

Criticism was also levelled at the format of the show, which was considered outdated. In 2003, journalist Pat Stacey felt the show in its current form was redundant, while acknowledging it was still a 'cash cow' and a 'recognised brand name', still regularly commanding an audience in excess of half a million people. Like many critics at the time, she felt the show was a relic of a bygone age, a painful hangover from a lost and unlamented Ireland. *The Late Late Show* with Pat Kenny was seen as no more than 'an over-inflated talk show' that frequently struggled to fill its two-hour running time.[14]

Seven years into his role as host of the show, media commentators were still not convinced of Kenny's suitability for the job. In her *Sunday Independent* article entitled 'Sorry, Pat, but

---

[12] 'Late Late should retire gracefully with Gaybo', *Connacht Sentinel*, 13 April 1999.

[13] 'Dull and duller', *Sunday Independent*, 7 May 2008.

[14] 'Will Dunphy put the boot to the lamentable Late Late?' *Irish Independent*, 17 May 2003.

you're no Gay Byrne. You never will be. And you know it,'[15] Eilis O'Hanlon harshly criticised Kenny for not accepting complaints about his handling of the show:

> Has he [Kenny] ever considered the possibility that the reason many people don't like what he's done to *The Late Late Show* isn't because they object to being challenged, or are afraid of change, but because they genuinely think that, in his seven-year tenure, he has performed the broadcasting equivalent of drawing a felt-tip moustache on the Mona Lisa?[16]

O'Hanlon goes on to criticise Kenny's interviewing style, in particular his clumsy style of 'exaggerated mateyness' with the studio audience, which she believes made Kenny 'look like the class geek who's desperate to be seen as one of the lads.'[17]

Broadcaster and journalist Vincent Browne was somewhat kinder in his assessment of Kenny on the occasion of the latter's sixtieth birthday.[18] Browne believed Kenny suffered from the contrast between 'his stiff, awkward style' compared with Gay Byrne's 'easy mastery' of that genre. Browne also points to Kenny's 'celebrity susceptibility' where the 'embarrassing air-kissing of celebrity woman participants' was excruciating at times. But, he adds, 'for someone burdened with degrees in chemical engineering from UCD and the Georgia Institute of Technology in Atlanta, this was quite an achievement.'[19]

Interesting comparisons have been made between Kenny's intellectualism and Byrne's almost anti-intellectualism. Journalist Liam Fay is generous in his praise of Kenny as a radio host. He believes Kenny is excellent on the radio doing current

---

[15] Eilis O'Hanlon, 'Sorry, Pat, but you're no Gay Byrne. You never will be. And you know it', *Sunday Independent*, 27 August 2006.
[16] *Ibid.*
[17] *Ibid.*
[18] 'Pat Kenny at 60', *Village Magazine*, 31 January 2008.
[19] *Ibid.*

affairs. However, regarding his role as host of *The Late Late Show*, Fay makes the following comments:

> Most of the time people end up watching him in horror, through their fingers, on *The Late Late Show*. He's just somebody who shouldn't have made the switch.[20]

Many critics felt that the show would not survive under Kenny in the digital age because it was not encouraged to be controversial. RTÉ bosses seemed happy for it to remain blandly entertaining. In 2009, the then Director General of RTÉ Cathal Goan and Director of News Ed Mulhall revealed they were 'uneasy' about a segment of the show in which commentator Eoghan Harris and television pundit Eamon Dunphy engaged in a heated pre-election discussion 'about the media, Bertie Ahern and the Mahon tribunal leaks.'[21] For viewers, the debate was a wonderful piece of television, reminiscent of the good old days with Gay Byrne when anyone could deliver a broadside from the audience and stir up high drama and passions.

In 1997, when Gay Byrne was still hosting *The Late Late Show* and Pat Kenny was host of *Kenny Live*, a nationwide survey was conducted by this author to garner public attitudes towards both hosts.[22] The survey encompassed aspects of both qualitative and quantitative research and took the form of a nationwide questionnaire.[23] The questionnaire was formulated with two purposes in mind: the first purpose was to elicit

---

[20] *Sunday Independent*, 18 May 2008.

[21] 'Debate on Late Late makes RTÉ feel "uneasy"', *Sunday Independent*, 2 March 2008.

[22] The survey, 'Attitudes to Two Talk Shows', focused on the views of audiences regarding *The Late Late Show* and *Kenny Live*, a talk show hosted by Pat Kenny on RTÉ television on a Saturday night. The questionnaire was devised by this author in 1997, and the audience research was conducted by the marketing group, AGB Adelaide.

[23] Viewing figures for *The Late Late Show* were correlated with the gender, age and demographic details of the respondents – 1,101 in total, from the six main geographical regions of Dublin, Leinster Urban, Leinster Rural, Munster Urban, Munster Rural and Connaught/Ulster Urban.

opinions to general questions on the frequency of viewing *The Late Late Show* in comparison to *Kenny Live* and the entertainment value of each show. The second purpose was to elicit personal and individual opinions from respondents on issues such as why they liked or disliked Byrne or Kenny and the format of their respective shows. Although the survey is not intended to justify any analysis of Byrne and *The Late Late Show*, it is nevertheless a useful resource for historical research.

Data from the survey findings indicated that the viewing frequency of *The Late Late Show* was highest in the 35–64 age bracket and lowest amongst 15–24-year-olds. It could be inferred that in the mid-1990s, with fewer television sets per household, the viewing preferences of the older age groups took precedence regarding programme viewing. Survey findings also indicated that an overwhelming 82 per cent watched *The Late Late Show* on a regular basis, pointing to a more settled, terrestrially loyal profile amongst its audience, a profile that is now almost impossible to attain in the age of digital TV.

The format of *The Late Late Show* was generally liked by respondents. Top of their list of preferences were the interesting mixture of guests, the annual Toy Show and the Antiques Show (this no longer forms part of the current show's format) and, of course, the free giveaways to the audience. The data from this survey also indicated that 56 per cent of respondents tended to agree that Byrne was generally better than other talk-show hosts, and 64 per cent disagreed that Byrne should retire.

In response to the question, 'What do you like (if anything) about Pat Kenny,' answers predominantly mentioned his good looks and his professionalism. On the other hand, when asked what they disliked about Kenny, respondents' answers included that he was 'dull', 'yuppish'[24], 'a bit stuffy', 'looks too perfect' and tended to ask rhetorical questions to display his

---

[24] 'Yuppie' was a pejorative term used frequently in the 1990s to describe a 'young urban professional'.

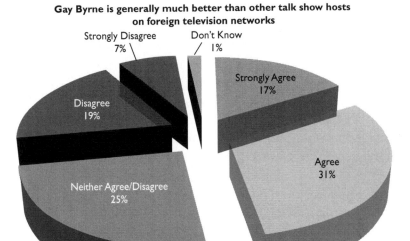

Gay Byrne is generally much better than other talk show hosts on foreign television networks

Strongly Disagree 7%
Don't Know 1%
Strongly Agree 17%
Disagree 19%
Agree 31%
Neither Agree/Disagree 25%

48% of respondents are in some form of agreement with this statement, 25% neither agree nor disagree, while 26% are in some form of disagreement with this statement, indicating that Gay Byrne is generally perceived as much better than other talk show hosts on foreign television networks, although there is also a high % of neutral responses at 25%.

Source: Finola Doyle O'Neil UCC. Source survey data collected and prepared by AGB Adelaide, graphical presentation by Envisage HPC. All rights reserved.

intellect. Furthermore, many agreed that Kenny was better on radio than on television.[25]

Pat Kenny exited *The Late Late Show* in May 2009, claiming he was happy he had succeeded in 'keeping the brand alive' and that the show, throughout the 2009 season, had an average audience of 682,000 – more than at any other time over the previous ten years.[26] Kenny went on to become host of a high-profile current affairs television programme, *The Frontline*, broadcast on RTÉ One from 2009 to 2013. He left RTÉ in 2013 and moved to the independent national radio station Newstalk to host his own daily radio show.

He performed well in the Joint National Listenership Research (JNLR) figures within the first two years of the show, pitted

---

[25] 'Attitudes to Two Talk Shows', *op. cit.*, survey conducted in 1997.
[26] *RTÉ Guide*, 23–9 May 2009.

against his former RTÉ Radio 1 colleague Sean O'Rourke.[27] Kenny also started a new television talk show, *Pat Kenny in the Round*, for UTV Ireland in May 2015, proving in spite of his critics that he still has a career in television.

Commenting on his move to UTV Ireland (an independent commercial television station), Kenny, who spent 41 years with RTÉ, said he firmly believes the Irish media landscape has changed irrevocably. 'It was the art of the possible,' says Kenny of the move. 'It showed that there is an alternative market.'[28]

In the UK, that 'alternative market' has always offered a wide-ranging choice of talk-show host. Though Gay Byrne was an iconic host in Ireland, he was not, according to British journalist Roy Greensdale, 'A Johnny Carson or a Michael Parkinson.'[29] Although celebrities did appear on *The Late Late Show*, it wasn't its *raison d'être*. Greensdale felt *The Late Late Show* dealt with 'real issues and real people' and that 'it mattered' and 'couldn't be ignored'. Greensdale believed that Gay Byrne was 'embedded within Ireland and its society'. He believed that *The Late Late Show* with Byrne as host 'could not be exported', and it was 'impossible to compare with any British programme.'[30]

US and UK Talk Shows Versus *The Late Late Show*

The Late Late Show was wholly unlike American and British talk shows, adapted as it was to an Irish audience. The American talk show, for example, is more intimate in its approach than the Irish version. Complex human experiences are discussed, and the guests often appear bruised and emotionally bereft after each interview. However, one of the most essential differences between *The Late Late Show* and US/UK talk shows is that the latter are shown predominantly during the day, and

---

[27] Sean O'Rourke is a radio presenter on RTÉ Radio 1, hosting *Today with Sean O'Rourke* on weekdays.
[28] 'Back in the Arena', *RTÉ Guide*, 9–15 May 2015.
[29] 'So much more than just another chat show', *Irish Times*, 5 May 1999.
[30] *Ibid.*

audiences are made up largely of women. American day-time talk shows such as *Ricki Lake, Geraldo, Jerry Springer, Monroe* and *Steve Wilko* – all of which are available via satellite to Irish audiences – are strong on empathy and human suffering. Many of these shows have no agenda other than to express feelings, making no attempt to resolve or change situations.

US and UK talk shows have become increasingly unorthodox and eclectic. They have been vilified by critics who suggest 'the culture's preoccupation with victimization' is leading to 'the general decline of social discourse'.[31] In the US, the style of talk show led to the fatal shooting of Scott Amedure after he appeared as a guest on the *Jenny Jones* show. On the show Amedure revealed that he was attracted to a male acquaintance. After the show aired, the acquaintance shot Amedure for humiliating him on national television.[32]

Also at this end of the eclectic and eccentric spectrum was a *Jerry Springer* show centred on a husband's infidelity with the babysitter while his wife was in hospital having the couple's baby.[33] Such shows offer a distorted vision of America, but many viewers nevertheless claim that the American daytime talk show, and its preoccupation with sex, race and family dysfunction, is the only forum where these issues are discussed on television. In contrast, *The Late Late Show* has maintained consistent viewing figures with material that is of a general interest to the majority of Irish audiences, without being tasteless.

In real terms, the versatility of the talk show is its ability to straddle virtually the whole of television, from journalism to soap opera to sports. The format of the television talk show is also technically and financially undemanding. Over the years RTÉ has grossly overused this genre of talk TV, allowing *The Late Late Show, The Saturday Night Show*[34] (which ended its five-year stint in 2015 in spite of overtaking Ryan Tubridy's version

[31] Steven D. Stark, *Glued to the Set* (Dell Publishing: New York, 1977), p. 371.
[32] *The Jenny Jones Show*, NBC Network, 6 March 1995.
[33] *The Jerry Springer Show*, RTÉ 2, 7 March 1998.
[34] A Saturday-night talk show presented by Brendan O'Connor on RTÉ One.

of *The Late Late Show* in April 2015[35]), and the summer-filler *Tonight With Miriam*[36] to dominate peak-time weekend viewing.

There is also a virtual graveyard of unsuccessful former talk-show hosts, including Carrie Crowley,[37] Mary Kennedy,[38] Clare McKeon,[39] Gerry Ryan,[40] Lucy Kennedy[41] and Craig Doyle.[42] In the 1990s, Pat Kenny's *Kenny Live* for a time rivalled Byrne's *The Late Late Show,* while Ryan Tubridy's *Tubridy Tonight*[43] also proved a success. Both shows ended when Kenny and Tubridy, in turn, took over as host of *The Late Late Show.*

Ireland's first commercial TV broadcaster, TV3, also attempted to compete in the talk-show wars when it launched *The Dunphy Show* in 2003, hosted by soccer pundit Eamon Dunphy. The show aired for just one series and was cancelled after three months. Dunphy acknowledged his losing battle with *The Late Late Show* when he signed off on his last show with the words: 'I fought the law, and the law won.'[44]

The Future of Television Talk in Ireland and the Rise of Social Media

In May 2009, 35-year-old Ryan Tubridy was announced as the new host of *The Late Late Show.* Tubridy had made his broadcasting debut doing children's book reviews on Radio 2 in 1985, along with an occasional spot on *The Gerry Ryan Show.*[45] By

---

[35] Television Audience Measurement (TAM) Ireland, www.tamireland.ie, 9 July 2015.

[36] A Saturday-night talk show scheduled during the summer months, presented by Miriam O'Callaghan on RTÉ One.

[37] *Limelight*, RTÉ One, 1997.

[38] *Kennedy*, a summer-filler on RTÉ One from June to August 1997.

[39] *Later with Clare McKeon*, a women's talk show on RTÉ 2, 1997–2000.

[40] *Ryantown*, RTÉ One, 1993–94; *Gerry Ryan Tonight*, RTÉ One, 1995–97; and *Ryan Confidential*, RTÉ One, 2004–10.

[41] *The Lucy Kennedy Show* lasted just five episodes from January to February 2009.

[42] *Tonight with Craig Doyle*, RTÉ One, 2010.

[43] *Tubridy Tonight*, a Saturday-night talk show hosted by Ryan Tubridy from 2004 to 2009 on RTÉ One.

[44] *The Dunphy Show*, 12 December 2003.

[45] 'Will it all start again on the Late Late Show?' *Irish Examiner*, 16 May 2009.

May 2009 his early-morning radio programme, *Today with Ryan Tubridy*, had a daily listenership of 330,000, making it one of the most popular programmes on RTÉ Radio 1.[46]

Prior to taking up his role as host of *The Late Late Show*, the media was awash with advice for Tubridy, including some words of wisdom from former host Gay Byrne:

> Off you go, young Tubs; get yourself a good producer who's a grafter and a forager, and who is trustworthy. After that it's research and ideas. And then more research and ideas.[47]

In terms of advertising appeal, Tubridy was an attractive option, as he reached out to all demographics. His Saturday-night talk show on RTÉ One television was hugely popular, garnering an average audience of 464,000[48] right up to the demise of the show. It was this popularity that emboldened RTÉ to seek a €1.2 million sponsor for the first season of *The Late Late Show* with Tubridy as host. It was announced in August 2009 that one of the most famous names in Irish business, the Quinn Group, would begin a two-year sponsorship deal of the show. The fact that the owner of the Quinn Group, Sean Quinn, and his family lost over €1 billion in the Anglo Irish Bank debacle, which scuppered the Irish banking sector, led to accusations of a conflict of interest when the banking crisis was to be discussed on the show. Many commentators felt that the Quinn sponsorship deal 'could have a fundamental effect on choosing topics for discussion.'[49]

In Pat Kenny's final season as host, *The Late Late Show* was unable to attract a sponsor, despite Kenny having the best

---

[46] 'It's a long time since I've been this happy', *Sunday Independent*, 17 May 2009.

[47] Gay Byrne, 'A Log', *Sunday Independent*, 17 May 2009.

[48] 'Most Watched: TAM Viewing Figures', *RTÉ Guide*, 23–9 May 2009. (Up to December 2014 the *RTÉ Guide* provided TAM viewing figures for RTÉ television programmes on its inside cover page with the title 'Most Watched'.)

[49] 'Conflict of interest in Late Late's Quinn deal', *Sunday Independent*, 16 August 2009.

performing year of his ten-year tenure, with audiences averaging 683,000 per programme.[50] However, this was not seen as a deterrent by RTÉ. According to Nielsen Media Research, the 2008/09 series reached 93 per cent of all adults in the country and 98 per cent of all parents.[51]

The predictions were that Tubridy would do well to maintain these percentages and that he was more likely to attract younger, more affluent consumers. However, that same group typically socialises on weekends, and thus his appeal might not necessarily translate into healthy audience figures. According to journalist Shane Hegarty, 'moving Tubridy from a Saturday night slot to Friday solves the problem of having two talk shows each weekend in a landscape saturated with talk shows.'[52] This observation went unheeded by RTÉ when it launched the *Saturday Night Show*, hosted by Brendan O'Connor, just a year later in 2010. The pool of interviewees for two Irish talk shows is difficult to sustain. Moreover, the cult of celebrity is now very much diminished, and talk shows have become little more than conduits for celebrities to sell their latest product. According to one media pundit, in order to succeed, Tubridy would have to 'jettison the last ten years of *The Late Late* and go back to the future when missing the show meant missing a slice of Irish life.'[53]

To date, the programme with Tubridy as host has yet to prove that it is a viable example of public service broadcasting at its most interesting and challenging. The current *Late Late Show* has not been without controversy, however. On 4 September 2009, Tubridy hosted his first show of Europe's longest-running talk show, capturing 1.6 million viewers.[54] Reminiscent of the Byrne years, his handling of an interview with former Taoiseach Brian Cowen received an avalanche of comments. Many viewers took

---

[50] 'Late Late to seek €1.2m sponsor deal', *Sunday Independent*, 28 June 2009.

[51] *Ibid.*

[52] 'The making of a chat show host', *Irish Times*, 16 May 2009.

[53] *Ibid.*

[54] '1.6m tune in to watch Ryan's Late Late Show', *Irish Examiner*, 8 August 2009.

time to voice their opinions on the interview in the letters page of the *Sunday Independent*:

> Sir,
>
> As a result of Ryan Tubridy's ugly, rough treatment of Brian Cowen I compare this *Late Late Show* persona to the *Sun*, while Pat Kenny is comparable to the *Examiner* and Gay Byrne to the *Independent*.[55]

> Sir,
>
> The idea of an interview of the most powerful politician in the land on a TV show being declared 'outrageous' is ludicrous in a democracy, no matter how hard the questions or how brief the answers.[56]

However, despite the initial promise of Tubridy as host, viewing figures have declined over his tenure, with the standard exception of the Toy Show, which garnered a total of 1,594,000 viewers in 2014, approximately 20,000 more than 2013.[57]

The Battle for Viewers

How can one account for the longevity of *The Late Late Show*? Is it feasible to still assume that its structure and content continues to somehow tap into the Irish psyche in a way that is unique? Or rather, is it the case that, without Byrne, it is simply a tired re-creation of a lucrative brand, with a talk/entertainment format that is cheap and unchallenging?

The media landscape in Ireland has certainly changed dramatically from Byrne's halcyon days as a broadcasting heavyweight. Twenty-first century consumers are now being offered

---

[55] Letters to the Editor, *Sunday Independent*, 13 September 2009.

[56] *Ibid.*

[57] Television Audience Measurement (TAM), March 2015.

a plethora of choice regarding information and entertainment. On-demand viewing and social media are changing the way audiences interact with and experience television. Figures for the first quarter of 2015 show that over 85 per cent of all Irish Internet users used social network sites such as YouTube, Facebook, LinkedIn and Twitter.[58]

In terms of television broadcasting, Ireland has also seen dramatic change. For over 40 years Ireland had broadcast television services from a terrestrial network on an analogue basis, but in 2012 all terrestrial channels were converted to digital. Such technological changes are light years away from the one-television channel of Gay Byrne's *Late Late Show* throughout the 1960s and 70s.

Viewer loyalty to *The Late Late Show* was already in question when audience figures for the show fell from over a million in 1991 to just above seven hundred thousand on 5 May 1998.[59] This gradual fragmentation of the show's audience is indicated in a survey conducted by this author that revealed 77 per cent of viewers had multi-channel television access by the late 1990s.[60] This presented its own problems to advertisers. In 1985, a commercial during *The Late Late Show* reached a captive audience of well over 1.5 million. By 1999, the same commercial reached only 780,000 people,[61] with the exception of the last edition of the show with Gay Byrne, which attracted over 950,000 viewers.[62]

The current battle for viewers is even more intense. RTÉ is now broadcasting to a multicultural society. In its 2013 annual report it claims its aim is to 'nurture and reflect the cultural and regional diversity of all the people of Ireland' and to 'provide distinctive programming and services of the highest quality

---

[58] Irish Social Media Statistics (May 2011), www.neworld.com, accessed 3 May 2011.
[59] *RTÉ Guide* TAM figures compared by the author from April/May 1991 and April/May 1998.
[60] 'Attitudes to Two Talk Shows', *op. cit.*, survey conducted in 1997.
[61] 'Most Watched: TAM Viewing Figures', *RTÉ Guide*, 23–9 May 2009.
[62] Nielsen, *Republic of Ireland TV Review*, May 1999.

with the emphasis on home production.'[63] There is an acknowl-edgement by RTÉ that 'much like Ireland itself is changing, RTÉ must change, and change quickly.'[64]

The *Reality Bites* series of one-off, non-judgemental slices of Irish life is just part of the current direction taken by RTÉ away from packaged descriptors of 'Irishness'. Some RTÉ pro-grammes, out of necessity, appear to have adopted an American gloss in order to attract younger viewers. However, within this Americanisation, a handful of programmes still manage to keep issues pertinent to an Irish audience. These include *Would You Believe?*, a series profiling ordinary and extraordinary Irish people and their beliefs; *Who Do You Think You Are?*, where well-known Irish people trace their ancestry; and *The Investigators*, a programme which documents the work of Irish scientists at the cutting edge of technology. RTÉ's impressive range of home-produced programmes also covers areas such as health and lifestyle, in *Operation Transformation*, and a host of cookery programmes.

Back in 1988, Irish cultural theorist and philosopher Rich-ard Kearney argued that a distinctive identity would surface quite naturally if an artist spoke with his or her voice about his or her own experiences and environment.[65] Some claim that the earlier success of *The Late Late Show* was primarily due to this airing of personal experiences publicly on live television. Yet, the viability of *The Late Late Show* will centre around an acknowledgement by RTÉ that Ireland has become a pluralist society, host to several religions and diverse cultures. Though it may appear that the State broadcaster is aware of its role as the promoter of an indigenous Irish culture, it remains to be seen whether it has done enough to adapt its programming to the seismic shift in Ireland's cultural landscape.

---

[63] *Annual Report 2013*, RTÉ Publications.

[64] *Ibid.*

[65] Richard Kearney, *Across the Frontiers: Ireland in the 1990s* (Wolfhound Press: Dublin, 1988), p. 79.

In 1973, historian Desmond Fennell attempted to outline the features that would characterise successful RTÉ programming:

> It takes place in Ireland. It is predominantly urban. It is religious and its religion is Roman Catholic. It is culturally English in an Irish Catholic mode, with some Gaelic memories. It has its own politics.[66]

In twenty-first-century Ireland many of these characteristics are virtually unrecognisable. RTÉ no longer addresses a homogenous audience united by its Catholic nationalist culture. Indeed, some critics would claim RTÉ is still quite insular and those 'Gaelic memories' of which Fennell spoke in 1973 have now taken centre stage in a culture struggling to define itself, sandwiched as it is between the broadcasting cultures of Anglo-America. Furthermore, *The Late Late Show* should not be the sole flagship of that diversity, as has been the case since its inception. Nevertheless, the fiftieth anniversary special of the show in 2012, *The Late Late Show 50*, on which Byrne, Kenny and Tubridy all appeared in studio, garnered 1.6 million viewers, making it the most-watched show that year.[67]

While RTÉ One continues to be the most dominant Irish station, particularly with older audiences, a growing number of extra channels have diminished its share of the market. TV3 has seen a huge growth in viewing figures in the 15–44 age bracket. This is due to the popularity of shows such as *The X Factor, The Apprentice, Tallafornia* and *Come Dine with Me Ireland*. Irish audiences' insatiable appetite for current affairs also helps *Tonight with Vincent Browne* to a nightly audience of more than two hundred thousand viewers. The percentage of home-produced content on TV3 reached 37 per cent in 2011, helping to increase its market share that year.[68] Its sister channel 3e has become the most-viewed digital-only channel in Ireland, ahead of Sky One

---

[66] Desmond Fennell, 'Successful programming', *Irish Press*, 3 February 1973.
[67] www.digitaltimes.ie, accessed 4 February 2012.
[68] *Ibid.*

and E4.[69] TV3 has also invested in local talent with inexpensive studio-based talk programmes such as *Ireland AM, Midday* and *Late Lunch Live,* all of which are intent on keeping the nation talking.

Despite all the home-grown shows being produced in Ireland, our proximity to Britain continues to impact on our programme preferences. It is self-evident that Britain's media culture will, to a certain degree, dilute and shape that of Ireland. The most popular station broadcasting into the Republic from beyond it in 2014 was BBC One Northern Ireland, with a 4.5 per cent market share.[70] This channel was watched on average by one in twenty viewers at any point. UTV took second place in this category and has since launched a new television station in the Irish Republic, leading to further fragmentation of the Irish television audience.[71]

The combined impact of Sky Television, MTV, E4, Nickelodeon and Paramount on Irish viewing figures indicates that these channels have instigated a gradual and continuous trend away from Irish television stations. This will undoubtedly have implications for Irish culture and politics in the future, as particularly younger adult viewers move away from terrestrial channels and indigenous culture and viewpoints.

The Irish Television Talk Show as Social Historian

The notion of television talk shows in the 1990s as powerful cultural institutions and leading forums for evolving national values and ideas was challenged with the advent of the 'new media' of the twenty-first century. Viewers have now become netizens, as they engage online with television. Recent studies have shown

[69] '"Byrne factor" helps TV3 Group to bounce back from loss to profitability', *Irish Times*, 2 December 2011.

[70] AGB Nielsen viewing share from 2014.

[71] The advent of UTV into the Irish TV market particularly affected TV3, which held the franchise to broadcast into the Republic of Ireland soap operas such as *Coronation Street* and *Emmerdale*. The franchise is owned by UTV and was added to its own programming schedule when it launched UTV Ireland in January 2015.

that at least two pivotal moments in Egypt's 2011 Arab Spring Revolution took place on talk shows on the country's private satellite channels, primarily due to a synchronisation of new social media and satellite media. Popular mobilisation through Facebook and Twitter, along with the more traditional mass media, featured prominently in the eighteen-day uprising that toppled Egypt's President Hosni Mubarak, under whose rule Egyptian television was heavily censored. This was perhaps the first glimpse of the disintegration of the satellite/Internet divide and the demise of the centrality of the day-time talk show.

For television viewers in Ireland and the UK, the love affair with the day-time talk show is over. Choosing a random day in May 2015 from the programme listings in the *RTÉ Guide* to illustrate this argument, just one talk show featured – *The Jeremy Kyle Show*. Moreover, this had been relegated to a 10 a.m. slot on TV3, 9.25 a.m. on UTV Ireland, and 2 p.m. on 3e.[72] It seems the glory days of wall-to-wall day-time talk shows are long gone. They have been supplanted by a proliferation of reality shows and lifestyle and makeover programmes.

In contrast, the late-night talk show, in the US in particular, is still a powerful monitor of public opinion. These shows continue to have popular appeal, and their hosts remain influential. From Carson to Cordon, and from Byrne to Brendan O'Connor and his replacement Ray D'Arcy, talk-show hosts speak to cultural ideals and ideas as forcefully as politicians. National talk-show hosts like Byrne became surrogates for the viewer/citizen, interrogating and deliberating on public affairs and national concerns. Moreover, talk shows can be valued as social texts, highly sensitive to the topics of their social and cultural moment and important barometers of public opinion. References to the O.J. Simpson case[73] on US talk shows in the mid-1990s, for example, reflected a preoccupation in that

---

[72] *RTÉ Guide*, 9–15 May 2015.

[73] In 1995, O.J. Simpson, a retired American football player, was acquitted of the 1994 murder of his ex-wife, Nicole Brown Simpson, and Ronald Goldwin, after an internationally televised criminal trial.

country with domestic violence and issues of gender, race and class. In Ireland, in a similar way, Byrne's *Late Late Show* channelled and challenged the issues of the day, making it, and indeed the talk show generally, an important social historian of its time.

Will the television talk show remain a significant sociohistoric indicator of a nation's indigenous culture? In Ireland, for instance, its vulnerability to exogenous cultures is diluting the influence of the nation's broadcast media. In an attempt to counteract the effects of Anglo-American media, the Broadcasting Bill of 2008 recommended wide-reaching changes to assist RTÉ in its role in promoting Ireland's unique indigenous culture.[74] Yet, in spite of this competitive broadcasting world, the Irish talk show and talk-show host have survived. Byrne himself has stated that there 'is always a place for a talk show, human nature doesn't change,' adding that the host has now become 'more important than any guest'.[75]

In spite of the proliferation of social media, Irish audiences are quite unique in that they still like to consume their television live. A survey conducted by Television Audience Measurement (TAM) Ireland in March 2015 revealed that 89 per cent of Irish viewers watch their favourite shows live, highlighting perhaps that the immediacy of a television talk show has more appeal than a later viewing.

Nonetheless, viewing figures for *The Late Late Show* in the first half of 2015 were not encouraging.[76] Apart from the annual Toy

---

[74] Many of the proposals deviated considerably from existing regulations. Under the Bill, a newly formed body – the Broadcasting Authority of Ireland (BAI) – replaced both the Broadcasting Commission of Ireland and the Broadcasting Complaints Commission. In terms of a commitment to addressing the fragile status of Irish culture and the role of the public service broadcaster, the Bill recommended the requirement that every five years public service broadcasters draw up a charter of commitment that would be reviewed by the Minister and the BAI. Also proposed were 'more qualitative measures and an assessment from the audience' to help gauge the value from the licence fee and to produce 'better content in a broadcasting world that is becoming far more competitive.'

[75] Gay Byrne on the *Saturday Night Show*, RTÉ 1, 12 May 2012.

[76] TAM Ireland LTD/Nielsen, 6 May 2015.

Show, which showed an increase of viewers in its December 2014 show, it seems that Byrne's legacy as longest-serving host of *The Late Late Show* – a record 37 years – is safe. His longevity as host has prompted some observers to compare him to one of Ireland's most iconic historic figures, Éamon de Valera. Kevin Myers, in his column *An Irishman's Diary*, claims that Byrne 'was the finer man by far.'[77]

In response, Roy Greensdale of *The Guardian* has stated that he balks at agreeing with Kevin Myers's hyperbolic view that history will rank Byrne alongside, maybe even above, Éamon de Valera, adding:

> Byrne has helped to dismantle the society envisaged by Dev. He has challenged his taboos, and, as a professed Catholic conservative, has been able to do so without the kind of hostility which would have probably scuppered an atheistic liberal.[78]

The comparison of Byrne to de Valera is not without its ironies. The closed, insular society created by Éamon de Valera was ripped open by the searing searchlight of Gay Byrne and his television and radio shows. Yet, while television talk shows may have come full circle, radio talk shows have become increasingly significant as purveyors of popular culture. In Ireland, the evolution of the radio talk show can be attributed to the influence of Byrne's pioneering radio show, *The Gay Byrne Show*. Talk radio is central to our public discourse. With over 80 per cent of the Irish population listening to radio on a daily basis,[79] the talk-radio show – the history and significance of which is discussed in the next chapter – has become an important barometer of Irish life and culture.

---

[77] Kevin Myers, 'An Irishman's Diary', *Irish Times*, 3 April 2000.

[78] Roy Greensdale, 'Goodbye Gaybo', *Guardian*, 14 May 1999.

[79] Joint National Listenership Research (JNLR), July 2014–June 2015, Broadcasting Authority Ireland (BAI).

8

From Gaybo to Joe: Talk Radio in Ireland

Simultaneous to the decline in cultural impact of the television talk show in Ireland, the talk-radio genre has evolved into a significant indicator of popular culture. With its link to the greater community, radio is a place 'where the nation meets',[1] and one of the most popular forms of media in Ireland today. More than 80 per cent of adults in Ireland tune into radio on a daily basis.[2] This often overlooked medium has become something of a cultural phenomenon within the Irish commercial media landscape. The notion of talk radio as an ersatz confession box is one that originated with *The Gay Byrne Show*. For a programme that began in a quiet way, specialising in completing sets of china and offering advice on tourist attractions,[3] it evolved into one of the most influential radio shows of its genre.

Yet, *The Gay Byrne Show* does not fall neatly into any category of talk-radio show. Most research in this area has focused on characteristics such as keeping listeners up to date on political issues and providing them with a forum where these issues can be discussed by ordinary people. This descriptor could apply in

---

[1] Joint National Listenership Research (JNLR)/Broadcasting Authority of Ireland (BAI), 15 July 2014–15 July 2015.

[2] JNLR 2015, *ibid.*

[3] 'Radio Review', *Irish Press*, 7 April 1973.

some degree to Joe Duffy's radio phone-in show, *Liveline,* on RTÉ Radio 1. Here, callers can 'talk to Joe', allowing them a forum for social criticism, an almost 'instant complaint channel'.[4] In contrast, *The Gay Byrne Show*, due to its predominantly female listenership, was what researchers Harriet Tramer and Leo W. Jeffers termed 'a forum and a companion'.[5] One could argue that the show was used by women in the same way as they viewed television soap operas – 'as an escape outlet'[6] and as a source of information about everyday problems.

Radio History

In Ireland, the transformation of radio into a vibrant cultural force has been a long and arduous journey. Its roots extend right back to the foundations of the State. The messages sent across the airwaves from the School of Wireless Telegraphy in Dublin's GPO to announce the Easter Rising in 1916 marked not only the birth of the Irish Republic but also the inauguration of broadcasting. From its moment of inception, the primary function of Irish radio broadcasting was to defend the cultural autonomy of Ireland and to revive the national spirit. The first actual radio broadcast service in Ireland (on 2BE) began in Belfast in 1924 from the BBC studio. It was not until 1926 that the Irish Free State launched its own national radio service, 2RN, later to become Raidió Éireann.

In the early days, with no other radio stations to mask their frequencies, the inexpensive crystal radio sets could pick up signals from London and beyond. Those who possessed the more expensive valve radios could tune into a babble of voices from all over the world. All this changed, however, when former telegrapher and Minister for Post and Telegraphs J.J. Walsh regulated

---

[4] Norma Ellen Verwey, *Radio Call-ins and Covert Politics* (Averbury: Wiltshire, 1990), p. 10.

[5] Harriet Tramer and Leo W. Jeffers, 'Talk Radio—Forum and Companion', *Journal of Broadcasting* (27(3), 1983), p. 61.

[6] *Ibid.,* p. 64.

radio in Ireland in 1926.[7] Many were not happy with the loss of radio stations, and the Minister was accused of deliberately placing the new station, 2RN, on frequencies that blocked out signals from Manchester and Bournemouth, both of which were very popular with Irish listeners.[8] From the very start, Walsh ensured Irish radio would not assume any of the internationalism proposed by the BBC's first Director General, Lord Reith, whose welcoming letter to the new station spoke of 'a free exchange of thought and culture between all nations.'[9] Instead, Irish listeners had to be content to talk amongst themselves, with a radio schedule that remained largely unchanged until the 1960s.

Lord Reith passionately believed in the cultural rather than the commercial role of radio. Thus, in 1927, when the BBC became a corporation, it was allowed the autonomy of a public service broadcaster. In contrast, the nationalised radio service in Ireland had far less autonomy, being closely aligned with and controlled by the State.[10] Furthermore, the Irish radio service was a monopoly financed from domestic radio licence sales and from advertising revenue. During the earlier years of 2RN (the name is a pun on the song, 'Come Back to Erin'[11]) sponsored programming was the norm. Irish radio did not fully reflect popular culture of that time, but rather adhered to the Reithian principle of giving the people not what they wanted, but what the State felt they needed – information, education and some rather high-brow entertainment.

And so there were army bands, traditional musicians, programmes in Irish and programmes aimed at teaching Irish. Back then the schedule was predictable and safe, displaying little evidence of cultural energy or innovation. Instead, it

---

[7] Richard Pine, *2RN and the Origins of Irish Radio* (Four Courts Press: Dublin, 2002), p. 13.

[8] Christopher Morash, *A History of the Media in Ireland* (Cambridge University Press: Cambridge, 2010), p. 137.

[9] Quoted in J.C.W. Reith, 'A message from 2LO', *Irish Times*, 11 November 1925.

[10] Lance Pettit, *Screening Ireland: Film and Television Representation* (Manchester University Press: Manchester, 2000), p. 142.

[11] Pine, *op. cit.*, p. 3.

reflected a Catholic, homogenous, Gaelic-imbued culture with enthusiastic coverage of the Gaelic Athletic Association (GAA) and its games of hurling and football, and national religious feast days. During World War II restrictions were placed on news and weather reporting, or on anything controversial that might aid the Nazi cause. Thus, the dominant feature of the station was one of bland predictability, offering little in the way of listener interaction.

In addition, the culturally pretentious admix of Edwardian drawing music and céilí bands encouraged many to tune into the BBC and Radio Luxembourg services, which could still be accessed from within Ireland. By 1966, Raidió Éireann became Raidió Teilifís Éireann, acknowledging the advent of television in Ireland and forcing radio to compete with its more glamorous rival.

Nonetheless, there were some highlights in the radio schedule, most notably the general knowledge quiz show, *Question Time*, launched in 1938. This allowed for the first time a degree of audience participation, prefiguring the possibilities of radio as an interactive medium. It enabled listeners not only to play along at home, but it also lured them to the broadcasting site at the local town hall, making them integral to the production process. The show's ability to elicit impromptu political remarks from contestants made it a more emboldened and livelier programme than others at that time. The unscripted nature of the programme, later the hallmark of the talk-radio genre, eventually led to outrage when the show visited Belfast in 1948.[12] There the host asked a competitor the name of the world's best-known teller of fairy tales. The anticipated reply was Hans Christian Anderson. Instead, the contestant replied, 'Winston Churchill' – a breach of political protocol that delighted nationalists in the audience but very much perturbed officials in Belfast and London, ensuring the programme was never re-invited across the border.

---

[12] Eileen Morgan, 'Question Time: Radio and the Liberalisation of Irish Public Discourse after World War II', *20th Century Contemporary History*, Issue 4, Winter, 2001, Volume 9.

In addition, there was the excellent *Thomas Davis Lectures* series. These were half-hour broadcasts, delivered by established scholars who sought to provide sustained academic debate on subjects of Irish interest. Though scripted, these also provoked controversy, offering debate in the form of divergent historical interpretations and prompting listeners to respond with their own viewpoints. In essence, before the advent of the radio talk show in Ireland, both *Question Time* and the *Thomas Davis Lectures* played a significant role in facilitating national dialogue, thus paving the way for the expansion of public discourse through radio. Although it was oftentimes referred to as the Cinderella of the broadcasting service, Raidió Éireann in fact performed the thankless task of preparing the way for the talk-show radio genre and its subsequent reincarnation on television.

'Dear Frankie' and Talk Radio in Ireland

In contrast to the television sector, Raidió Éireann was not, and is still not, vulnerable to the influence of foreign broadcasters. While the Irish Government tolerated the growth of cable systems relaying British television into Ireland in the late 1960s, Irish radio endured no such competition. This monopoly position remained intact until the licensing of commercial radio stations in 1990. Raidió Éireann has never had to contend with exogenous radio stations, but rather with indigenous local radio, allowing it a virtual dominance for over 65 years. During the 1970s, when *The Gay Byrne Hour* first aired, RTÉ had evolved from a defender of national culture into a semi-commercial multi-media corporation. With the launch of the pop station 2fm in 1979, few saw the difference between this national radio station and the so-called 'superpirate',[13] both of which played pop music and were funded by advertising.

---

[13] The 'superpirates' were the larger, illegal commercial radio stations which were attracting a lot of advertising revenue away from RTÉ.

The successful adoption of commercialism by RTÉ from the very onset[14] opened the way for a fully independent commercial broadcasting sector in the Republic. It wasn't long before the Scottish Media Group took ownership in 2001 of the first commercial national radio station, Today FM, along with other regional stations. The country's third commercial national radio station, Newstalk, established in 2006, is at present wholly controlled by Irish interests. Currently, in the interests of a competitive market, media operators are prohibited from having more than a 27 per cent share in any broadcasting company.[15] There is a watching brief on this current percentage, bearing in mind the return of a more buoyant broadcasting landscape that skilfully survived the recession years of 2008 to 2013.

Much of this survival was due to the penetration of local radio stations into the hearts and minds of regional audiences, many of whom were starved of local references and resonances. During the 1980s the Irish authorities tolerated the existence of countless pirate stations, such as Dublin's Radio Nova and Cork's ERI. These thrived in the music vacuum left by RTÉ Radio 1 and its younger sibling, RTÉ Radio 2 (now 2fm). The diversity of culture in Ireland was immediately apparent as listeners tuned into their own local station to discuss the problems and issues specific to their locality.

No such diversity existed when *The Gay Byrne Show* began in 1973, broadcasting primarily to the nation's stay-at-home women. Irish comedienne Rosaleen Linehan once commented:

> Gay Byrne was the Irish woman's first affair. The smelly husband who didn't wash. He went out at 8 o'clock in the morning and Gay came in.[16]

---

[14] RTÉ Annual Report, 2014.

[15] John Horgan, Paul McNamera and John O'Sullivan, *Mapping Irish Media, Critical Explorations* (UCD Press: Dublin, 2007), p. 35.

[16] 'Dear Frankie', *Irish Independent*, 19 December 1998.

Unlike many of today's talk-radio programmes, *The Gay Byrne Show* was never openly confrontational. It was, in principle, not a talk-radio show, but a radio programme which facilitated talk, and with it emerged the phenomena of the public confessional.

Prior to Gay Byrne, however, there was Frankie Byrne, Ireland's first radio agony aunt and no-nonsense relationships advisor. Her show's opening words were always, 'Welcome to *Woman's Page*, a programme for and about you.' It was more colloquially known as *Dear Frankie*, as this was the opening line of each letter sent to the show. The programme (which formed the basis of a play by Niamh Gleeson in 2010[17]) was broadcast from 1963 to 1984. It had started out as a fifteen-minute domestic science question-and-answer segment, but soon turned into compelling radio. People all over Ireland sat in their kitchens, workplaces or boarding schools during their lunch break, listening in silence as letter writers shared problems of jealous husbands and lovelorn teenagers.

The most important feature of the programme was the fact that it was the first of its kind on radio to set people talking, and it helped begin a national conversation on the lonely struggles of generations of Irish women. The show is remembered fondly today by a cohort of listeners who lived through a time of no Internet, in an era when self-help books on issues of love and more daring intimacies were stored in a section of the town library, where everybody knew your name, thus limiting their appeal.

For twenty years Frankie solved the relationship problems of a nation, while living a life of turmoil herself.[18] With her distinctive husky voice, she became a household name in Ireland as the woman who found solutions to problems in a witty yet warm way. The letters sent to her, mainly by women, showed Ireland in a more innocent time. Letter writers wanted to know how to prod a reluctant boyfriend into popping the question or

---

[17] Niamh Gleeson, Clontarf playwright, author of the play *Dear Frankie*, first performed by the Five Lamps Theatre Company in Liberty Hall Dublin, October 2010.
[18] *Ibid.*

how to get their husbands to help out in the home. One such letter, which is certainly reflective of Ireland in a more innocent era, was sent by a woman asking if 'she could get pregnant by sitting on her boyfriend's knee.'[19] Frankie advised her to have a chat with her mother.

When Frankie gave advice it was according to the Raidió Éireann guidelines of the time. The establishment thinking of the 1950s and 60s came up with the view that single mothers, abortion, rape and marital infidelity were unfit for discussion on air, even though they might have taken up a huge part of people's lives. Equally unappealing were queries regarding mental illness, alcoholism, instability or tuberculosis in a family. Those whose questions touched on such matters did not have their problems answered on air.

In a rare interview with *The Irish Times* in 1993, Frankie spoke of how heartening it was to see 'the thick fog of hypocrisy lessen'.[20] However, she was sad to note that people's problems seemed to have remained the same, even though they could now be discussed in public. She spoke of 'the amazingly revealing interviews on *The Gay Byrne Show*,'[21] where women would ring in and tell the innermost secrets of their lives. Frankie would listen to these interviews and marvel at how things had changed. A lot of the people who had written to her show over the years did so in despair. They would print their letters for fear of recognition and some would even travel to different parts of the country to post them so they could not be traced.[22]

Frankie was herself a victim of the times, having given her child up for adoption in the 1950s.[23] She died in 1993 at the age of 71. Tributes were led by Gay Byrne, who said that for over 'twenty years Frankie Byrne was a national institution who

---

[19] *Ibid.*

[20] 'Ireland's Agony Aunt', *Irish Times*, 18 December 1993.

[21] *Ibid.*

[22] *Ibid.*

[23] *A Programme For and About You*, documentary by Collette Kinsella broadcast on RTÉ Radio 1, 22 October 2012.

had been loved by everyone.'[24] At its peak, her radio show was receiving one hundred letters from listeners. In more than one thousand programmes, in which she never missed a week,[25] Frankie was often quoted as saying that what her listeners wanted was not so much an agony aunt but a witch doctor with a potion that said 'how to make him love you and stay with you' on the bottle.[26]

In essence, it was Frankie Byrne's show that provided the template for not only *The Gay Byrne Show* but also *The Gerry Ryan Show* and RTÉ Radio 1's *Liveline* with Joe Duffy.[27] *Dear Frankie* played an important part in opening the doors for women's concerns to be heard more widely. Gay Byrne, in turn, became a companion and a listener for women of all ages, all over the country. According to former RTÉ broadcaster Doireann Ní Bhriain,[28] if he was accused of being occasionally, and perhaps unconsciously, somewhat patronising or chauvinistic, he wasn't alone amongst men of his generation in exhibiting these attitudes. Byrne had an unerring feel for what made good radio, and he and his programme teams were quick to respond to their women listeners' needs.

Prior to the advent of *The Gay Byrne Show*, Ní Bhriain points to the important change that had taken place in RTÉ with the introduction of daytime radio in 1968. Before then, the station used to stop broadcasting at 10 a.m., and didn't resume broadcasting again until lunchtime, with news and sponsored programmes. The early days of morning radio consisted of music programmes with titles like *Housewives' Choice* and *Rogha na mBan*, but these were eventually replaced with programmes

---

[24] 'Ireland's Agony Aunt', *op. cit.*

[25] 'Frankie loved by all', *Irish Independent*, 19 November 1980.

[26] 'Ireland's Agony Aunt', *op. cit.*

[27] *The Gerry Ryan Show* on RTÉ Radio 2 (later 2fm) ran from 1988 to 2011. *Liveline* with Joe Duffy has been broadcast on RTÉ Radio 1 from 1998 to the present.

[28] Doireann Ní Bhriain, in interview with the author, 20 September 2014. Doireann Ní Bhriain generously gave much of her time during a series of wide-ranging interviews (July–September 2014) with the author, including her views on the role and impact of *The Gay Byrne Show* and *Women Today*.

like *Here and Now*, a daily current-affairs and features show which began in 1971. *Here and Now* was succeeded by *Day by Day* in 1972, a daily current-affairs show that was willing to give airtime to what were finally beginning to be called 'women's issues'. Slowly but surely the agenda being set by the women's movement was finding its way into programmes like this, with space being provided for debates on subjects like contraception, which throughout the 1970s was still illegal in the Republic.

For many women *The Gay Byrne Show* became their lifeline to the outside world. There was no competition from daytime television – at least in Ireland at any rate – or from local or other national stations. They were, in effect, a captive audience, but they began to recognise the value of the access radio gave them to a wider world than the one in which they lived.

Women on Air: The *Women Today* Programme

The Gay Byrne Show heralded the beginning of the radio phone-in show in Ireland. For the first time the listener became an audible presence in the medium, not as a result of having her letter read out on air or going into studio but 'spontaneously and away from broadcasting equipment, in her own home or local telephone box or at her place of work.'[29]

Radio talk shows often provide political information to listeners and serve as a forum to criticise the Government,[30] and *The Gay Byrne Show* was no exception. Byrne endlessly criticised the Government and its running of the country. Yet, unlike talk-radio hosts in America, Byrne didn't really wish to talk about politics. He preferred to use the intimacy of radio to allow his listeners to confide in him. As discussed previously, it was his programme's broadcasting of personal stories that connected so well with listeners.

---

[29] Andrew Crisell, *Understanding Radio* (Sage Publications: London, 1986), p. 384.
[30] *Harvard International Journal of Press/Politics*, Volume 4, Issue 1 (Sage Publications: London, 1991), pp. 57–79.

Throughout the 1970s, the impact of the women's liberation movement began to be felt in Irish society. Women's voices were being heard in public in a way that they had never been heard before. The voices of Irish women campaigning for change were heard in the streets and in the newspapers. They demanded the right to equal pay for equal work, access to contraception and representation in political life. The veil was being drawn back over areas of life that had long been suppressed by social, political and religious attitudes that discouraged revelations of discontent or questioning of any kind.

Radio broadcasting, albeit in a more gradual way than television, began to open the airwaves to reflect the existence of women in roles other than those of homemaker and housewife. The marriage bar was finally removed in 1973, and a gender balance in terms of voices and views began to emerge. In 1979, a group of people in RTÉ radio decided the time was ripe for a programme devoted specifically to women listeners, featuring topics of particular interest to them. Launched in the year Pope John Paul II visited Ireland, the mass display of Catholic devotion that surrounded that event contrasted sharply with the issues dominating the airwaves on *Women Today*, as it captured the tensions and turbulence of Irish feminism. Marian Finucane, the show's first presenter, with a voice as husky and low-pitched as Frankie Byrne's, was also allied to the women's movement. The show was produced by Clare Duignan and first broadcast on 31 May 1979, the same day as the launch of RTÉ Radio 2, now 2fm.[31]

Besides Finucane and Duignan, there was also producer Betty Purcell, reporter Hilary Orpen, and researcher Patrick Farrelly. Here at last was the reflection on radio of the clamour for change being heard all over Ireland and elsewhere.[32] The show was scheduled for 2 p.m., a time when, for women at home, children had not yet got back from school, and when women at work might still be on a lunch break. According to

---

[31] RTÉ Tapes Archive, Donnybrook, Dublin 4.
[32] Doireann Ní Bhriain, in interview with the author, 20 October 2013.

Ní Bhriain, 'It took on, head first, some of the basic women's rights issues of the day.'[33]

Clare Duignan has spoken of the pioneering content of its first programme.[34] It was a debate on the question of whether women ought to work outside the home. Legislation on equal pay had yet to come from Europe, and contraception was still illegal. Politics, education, social justice, employment and unemployment, health, sexuality, sport, the arts – they were all on the agenda, and all examined from a woman's perspective. Both Ní Bhriain and Duignan recall that some listeners found the very idea of discussing anything to do with sex on the radio anathema, and those listeners wrote in great numbers to the programme to complain.[35] To others – those who wanted and needed to hear sexual matters talked about and, in many cases, explained – it was a liberation and an education.

Ní Bhriain recalls that *Women Today* encouraged women to talk. She recalls their stories of the joys and pains of pregnancy and childbirth, the misery of difficult marriages, the exhilaration of sporting achievement, the pleasures and pains of artistic creativity, the frustrations of trying to break the male mould in traditional politics and the delight in succeeding, the unfairness which still caused women to be treated as unequal to men in so many spheres. And they and the programme were accused of undermining family values, and of being a danger to society.

The *RTÉ Programme Policy Committee Meeting Notes* regarding the show highlight the almost heroic efforts of Michael Littleton, Head of Features and Current Affairs in RTÉ, to shield his team from the disquiet directed at the programme. His defence of the programme started from his very first encounter with a young Betty Purcell (later to become series producer), when he offered her a job on the show. He told her to 'do the best programme'

---

[33] *Ibid.*

[34] Clare Duignan, in interview with the author, 15 June 2014.

[35] Ní Bhriain has kindly donated copies of some of these letters to the author, forming the genesis of a further study on women and radio in Ireland.

she could and he would 'back her up'.[36] *Women Today* met with an avalanche of criticism, including from former GAA President and RTÉ Authority member Con O'Murchú, who accused the show of becoming 'obsessed with sex and obscenity',[37] an accusation that had been levelled at *The Late Late Show* some years previously.

Yet, in spite of all the talk the show generated, *Women Today* was not a talk show as such. Letters were central to its modus operandi, but unlike on *The Gay Byrne Show* where letters to an extent dictated the programme format, the letters written to *Women Today* were precipitated by topics discussed on the show.

If the 1970s gave a voice to women through the Women's Liberation Movement and through the quietly revolutionary efforts of the Irish Country Women's Association (ICWA), the 1980s heralded the confessional era. The airwaves were filled with stories of institutional abuse and intimate sexual stories, and *Women Today* was at the coalface of all these revelations. In a much more direct and forthright fashion than *The Gay Byrne Show*, it provided the platform for these emerging stories.

The show ultimately ran from 1979 to 1984. Though not always directly through the channels of phone-in radio, which was still in its infancy in Ireland at that time, *Women Today* nonetheless inspired the setting up of women's support groups throughout the country. By putting women in touch with each other, providing information they could not otherwise have found easy access to, and boosting their confidence, the show helped women to realise they were not alone and provided them with a real lifeline.

The ultimate agenda of *Women Today* was to ensure women's concerns gained as much attention as men's. By the mid-1980s this was finally beginning to happen in broadcasting. What would heretofore have been considered 'women's issues' were beginning to find their way into mainstream politics and public life. According to Ní Bhriain, the real victory for the

---

[36] Betty Purcell, *Inside RTÉ: A Memoir* (New Island: Dublin, 2014), p. 44.

[37] RTÉ Authority Minutes, 7 April 1980.

campaigning broadcasters who had initiated the programme was the knowledge that by the time it went off the air in the mid-1980s, it was no longer needed,[38] in particular with the arrival of *The Gerry Ryan Show*.

Gerry Ryan and Talkback Radio

When former *Gay Byrne Show* producer John Caden commented that he was 'absolutely convinced' that there was an 'insatiable desire' in Ireland for serious, well-conducted, lively entertaining debate,[39] he was referring of course to *The Gay Byrne Show*. Yet, his comments were equally pertinent to that other morning radio talk show, *The Gerry Ryan Show* on 2fm.

The show was launched in 1988 and hosted by 'the brash and boorish'[40] Ryan, or 'Lambo' as he came to be known following a report he filed on *The Gay Byrne Show* in 1987.[41] In a segment intended to see how a group of people could subsist in the wild with nothing but a recent book on survival to guide them, Ryan and some volunteers were deposited in the wilds of Connemara. They had to survive without materials or money. Ryan sparked national controversy when he claimed on the show that he and his crew had killed and eaten a lamb. The incident, and Ryan, subsequently became known as 'Lambo', pre-figuring not only reality TV and media feeding frenzies but, more immediately, the uniquely outrageous content of *The Gerry Ryan Show* which made Ryan a household name in Ireland.

Ryan has been credited with metaphorically removing the grill in the confession box that separates the priest and the penitent,[42] using the intimacy of radio as a substitute for the public discourse Irish people never had. Ryan's style of broadcasting, briefly referenced in a previous chapter, can be further

---

[38] Ní Bhriain, 20 September 2014, *op. cit.*

[39] 'GBS still popular with listeners', *Sunday Independent*, 6 April 1997.

[40] *Ibid.*

[41] 'Is Ryan for Real?', *Sunday Independent*, 1987.

[42] 'Gerry Ryan: Ireland's cleverest interviewer', *The Sunday Times*, 2 May 2010.

sub-divided into a genre known as talkback radio. Talkback radio is a particular phenomenon of American and Australian radio, and Ryan adapted much of its characteristics. In contrast to *The Gay Byrne Show*, which did not intentionally invite confrontation or debate, *The Gerry Ryan Show* provided an opportunity for callers to state their opinions on air, the focus being primarily on entertainment rather than any real sense of social responsibility. The talkback radio audience is a community of listeners who are brought together by a programme or host as a result of the conversational exchanges between host and callers.

Ryan's listeners called the show for a variety of reasons, including as a form of compensation for a lack of social activity or other interpersonal communications. Social scientist Sara O'Sullivan's study on callers to the Ryan Line showed he had a younger audience than Gay Byrne, but the majority of his callers were also women.[43] O'Sullivan also makes the point that despite RTÉ's role as a public service broadcaster, more than half of its revenue is obtained through advertising. Thus, the main purpose of *The Gerry Ryan Show* was to attract as many listeners as possible rather than to provide a forum for debate.[44] Despite this, Ryan did challenge the public–private divide by using his own personal experience and that of his listeners to legitimise topics belonging to both spheres.

One of the more defining moments of the Ryan Line came in 1993, when rape victim Lavinia Kerwick rang in to air her feelings on the suspended sentence of her attacker.[45] In waiving her anonymity, Kerwick became the first Irish victim of rape to go public, using the radio talk show as her vehicle of response. Here the notion of the radio talk show as a forum where ordinary people could use their own experiences to bring the

---

[43] Sara O'Sullivan, 'The Ryanline is Now Open', *Media Audiences in Ireland: Power and Cultural Identity* (UCD Press: Dublin, 1997), p. 168.

[44] *Ibid.*, p. 169.

[45] *The Gerry Ryan Show*, 2fm, 11 April 1993.

powerful to task – forcing women's private issues into a very public arena[46] – had become very real.

Ryan's show also introduced another broadcasting talent, Terence the agony uncle, who further fuelled the notion of radio as a form of confessional. Described, tongue-in-cheek, by *Irish Times* radio critic Michael Foley as a cross between 'Woody Allen, Liberace, Max Headroom and Frank Spenser of *Some Mothers Do Have 'Em*,' this 'flamboyant but tragic Chaplinesque figure on the broadcasting landscape'[47] rose to prominence while still working as a hairdresser in Cork. He would phone into *The Gerry Ryan Show* and simultaneously regale and entertain listeners with advice and absurd opinions. Terence, alias veteran Irish broadcaster John Creedon, was the radio doppelgänger of the BBC television drag queen Dame Edna Everage, but more lovable and more endearing, with his childlike catchphrase: 'We're all God's children.' For radio listeners in Ireland in the late 1980s, Terence was the champion of the underdog, as he meted out questionable advice to his chosen target audience – housewives and the unemployed. He was an entertaining interlude in an Ireland not yet gripped by the sophistication that the Celtic Tiger would herald. When the 1990s did come around, Terence and his simple childlike philosophy soon became redundant.

For some, the late Gerry Ryan, the 'titan of broadcasting', remains irreplaceable. Ryan's show offered something that no other radio host's offered: his larger-than-life personality and his heady, seemingly effortless mixture of sensitivity and laddishness was, according to broadcaster Darragh McManus, what made him so 'compelling and authentic and annoying and clever and you never knew what was coming next.'[48] Some critics, like McManus, have expressed doubt about the survival of 2fm's morning talk show with Ryan Tubridy, with JNLR

---

[46] Sara O'Sullivan, *op. cit.*, p. 168.

[47] 'Radio Review', *Irish Times*, 14 October 1989.

[48] 'How do you replace the irreplaceable?', *Sunday Independent*, 24 April 2015.

figures showing he was haemorrhaging listeners.[49] Tubridy has now moved to RTÉ Radio 1 as host of the 9–10 a.m. slot. Nevertheless, talk radio is alive and well in Ireland, as evidenced by the continued popularity of Joe Duffy's show *Liveline*.

Irish Talk Radio Today: Talk to Joe on *Liveline*

When *Women Today* ended in 1984, Marian Finucane (who had temporarily left the programme to edit *Status* magazine,[50] a publication aimed primarily at women) became presenter of *Liveline*, a title dreamed up by former *Women Today* presenter Hillary Orpen and editor Ed Mulhall.[51] With a daily 2–3 p.m. slot, the show kept many of the elements and staff of *Women Today*, and most of its focus in the early days was on the empowerment of women.

In 1997 Finucane left to present her own weekend show, *The Marian Finucane Show* on RTÉ Radio 1,[52,53] and Joe Duffy took over as presenter. Duffy's *Liveline* is currently Ireland's most listened to talk-radio show.[54] The success of the show confirms that talk radio is still a phenomenally popular choice of public discourse in Ireland, and its origins can be traced right back to *Women Today* and *The Gay Byrne Hour*.

When Joe Duffy took over as presenter of the show he acknowledged that Finucane and her production team had already established *Liveline* at 'the centre of Irish life' and 'at the heart of national discussion'.[55] The phone-in element had become central to the show, with reports and studio guests gradually phased out to accommodate the unending stream of

---

[49] *Ibid.*

[50] *Status* magazine, published from March–December 1981 with ten issues in all, was part of the *Sunday Tribune* newspaper.

[51] Joe Duffy, *Just Joe: My Autobiography* (Transworld Ireland: Dublin, 2012), p. 330.

[52] 366,000 listeners in JNLR 2014.

[53] 'Listeners "tuning out" of popular radio shows', *Irish Examiner*, 26 December 2012.

[54] 431,000 listeners in JNLR 2014.

[55] Duffy, *op. cit.*, p. 314.

listener interaction. With Duffy as host, *Liveline* has mediated over a new Ireland, and its success has been in part due to the explosion in social media. Callers engage with its performative role as a vehicle for the expression of everyday experiences and as a voice for the marginalised.

Yet, the reasons why people call radio talk shows is still a potentially rich area of unexplored research. O'Sullivan found that talkback radio has a therapeutic quality for some callers, legitimising their troubles and enhancing their self-esteem.[56] Certainly the notion of sharing and legitimising a viewpoint was evident in 2007 when prisoner John Daly spoke to *Liveline* from his cell in Portlaoise, prompting outrage from the Minister for Justice that RTÉ had allowed the call live on air.[57] The ownership of a mobile phone in a prison cell was a hugely contentious issue. A security sweep of the prison services some weeks later saw the confiscation of hundreds of mobile phones, 'along with plasma TVs, and various other treasures, including a budgie!'[58] When Daly was murdered shortly after being released from prison, Duffy wondered if the phone call from his prison cell had somehow contributed to his murder.[59]

More outrage followed from ministerial quarters in 2008 when *Liveline* discussed the banking crisis and the queues forming outside local post offices and bank branches, as people queued in their thousands to withdraw their money. Described as 'the most destructive broadcast ever' by a senior bank official,[60] the Minister for Finance Brian Lenihan alleged the broadcast had caused huge panic in the financial systems.[61]

Talk radio has many incarnations. Sociologist Ike Hutchby has called radio conversations 'confrontation talk' – a reflection

---

[56] Sara O'Sullivan, 'The Whole Nation is Listening to You: The Presentation of the Self on a Tabloid Talk Radio Show', *Media, Culture and Society* (25(5), 2005), pp. 719–38.

[57] *Liveline*, RTÉ Radio 1, 4 May 2007.

[58] Duffy, *op. cit.*, p. 375.

[59] *Ibid.*

[60] *Liveline*, RTÉ Radio 1, 22 September 2008.

[61] Duffy, *op. cit.*, p. 405.

of our perceived need to argue.[62] On *The Gay Byrne Show* there was little by way of confrontation, just revelation and confession in its purest form. Now, in the form of *Liveline*, talk radio may be viewed as both a form of resistance and as an attempt to create a community. It can also be said to encourage a community of the disaffected, as it offers solidarity and reinforcement for those alienated from power.[63] Duffy has revealed that of all the stories concerning political, judicial and social issues discussed on *Liveline*, it was in fact the stories of 'scams, rip-offs and double-dealing' that proved the most enthralling for listeners.[64] Duffy regards the function of the programme as providing a 'voice for the voiceless'.[65] For him, what distinguishes *Liveline* from other radio programmes is its insistence that 'those who would not normally have a voice are given priority.'[66]

Another attractive aspect of talk radio for those who feel frustrated with not being able to be heard by those in power is the immediate gratification that it provides. Listeners to *Liveline*, or the regionally based phone-in shows throughout Ireland, know instinctively that they have a platform to vent their ideas, to praise, to gripe or to criticise to an audience of like-minded souls, making them feel uplifted and empowered. Nevertheless, most people who listen to talk radio never call the programme, the main exception being with regard to sports-talk programmes. Studies in the US on sports-talk radio reveal that if a listener hears another person air a point of view during a call which is similar to their own point of view, a bond begins to exist between that listener and the caller.[67] This para-social interaction builds affinities between hosts and callers and among other

---

[62] Ike Hutchby, *Confrontation Talk: Arguments on Talk Radio* (Mahwah NY: New York, 1996), p. 11.

[63] M.T. Levin, *Talk Radio and the American Dream* (Lexington Books: New York, 1992), p. 78.

[64] Duffy, *op. cit.*, p. 325.

[65] *Ibid.*, p. 326.

[66] Duffy, *op. cit.*, p. 325.

[67] Peter Haag, 'The 50,000 Watts Sports Bar: Talk Radio and the Ethic of the Fan', *South Atlantic Quarterly* (Volume 9, Issue 95, 1998), pp. 453–71.

callers in the community. Sports-talk radio, though still very much in its infancy in Ireland, can be seen as a uniquely democratising force, helping people satisfy their need to be thrown together in unexpected, impassioned, even random social communities in order to 'mix with people they have nothing but sport in common with.'[68]

Talkback Radio and the Local Community

Today, the 21 commercial radio stations dotted throughout Ireland help to build a very positive sense of community through talkback radio. In an environment which consists of an increasing networking of content and decreasing opportunities for news about events and issues pertinent to the local community, talkback radio shows on local radio stations have successfully evolved into a purveyor of specialised community reports. They range from weather and traffic updates to local events and issues targeted at listeners in specific geographic locations. In essence, the function of the daily talk show on local radio is to provide its listeners with a map of local life, revealing the inner sanctum of a community, fulfilling a role that national radio stations cannot. Furthermore, local talkback radio programmes allow listeners to respond to issues and events that might directly affect them.

In Dublin, 98FM's daily phone-in show *Dublin Talking* is showing huge increases in audience figures by virtue of its listener-driven format, which allows for a diverse range of views from 'ordinary' listeners. So, too, are the highly regarded mid-morning talk shows on stations such as Radio Kerry, Cork's 96FM and Red FM, Highland Radio in Donegal, and the hugely popular Clare FM, all of which interact on a daily basis with members of the local community. In contrast, neither of the two national morning shows, *The Pat Kenny Show* on Newstalk and *Today With Sean O'Rourke* on RTÉ Radio 1, involve any interaction from the 'ordinary' listener, focusing instead on live

---

[68] *Ibid.*, p. 459.

interviews with studio guests/experts or pre-selected phone interviewees.

In 2015, Today FM lost one of its most popular radio stars, Ray D'Arcy, who moved to RTÉ Radio 1, where he now presents a genial mix of afternoon banter and eclectic interviews, with little in the way of listener interaction.

Conclusion

That Irish people appear to desire a sense of community and belonging in radio is evident in the choice of talkback radio programmes scheduled on prime mid-morning slots on local radio stations throughout the country. Gay Byrne could not have foreseen that his casual conversations with callers to *The Gay Byrne Show* would set a template for talk radio in Ireland, with its sub-genres of phone-in shows and talkback radio. *The Gay Byrne Show* was for many years the conduit through which the Irish nation spoke to itself. To a certain extent, Byrne's former protégé Joe Duffy, in his role as presenter of *Liveline,* is simply emulating his mentor. However, back in Gay Byrne's day it was the pen, rather than the phone, that reigned supreme.

But who is Gay Byrne? The facilitator of change, the host to the nation, the lone voice in those early years of radio and television who dared to challenge Irish society? The final chapter attempts to answer some of these questions and assesses the appeal of Byrne and his continuing presence in Irish life.

9

Conclusion: The Byrne Legacy

In 1983, broadcaster and historian John Bowman made the following comments regarding *The Late Late Show*:

> Jack Dowling[1] likened *The Late Late Show* to the Shannon Scheme in terms of its impact on Irish life; Conor Cruise O'Brien[2] made the point that Irish democracy's debt to the programme had yet to be appreciated; may I conclude by suggesting that radio's current affairs service is also indebted to *The Late Late Show* for its initial expansion of the permitted areas for public debate on the Irish airwaves. It is a point which the next historian of Irish broadcasting should not ignore.[3]

Though not assuming to be 'the next historian of Irish broadcasting', it is certainly significant that *The Late Late Show*, with Byrne as host, excavated areas of Irish life that had not yet been

---

[1] Jack Dowling is a former RTÉ producer who resigned from RTÉ in 1969 – along with producers Lelia Doolan and Bob Quinn – in protest over the station's perceived inability to confront current events.

[2] Conor (the 'Cruiser') O'Brien (1917–2008) was an Irish politician, writer, historian and academic. He was former Editor in Chief of the *Observer* newspaper in Britain from 1978–81.

[3] John Bowman, 'Radio in a TV age', *Irish Broadcasting Review*, Spring, 1983.

explored. Byrne and his broadcasting style were important to Irish society, particularly in the 1960s and early 70s, because he asked the questions that the audience at home wanted to ask but would not dare articulate. On both *The Late Late Show* and *The Gay Byrne Show,* he staged the great drama of Irish life, performing the vital role of convivial ringmaster as he mediated and negotiated the chasm between the insular, established Ireland and an emergent, more outward-looking nation.

His was the best-known face and voice in Ireland. He was the man in the street, a very private person, a master showman and shaman in Irish life for almost four decades. This morass of contradictions made him perfectly placed to debunk the unsavoury aspects of Irish life. He somehow mirrored and shaped what we were. He was the Everyman and Nowhere Man of a modernising Ireland. He held right-wing views but appeared middle-class and conservative. He taught many Irish people everything they needed to know about sex but were afraid to ask. Yet, this trailblazer saw himself in an utterly different light:

> My world is bounded … I am not a man who wants to see the Amazon or to stretch myself with adventure … My mother was tough on all of us. Her influence has left me with a terrible Puritanism which I find very difficult to shake.[4]

This unadventurous, 'puritanical' broadcaster remarked quite early in his career that 'anybody in this type of job who expected to be universally loved is little more than a fool.'[5] He looked upon himself only as a 'pro-broadcaster', without 'any great talent' who at times became a 'facilitator and a conduit for open discussion.'[6] There is no doubt that he ever imagined his role as

---

[4] Gay Byrne with Deirdre Purcell, *The Time of My Life: An Autobiography* (Gill & Macmillan: Dublin, 1989), p. 30.

[5] 'Gay on Gaybo: I'm just dull, boring and shy', *Irish Independent*, 26 September 1984.

[6] Gay Byrne, in interview with Mary Fitzgerald on *Anything Goes*, RTÉ Network 2, 1984.

some liberalising innovator. He saw himself rather as the ring-master at one hell of a circus, where for over 37 years he had the whole of Ireland as his big top, making his guests jump through hoops to entertain and enlighten his audience.

John Ardagh, author of acclaimed works on French and German culture, has referred to Byrne as 'the boldest and brightest star of the media revolution.'[7] He once commented that Byrne, with his two-hour *Late Late Show* and *The Gay Byrne Show*, 'developed into a kind of conduit for the thoughts and feelings of the nation, a mirror of its conscience.'[8]

Upon Byrne's departure from *The Late Late Show,* journalist Vincent Browne made the following observation:

> There is nobody else in Irish life who has drawn so much on our collective affections and esteem, no politician, no liter-ary or theatrical figure, no business or trade union person.[9]

Byrne, who turned 80 in 2014, remains a source of fascina-tion for many. His ongoing one-man show, *Gay Byrne: Live on Stage*, is an exhilarating two-hour rollercoaster during which he reminisces about many of the extraordinary moments he has witnessed. This sell-out show, first devised in 2011 by *River-dance* co-founder and close friend of Byrne's John McColgan, is a testament to his enduring appeal. Indeed, Byrne has embraced all aspects of popular culture and, like the Rose of Tralee, he has himself become somewhat of an Irish institution. In 2012 An Post[10] commissioned a Gay Byrne stamp to mark the fiftieth anniversary of the first RTÉ broadcast.

But it wasn't just what Byrne talked about that made him a central figure in Irish culture for over 37 years, it was the fact that he created a collective discourse that had not existed

---

[7] John Ardagh, *Ireland and the Irish* (Penguin Books: London, 1995), p. 110.
[8] *Ibid.*
[9] Vincent Browne, 'Gay Byrne's departure marks end of an era', *Irish Times,* 26 May 1999.
[10] The Irish postal agency.

before, and perhaps never will again. He was the arbitrator, the facilitator, of all the talk that broke the endless silences in Irish life. According to former producer of *The Gay Byrne Show* John Caden, in the ephemeral world of television and radio 'it takes exceptional political and career management skills to stay at the top for 40 years ... And he did it by staying aloof from the management while staying closely in touch with his audience.'[11] Media critic Harry Browne concurs with this view and also attributes much of Byrne's success to the fact that 'Gaybo was and is inclined to think of himself as a robust outsider, who found himself inside but without being moulded to the contours of the institution.'[12]

Byrne was Ireland's first true star of popular culture. The public consumed him as they had no other figure before. His popularity was to become a form of entrapment. In his time presenting *The Gay Byrne Show* he was unable to take a break because it 'was just too difficult to explain why' and so he took only one day off in 26 years to attend a funeral.[13]

Things have changed dramatically since Byrne's golden era in broadcasting, yet he more than anyone else has contributed to this change. His showmanship, his penchant for the controversial, his instinct for the type of broadcasting that would capture the public's imagination, bought him the biggest audiences in radio and television. His fearlessness was formidable as he helped to expose the underbelly of Irish society, a society which spoke only in whispers of such things as incest, abuse and sad marriages.

Byrne was not a self-declared moral crusader. He did not set out to liberalise Irish society. He simply set out to entertain, to sometimes provoke, but primarily to put on a good show. The opening up of Irish society was a by-product rather than the main aim of his efforts. In this respect, his contribution was that

[11] John Caden, 'He reigned with a common touch', *Sunday Independent*, 16 August 1998.
[12] 'The honeyed tones of burning ambition', *Irish Times*, 11 August 2001.
[13] Gay Byrne, in interview with the author, 25 September 2008.

of an honest and straightforward broadcaster rather than that of a crusader against the establishment. However, the real magic that he brought to his professional technique was his unending fascination with the human condition, that along with his compassion that rendered interviewees readily responsive to his queries. Author Nuala O'Faolain put it more succinctly: 'People explained themselves to him because they trusted him.'[14] She understood this more than most, once describing her twenty-minute interview with Byrne on *The Late Late Show* as one of the highlights of her life because she 'reached down to a rare honesty for it.'[15]

For others, Byrne was as exasperating as he was entertaining. They have found his hypersensitivity and funny radio voices annoying. He was indeed idiosyncratic and, at times, irritating – qualities which he openly and honestly placed before his audiences.

In his personal life, Byrne holds a private pilot's licence. In his younger years, one of his main passions was to take his motorbike and go out to Dublin airport and look 'at the planes coming in and out and listen to them.'[16] A few years ago, he moved from his beloved Howth to an apartment in Sandymount with his wife of over 40 years, Kathleen Watkins, the former RTÉ continuity announcer. Of the move he says:

It's an insanity to think that I lived in Howth for 40 years and worked in Montrose and I drove in every day. Now that I'm retired out of Montrose, I'm living next door to it, and I could walk to it.[17]

This self-deprecating humour is evident in his journalistic writings for the *Sunday Independent,* where he recounts the myth

[14] 'Cherishing the honest impresario of hidden Ireland', *Irish Times,* 27 August 1993.
[15] Obituary of Nuala O'Faolain, *Irish Times,* 12 May 2008.
[16] 'Waking Hours Gay Byrne', *Life, Sunday Independent,* 12 December 2008.
[17] *Ibid.*

that he and Kathleen would issue invoices after attending parties or functions.[18] In spite of his apparent ordinariness, Byrne officially became a part of Ireland's history in 2000 when he made it onto the Leaving Certificate History syllabus.[19]

In 2006, just when it was thought that the broadcasting legend would vanish into a well-earned retirement, he was unveiled as the new Chairman of the Road Safety Authority, and continued to make headlines in this high-profile appointment. Even in 2009, a full decade after his departure from both *The Gay Byrne Show* and *The Late Late Show,* Byrne's high standing within the broadcast community was evidenced when he received an Outstanding Achievement Award at the Phonographic Performance Ireland (PPI) Awards for his work on classical music station Lyric FM, where he continues to indulge his long-term passion for jazz music. In 2011, Byrne's name was touted for candidature as the next president of Ireland, receiving a 28 per cent share of the vote in a national poll, slightly lower than that of Michael D. Higgins, the current incumbent.[20] Despite this, his potential candidature was not wholly agreeable to some, including the political correspondent of *The Irish Times*:

> It is hard to see how Gay Byrne is fitted for the job ... not only does he not have any political experience, he has spent his broadcasting career pouring scorn on politicians ... Byrne's hostility to the European Union and all that it stands for ... if he was elected president, would put him at loggerheads with the Government.[21]

Others, such as journalist Fintan O'Toole, were even less enamoured by the prospect of Byrne as the next president of Ireland:

---

[18] 'Was it true that whenever Gay and Kathleen go to a party anywhere, their hosts get an invoice the following week? Gay Byrne-A Log', *Sunday Independent,* 18 June 2006.

[19] 'It's now official: Gay Byrne is History', *Sunday Independent,* 27 August 2000.

[20] 'Presidency is a lot more than a PR gig with a nice house', *Irish Times,* 13 August 2011.

[21] *Ibid.*

> While the nation might be turning his lonely eyes to
> Dr Gaybo, the suave man who is above it all, it will first
> have to push past Mr Byrne, the mere mortal who votes
> Fianna Fáil, hates taxes, thinks Brussels is full of mad
> people and can get irritated by uppity women.[22]

Byrne, perhaps shaken by the hostile media attention, returned
to his role as the affable, veteran jazz-loving broadcaster, the
man who loves Laurel and Hardy movies, whose favourite pas-
time is walking, whose broadcasting hero is Eamonn Andrews,
whose favourite historical character is Jesus Christ, and whose
favourite poem is Philip Larkin's pithily composed diatribe on
parents.[23] It is hard to comprehend that this most extraordinar-
ily ordinary man has helped shape Irish popular culture for
almost four decades.

The Gay Byrne Show and *The Late Late Show* are synonymous
with Byrne. Both shows have publicly and unapologetically
questioned the morals and mores of Irish society. Yet, they have
been specifically Irish phenomena, whose remit included a conscious challenge to Irish people everywhere to reassess their
viewpoints on a wide range of issues.

The Late Late Show, because of its singular focus on Irish audiences, has adapted successfully to the simultaneous effects of
cultural homogenisation and social diversification. By consistently questioning the anomalies at the heart of Irish culture, the
show, in particular with Byrne as host, has provided the mirror
in which the socio-cultural changes of the past five decades
have been reflected. In celebrating national culture instead of
turning it into a select and formal necessity, *The Late Late Show*

---

[22] 'Gaybo's crafted persona and the man named Byrne', *Irish Times*, 12 August
2011.
[23] Quoted in Oliver O'Donohue's *Interviewers Interviewed* (Mercier Press: Dublin,
1996), p. 38:
They f— you up, your mum and dad,
They may not mean to, but they do,
They give you all the faults they had,
And add some extra just for you.

has done a considerable amount to promote Irishness and the country's rich cultural history.

The show has also mirrored the gradual attitudinal changes to sexuality and morality in Irish society and has not been afraid to challenge these areas in a forthright manner. Until the arrival of *The Late Late Show*, Irish broadcasting did not confront issues of sexual morality in current affairs or documentary programmes. Such topics were viewed as a threat to the Catholic Church and had traditionally been dealt with in an indirect manner.

By providing a public space for frank discussion, *The Late Late Show* is a prime example of the complex and profound effect of the media on Irish culture. Moreover, the televisual nature of *The Late Late Show* and the fact that it was broadcast at a peak viewing time initially on a Saturday night and, in the early years, had no competition from other talk shows, has helped earn it a place in Ireland's social history. The core issues in Irish life and current affairs at one time held centre stage on the show. However, it was the mixture of the old and the new, the safe and the controversial, and Byrne's cosy conversations with audience members intermixed with controversial guests on contentious issues, which made the programme such a vital catalyst for change in Irish life. For the show to continue to attract a wide demographic of viewers in the future, it needs – according to media advisor Terry Prone – some of that 'mad unpredictability, the wild surge of adrenalin, the lift-dropping terror of truly live TV.'[24]

In contrast, the radio show has not become as deeply rooted in Irish culture simply because it was a radio show, more intimate and less glamorous than its visual sister. Its mid-morning broadcast slot confined its market reach to a predominantly female audience, and the fact that it was a daily show meant that listeners dipped in and out, in contrast to the more focused viewership of *The Late Late Show*.

---

[24] Terry Prone, 'Ryan's greatest asset? He's not Pat Kenny...', *Evening Herald*, 3 June 2009.

Yet, *The Gay Byrne Show* is part of our socio-cultural history and is hugely important. It embraced and mourned the bleaker aspects of Irish life, while simultaneously revelling in its quirky, light-hearted moments. Its content reflected the diversity that existed in Ireland throughout the latter part of the twentieth century, and highlights the significance of the radio talk-show genre in accessing and assessing popular cultural trends. As the country moved towards the unprecedented prosperity of the 1990s, however, the show was no longer an essential forum for debate. Irish people had grown in confidence and could now confront the old order on their own.

In contemporary Ireland, radio continues to be a vehicle for disclosure and exposure of Irish life. *Liveline* on RTÉ Radio 1 is particularly adept at exposing new scandals. In the past decade there have been intimate phone-in tales of unmarried mothers who saw their babies wrenched from them in Church-run homes and offered up for adoption. Or who could not be moved by the plight of parents of children with cystic fibrosis who cried openly on the airwaves regarding the intransigence of the Irish healthcare services?[25] It was *The Gay Byrne Show* that provided the template for this and subsequent radio talk shows, all of which play a role in the development of a wider social discourse on popular culture, in particular surrounding attitudes to morality and to religion.

Journalist Harry Browne has claimed that despite the plethora of local radio stations 'there will never be another programme that will help Ireland imagine itself to the extent that *The Gay Byrne Show* did.'[26] According to former radio critic Tom O'Dea, people loved *The Gay Byrne Show* for what Byrne did and the manner in which he did it; others hated his affected mannerism and his patronising, condescending tone.[27]

---

[25] *Liveline*, RTÉ Radio 1, 18 January 2008.

[26] Harry Browne, 'Time for RTÉ and Gaybo to learn to let go', *Irish Times*, 1 January 1997.

[27] Tom O'Dea, 'Gay Byrne not just about opening Irish society', *Irish Times*, 12 August 1998.

Alex White, a former producer of the show, offers some insights:

> There has been much comment about the power and influence of *The Gay Byrne Show* in Irish society ... There has also been criticism of what has been described as Gay's various personal 'agendas' over the years; for example in the area of crime and taxation ... I accept that sometimes his comments were over the top, but I agree that *The Gay Byrne Show* had a significant influence, and Gay's own role has been a big part of this.[28]

Critic and journalist Bruce Arnold has said the following of Byrne on *The Gay Byrne Show*:

> The grandfather of the Irish talk-show invested the concept of 'Irish culture' with a new meaning. He raised topics not previously thought acceptable for the public airwaves, and he dealt with them in a uniquely popular fashion. He made it acceptable to discuss the intimacies of Irish life.[29]

According to Arnold, it was Byrne who made regular discoveries about what married couples wore – or didn't wear – in bed, the frequency with which they changed their underwear, made love, fought, argued and lived together. He lifted the taboos, and the listening public loved it.[30]

Launching forward from the final broadcast of *The Gay Byrne Show*, an over-crowded radio market now exists. Radio has become commodified to suit the ever-changing whims of its listeners. *The Gay Byrne Show* would not have survived a radio landscape boasting not only twenty-one local radio stations

---

[28] Alex White, 'Gaybo: Deeply compassionate... and so intelligent', *Irish Independent*, 15 August 1998.

[29] Bruce Arnold, 'Gaybo: There's good and bad in the legacy he will leave behind', *Irish Independent*, 15 August 1998.

[30] *Ibid.*

and five competing national stations,[31] but also an industry that is gradually turning digital. When *The Gay Byrne Show* was at its zenith, listeners were tuning into a brand-new wavelength called FM.[32] Today, RTÉ's four main stations – RTÉ Radio 1, RTÉ 2fm, RTÉ Lyric FM and Raidió Na Gaeltachta – are available on digital. This is in addition to four new digital stations: an all-new music station RTÉ 2xm, the classic music station RTÉ Gold, RTÉ Junior for younger listeners, and an RTÉ news bulletin service. However, the cost of digital audio broadcasting (DAB) may prove costly for not only the State broadcaster, but also for other commercial players, particularly if it remains unclear how long they will have to provide and pay for both the analogue FM service and the digital transmission.

The moot issue now is whether talk radio will continue to remain significant in the shaping of popular culture in Ireland. Many would claim local radio has lost its appeal for a younger, increasingly media-savvy youth market more comfortable with YouTube, Twitter and other social networking sites. These issues could provide the genesis for a much-needed book on Ireland's rapidly changing media environment.

Regarding television and *The Late Late Show*, RTÉ was barely six months old when the programme first went on air. It grew up in public, unashamedly showing all the cameras, the cables and the entrails of its TV studio long before it was fashionable. Byrne became the first undisputed king of an invisible empire.[33] He interviewed lesbian nuns, discussed condoms and abortion, and watched as singer Sinéad O'Connor appeared on the show dressed in clerical garb as Mother Bernadette Mary.[34]

Byrne withstood all the picketing and the posturing because he was a staunch defender of freedom of speech. When a young Brian Trevaskis called Bishop Browne of Galway a moron,

---

[31] 2fm, Lyric FM, Raidió Na Gaeltachta, Today FM and Newstalk are all national radio stations.

[32] FM is still the transmission frequency for all radio stations in Ireland.

[33] Michael Cunningham, 'Mr Plasticine', *Irish Times*, 30 July 1994.

[34] *The Late Late Show*, 8 March 1999.

Byrne invited the young lad back, only for Trevaskis to reiter-ate his criticism.[35] The package that was Byrne on *The Late Late Show* was a mixture of naivety and sophistication; the show was an artful piece of chemistry with Byrne at its core. He was rarely fazed, a consummate performer, playing simultaneously to the audience and the television cameras, a feat few presenters have managed to achieve.

Nonetheless, there are subtle differences between *The Gay Byrne Show* and *The Late Late Show*. The former, at its best, was quintessentially Irish, with its quirky native humour and its unique blend of urban and rural Irish culture. *The Late Late Show*, notwithstanding its native roots, has adapted elements of the Anglo-American talk show and used its open-ended format to probe and question some of the most entrenched and con-servative Irish values. Many would insist that it is now time to reimagine the format of the show once again and make it more relevant to a younger audience unwilling to endure a 90-minute live talk show.[36]

The longevity of *The Late Late Show* may be attributed to the fact that talk shows are cheap to produce. Even today, much of television generally is devoted to inexpensive studio debates or reality 'car-crash' TV. Notwithstanding this argument, *The Late Late Show* hosted by Byrne was a prime example of the tri-umph of studio-based debates and lengthy talk. John Ardagh has commented on the phenomena of the Irish talk show and its unique appeal to Irish audiences:

> These debates, including Gay Byrne's, tend to be so much lengthier and more rambling than British television would allow, but this is a deliberate choice and Irish audiences accept it. There is a strange informal intimacy about Irish television, relating maybe to the size of the country, also to the Irish love of being personal and gossipy, even with

---

[35] See Chapter 2 for more detail.
[36] Comments elicited from a second year UCC Media History class regarding the length of *The Late Late Show*, 11 March 2013.

strangers. It makes every studio chat seem like a family occasion.[37]

Ardagh's comments underline the fact that *The Late Late Show* is uniquely Irish. It was the innovations introduced for its target audience, the inflections given to the genre by its precise Irish context, which opened up the most valuable spaces for airing social issues.[38] It was precisely the sifting and processing of recalcitrant areas of social experience through its stylistic codes and narrative conventions which enabled *The Late Late Show* to challenge all aspects of Irish life since the launch of Irish television.

The current availability of cable, satellite and digital television has fragmented Irish audiences to the extent that the centrality of *The Gay Byrne Show* and *The Late Late Show* which once existed in Irish life is now unimaginable. When Byrne was host, Ireland was, for the most part, an homogeneous society. The late 1990s saw the onset of multiculturalism, and viewers were swamped with a plethora of television channels with provocative and wide-ranging international content. The iconoclasm of both shows was gone forever.

The digital platform has now replaced the satellite TV of the 1990s, and never has it been more important to promote and to nurture indigenous Irish programming. RTÉ may still well believe that by continuing with *The Late Late Show* in its current format it is fulfilling its remit as a public service broadcaster. Yet, its survival depends wholly on RTÉ's response to an increasingly dominant Anglo-American programming hegemony.

Canada, with a broadcasting situation analogous to that of Ireland, may well be used as a template for Irish broadcasters. Throughout its history, Canada has struggled with the overwhelming proximity of the US, and its radio and television airwaves are dominated by American programmes. Over three

---

[37] John Ardagh, *op. cit.*, p. 111.

[38] Luke Gibbons, *Transformations in Irish Culture (Critical Conditions: Field Day Essays and Monographs)* (Cork University Press: Cork, 1996), p. 131.

decades ago, social historian Anthony Smith commented that 'no country is more committed to the practise of free-flow in its country and no country is more completely its victim.'[39] Irish and Canadian viewers share many areas of communality. Both consume a remarkably high proportion of US broadcasts, and both countries have to confront the issue of bilingualism in their broadcasting policies.

In the case of Ireland, the launch in 1996 of the all-Irish television channel TG4 (formerly TnaG) to a certain extent appeased the audience sector who felt 'the right to communicate of linguistic minorities' was a civil liberty, but they remain 'unhappy with its level of Government funding.'[40] Almost two decades on, a report on RTÉ's Irish language output claims that the establishment of TG4 has meant a significant reduction in RTÉ's Irish language output, endorsing the view held by Irish language enthusiasts that the public broadcaster has effectively failed in its remit to promote all aspects of Irish culture by abdicating to TG4 and Raidió na Gaeltachta its responsibility to promote the Irish language.[41]

In Canada, its distinctly English–French cultural schism has seen both language communities opt out of French-Canadian and English-Canadian programmes to instead consume large amounts of American broadcasting. By the mid-1990s the Canadian Government was forced to counteract the high penetration of US imported programmes by introducing a slew of initiatives, including the 'Canada First' regulation. This meant that commercial operators (similar to TV3 in Ireland) were compelled to broadcast more local content in a bid to protect

---

[39] A. Smith, *The Geopolitics of Information: How Western Culture Dominates the World* (Oxford University Press: London, 1980), p. 54.

[40] Farrel Corcoran, *RTÉ and the Globalisation of Irish Television* (Intellect LTD: Bristol, 2004), p. 192. Corcoran has written of the very low level of funding for TG4 when compared to the large subventions received by the Welsh TV channel S4C.

[41] 'An Bealach ar Aghaidh: A proposed Strategy for RTÉ's Irish language Output' (Stillwater Communications, January 2012).

indigenous producers and broadcasters from the potential of US dominance of global broadcasting.[42]

Back in Ireland, the issue of the dual funding of RTÉ[43] and the survival of the national and commercial radio and television stations is a contentious one. Therefore, the 2013 proposal by the Broadcasting Authority of Ireland to increase funding to RTÉ's independent production sector to 'ensure creativity and innovation in the broadcasting sphere' is timely.[44] This additional funding may lead to the creation of more quality, indigenous programmes and may even produce more iconic shows like *The Late Late Show*.

Nevertheless, the current woes of Ireland's broadcasting sector are far removed from the heady monochrome days of 1960s Ireland, when *The Late Late Show* first emerged. There is, according to veteran broadcaster John Bowman, 'no programme in the world in the whole history of television that has ever played as important a role as *The Late Late Show* played in Irish society in the 1960s, 1970s and 1980s.'[45]

Yet, the real reason *The Late Late Show* and *The Gay Byrne Show* worked on our national consciousness was that Byrne was unthreatening. According to broadcaster Vincent Browne, this made it possible for him to become the effective 'mediator of change', the everyman who could 'challenge the conventions of our nationalist culture.'[46]

In 2015, the Irish nation went to the polls and voted overwhelmingly in favour of marriage equality. The minority 'no' voters who, for various reasons, were opposed to the notion of same-sex marriage, were quite harshly portrayed as intolerant homophobes, who may as well have been wearing 'an upside

---

[42] Colum Kenny, 'Maple and Shamrock: Seeking a Strategy for Survival in the Audiovisual Jungle', *Irish Communication Review*, Vol. 7, 1997.

[43] RTÉ, the national broadcaster, receives licence fee income as well as advertising revenue.

[44] 'Five Year Review of Public Funding for Public Service Broadcasters', Broadcasting Authority of Ireland (BAI), July 2013.

[45] 'Viewed from the inside: 50 years at RTÉ', *Irish Times*, 22 October 2011.

[46] 'Gay Byrne's departure marks the end of a unique era', *Irish Times*, 20 May 1999.

down crucifix'[47] on their lapels. Travel back over two decades to Gay Byrne's interview with gay rights activist David Norris, and the contrast is quite compelling. Norris was responding to a comment by the Archbishop of Dublin Dr Connell, who had referred to homosexuality as a disorder that could be remedied.[48] Norris's interview with Byrne provoked a deluge of letters from listeners, some supportive – albeit anonymously – of Norris. The majority were repulsed at the 'unnatural' and 'perverted act' of homosexuality, and Byrne's 'efforts to erode and undermine' the hearts of the Irish people.[49] Even in 1990s Ireland, Byrne was tackling sensitive issues and was at the forefront of concerns that would re-emerge in an Ireland that had changed irrevocably.

This enabling of a national dialogue on issues avoided in conventional discourse was the nexus of both *The Late Late Show* and *The Gay Byrne Show*. Both challenged, without fear or favour, traditional Irish values and helped modernise the views of audiences until issues that were deemed blasphemous or obscene became part of public discourse.

In contemporary Ireland, with the battle for ratings intense, one has to acknowledge that Byrne got out just in time. According to journalist Hilary Fannin, 'The days of a nation taking its emotional temperature with a televisual thermometer are over and we no longer need to look to a talk-show to impose a coherent narrative on our lives.'[50]

But who was Gay Byrne? The cheerful impresario in the Bing Crosby Christmas sweater on the annual Toy Show or the coldly cynical host who held a television masterclass in predatory interviewing, courtesy of former EU Commissioner Pádraig Flynn? Was the real Gay Byrne the convivial host of the Rose of Tralee or the misogynist interrogator of Bishop Casey's former

---

[47] 'Referendum 2015', *Sunday Independent*, 24 May 2015.
[48] *Ibid.*
[49] 'Gay's postbag and Ireland's prayers for the "perverts"', *Sunday Independent*, 17 May 2015.
[50] Hilary Fannin, 'Roll it again, Colette', *Irish Times*, 1 September 2007.

lover Annie Murphy? Or was he just simply 'Uncle Gaybo', the genial radio host who flirted in a priestly manner with the housewives of Ireland?

Byrne was the sum of all these diverse personas, an intensely private person,[51] a broadcast chameleon whose golden era is long gone. Former Taoiseach Bertie Ahern reiterated this point in his address to the Independent Broadcasters of Ireland in 2007:

> The simple fact is that there will never be another Gay Byrne but not because there are not other broadcasters as talented and as dedicated. No, there will never be another Gay Byrne because no one programme, no station or even any single medium of communication will ever again enjoy the same market dominance.[52]

Nowadays, Byrne's subversive and dangerous mixture of information and entertainment has been relabelled 'infotainment' and has become the standard fare of global television. Moreover, both radio and television audiences have become increasingly fragmented, so that feeling of *The Late Late Show* and *The Gay Byrne Show* as national events is gone forever. More important, of course, is the fact that the Ireland that shaped Gay Byrne, and which he in turn helped shape, is now long gone.

Yet, when Byrne departed *The Gay Byrne Show* in 1998, he was modest of its impact on listeners:

---

[51] Former *Late Late* researcher Myles McWeeney has stated that Byrne was 'the most private person I have ever encountered in my professional life' in his article 'Behind the scenes: the real Gaybo', *Irish Independent*, 23 September 2005. Also, Pan Collins, researcher and scriptwriter with the *Late Late* for 22 years, wrote in her book *It Started on the Late Late Show* (Ward River Press: Dublin, 1981): 'He is a very private man… I cannot really say I know him at all.'

[52] Address by the Taoiseach Mr Bertie Ahern TD at the AGM of the Independent Broadcasters of Ireland in Mount Juliet, Monday, 23 April 2007.

I annoyed them sometimes and I made them laugh sometimes and they cursed me sometimes. I was their outside
line to the world.[53]

Byrne hosted the nation through decades of social change. Like
a Greek chorus, both his radio and his television show mediated
and absorbed these changes and made them more comprehen-
sible to Irish audiences. Even so, Byrne's own response to the
grandiose notion of his significance in Irish life is as blunt and
as unequivocal as his broadcasting style:

If I ever begin to think of myself as important, it could be
self-destructive. I think it is much better to think, as I do,
that I am a popular entertainer, who happened to be there,
in the right place at the right time. I mean something to
Irish people merely because I am there.[54]

In spite of his own opinion, Byrne is widely regarded by his
broadcasting peers as one of the best talk-show hosts ever. Like
both his shows, he has been viciously criticised and lavishly
praised. His harshest critics were at other times his most ardent
admirers. Nonetheless, admired or reviled, the inimitable
'Uncle Gaybo' remains an indelible part of Ireland's broadcasting history, a unique broadcaster who helped to open up Irish
society and challenge the anomalies that lay within.

Leabharlanna Poiblí Chathair Baile Átha Cliath
Dublin City Public Libraries

---

[53] 'Gay Byrne – Filling the Hall', *Politico*, 1 January 1985.
[54] Quoted in Ivor Kenny, *In Good Company: Conversations with Irish Leaders* (Gill &
Macmillan: Dublin, 1997), p. 55.

Bibliography

Primary Sources

Interviews by the author with:

Gerry Adams
Gay Byrne
John Caden
Joe Duffy
Clare Duignan
Colm Hutchinson
Philip Kampf
Ronan Kelly
Mary Kenny
John Masterson
Nell McCafferty
John McColgan
Doireann Ní Bhriain
David Norris
Oliver O'Donohue
Alice O'Sullivan
Mary O'Sullivan
Julie Parsons
Helen Shaw
Alex White

Newspapers and Magazines

Business and Finance Magazine
Examiner
Guardian
Hot Press
Irish Independent
Irish Press
Irish Times
Kerryman
Magill
RTV/RTÉ Guides 1962–2012
Sunday Business Post
Sunday Independent
Sunday Tribune
Weekend magazine in the *Irish Independent*

Journals Consulted

Crane Bag, Vol. 8 No. 2, 1984
Furrow
Genders
Irish Communications Review
Irish Review
Journal of Advertising Research
Journal of Broadcasting
Journal of Communication
Journal of Royal Statistical Research
Media, Culture and Society

Official Government Publications/Reports

Active or passive? Broadcasting in the Future Tense, Green Paper on Broadcasting, Department of Arts, Culture and the Gaeltacht (Dublin, 1995).

Broadcasting Authority (Amendment) Act 1993, www.irishstatute-book.ie.

Fianna Fáil Position Paper on Broadcasting (Dublin, 1996).

Promoting Cultural Diversity in the Irish Broadcasting Sector: An Assessment of International Standards and Best Practises with a View to their Operationalization in an Irish Context, A Report for the Broadcasting Authority of Ireland, April 2010, www.bai.ie/publications.html.

Papers of Archbishop John Charles McQuaid, C.S.S.P. 1913–72. Ref: IE/DDA/ABB.

Teilifís na Gaeilge: Information Handbook (Dublin, 1996).

Television

Anything Goes, RTÉ Network 2, Gay Byrne in interview with Mary Fitzgerald, 20 November 1984.

Gaybo, RTÉ One, 13 and 20 September 2005.

Media Brief, RTÉ One, John Bowman in interview with Gay Byrne, 24 October 1974.

Miscellaneous episodes of *The Late Late Show*, 1962–2012 (RTÉ Archives).

Scoilnet: Look at History through the RTÉ Archives, Brian Trevaskis on *The Late Late Show*, 4 April 1966.

Radio

Gay Byrne on RTÉ Radio 1, *Conversations with Eamon Dunphy*, 27 February 2007.

Miscellaneous episodes of *The Gay Byrne Show* (1981–99), courtesy of RTÉ Tapes Library and Alice O'Sullivan, former researcher with *The Gay Byrne Show*.

What If?, presented by Diarmaid Ferriter, RTÉ Radio 1, Autumn 2003.

Unpublished Theses

Majella Breen, 'The Representation of Women in the Irish Radio Talk Show: Taking Sample Periods 1986 and 1996' (MA in Communications and Cultural Studies: Dublin City University, 1997).

John Caden, 'RTÉ's Coverage of the Campaigning on the Eight Amendment to the Constitution on Issues of Objectivity, Impartiality and Fairness' (Dublin City University, 2006).

Sara O'Sullivan, 'Understanding Irish Talk Radio: A Quantitative and Qualitative Case Study of the Gerry Ryan Show' (University College Dublin, 2000).

Secondary Sources

Nicholas Abercrombie, *Television and Society* (Polity Press: Cambridge, 1996).

Mark Abrams, 'The teenage consumer' in *London Press Exchange Papers*, Vol. 5 (The London Press Exchange Ltd: London, 1959).

Alison Anderson, *Media, Culture and the Environment* (UCL Press: London, 1997).

John Ardagh, *Ireland and the Irish: Portrait of a Changing Society* (Penguin Books: London, 1995).

Richard Barbook, 'Broadcasting and National Identity in Ireland' in *Media, Culture and Society*, Vol. 14 (Sage: London, 1992).

Brendan Bartley and Rob Kitchin (eds), *Understanding Contemporary Ireland* (Pluto: London, 2007).

John Bowman, *Window and Mirror: RTÉ Television: 1961–2011* (The Collins Press: Cork, 2011).

George D. Boyce, *Nationalism in Ireland* (Routledge: London, 1982).

Joe Broderick, *Fall From Grace* (Brandon Books: Dublin, 1992).

Mary-Ellen Brown, *Television and Women's Culture* (Sage: London, 1990).

Terence Brown, *Ireland: A Social and Cultural History* (Harper Perennial: London, 2004).

Milly Buonanno, *The Age of Television: Experiences and Theories* (Intellect Books: London, 2008).

Anne Byrne and Madeleine Leonard (eds), *Women and Irish Society: A Sociological Reader* (Beyond the Pale Publications: Belfast, 1997).

Gay Byrne, *To Whom it Concerns: Ten Years of The Late Late Show* (Torc Books: Dublin, 1972).

Gay Byrne with Deirdre Purcell, *The Time of My Life: An Autobiography* (Gill & Macmillan: Dublin, 1989).

David Carbaugh, *Talking American: Cultural Discourses on Donohue* (Simon and Schuster: New York, 1988).

Paddy Clarke, *Dublin Calling: 2RN and the Birth of Irish Radio* (Raidió Teilifís Éireann: Dublin, 1986).

Pan Collins, *It Started on The Late Late Show* (Ward River Press: Dublin, 1981).

Richard Collins, *Culture, Communication and National Identity: The Case of Canadian Television* (University of Toronto Press: Toronto, 1990).

Farrel Corcoran, *RTÉ and the Globalisation of Irish Television* (Intellect: Bristol, 2004).

Geoffrey Cox, *See It Happen: The Making of ITN* (Bodley Head: London, 1983).

Andrew Crisell, *Understanding Radio* (Routledge: London, 1986).

Clara Cullen and Margaret O'hÓgartaigh (eds), *His Grace Is Displeased: Selected Correspondence of John Charles McQuaid* (Merrion: Dublin, 2012).

James Curran and Michael Gurevitch, *Mass Media and Society* (Edward Arnold: Kent, 1991).

Oliver Donohue, *Interviewers Interviewed* (Mercier Press: Dublin, 1996).

Phil Donohue, *Donohue: My Own Story* (Routledge: New York, 1979).

Leelia Doolan, Jack Dowling and Bob Quinn, *Sit Down and Be Counted: The Cultural Evolution of a Television Station* (Wellington Publishers: Dublin, 1969).

Philip Drummond and Richard Paterson, *Television and its Audience* (BFI: London 1988).

Joe Duffy, *Just Joe: My Autobiography* (Transworld Ireland, London, 2011).

Ryle Dwyer, *The Rose of Tralee: Fifty Years A-Blooming* (O'Brien Press: Dublin, 2009).

Terry Eagleton, *Crazy John and the Bishop and Other Essays on Irish Culture* (Cork University Press: Cork, 1998).

Maurice Earls, 'The Late Late Show: Controversy and Context', in Martin McLoone and John J. McMahon (eds), *Television and Irish Society: 21 Years of Irish Television* (RTÉ/IFI: Dublin, 1984).

Brian Farrell (ed.), *Communications and Community in Ireland* (Mercier Press: Cork, 1984).

Desmond Fennell, *Nice People and Rednecks: Life in the 1980s* (Gill & Macmillan: Dublin, 1986).

Diarmaid Ferriter, *Ambiguous Republic: Ireland in the 1970s* (Profile Books: London, 2013).

Diarmaid Ferriter, *Occasions of Sin: Sex and Society in Modern Ireland* (Profile Books: London, 2009).

Diarmaid Ferriter, *What If? Alternative Views of Twentieth-Century Ireland* (Gill & Macmillan: Dublin, 2006).

Desmond Fisher, *A Policy for the Information Age* (Raidió Teilifís Éireann: Dublin, 1985).

John Fiske, *Television Culture* (Routledge: New York, 1988).

John Fiske, *Understanding Popular Culture* (Unwin: New York, 1989).

Louise Fuller, *Irish Catholicism Since 1950: The Undoing of a Culture* (Gill & Macmillan: Dublin, 2002).

Tara Gallagher, *100 Greatest Moments in Irish History* (Gill & Macmillan: Dublin, 2012).

Luke Gibbons, *Transformations in Irish Culture* (Cork University Press: Cork, 1996).

Elgy Gillespie (ed.), *Changing the Times: Irish Women Journalists 1969–1981* (The Lilliput Press: Dublin, 2003).

Maurice Gorham, *Forty Years of Irish Broadcasting* (Talbot Press: Dublin, 1967).

Jurgen Habermas, *The Structural Transformation of the Public Sphere* (Polity Press: Cambridge, 1989).

Stuart Hall, 'Culture, media and "ideological effect"' in Curran, J. et al. (eds), *Mass Communication and Society*, Vol. 3 (Taylor and Francis: London, 1977).

Andrew Hart, *Understanding the Media: A Practical Guide* (Routledge: London, 1991).

Mark Patrick Hederman and Richard Kearney, *The Crane Bag: Media and Popular Culture* (Blackwater Press: Dublin, 1984).

David Hesmondhalgh, *The Cultural Industries* (Sage: London, 2007).

David Holmes, *Communication Theory, Media, Technology and Society* (Sage: London, 2005).

John Horgan, Barbara O'Connor and Helena Sheehan, *Mapping Irish Media: Critical Explorations* (University College Dublin Press: Dublin, 2007).

John Horgan, *Broadcasting and Public Life: RTÉ News and Current Affairs 1926–1997* (Four Courts Press: Dublin, 2004).

John Horgan, *Irish Media: A Critical History since 1922* (Routledge: London, 2001).

Paddy Humphreys, *Mass Media and Media Policy in Western Europe* (Manchester University Press: Manchester, 1996).

Gemma Hussey, *Ireland Today: Anatomy of a Changing State* (Townhouse: Dublin, 1993).

Richard Kearney, *Transitions: Narratives in Modern Irish Culture* (Wolfhound Press: Dublin, 1988).

Mary Kelly and Barbara O'Connor (eds), *Media Audiences in Ireland: Power and Cultural Identity* (University College Dublin Press: Dublin, 1997).

Anne Karpf, *The Human Voice* (Bloomsbury: London, 2007).

Dermot Keogh, *Twentieth-Century Ireland* (Gill & Macmillan: Dublin, 1994).

Ivor Kenny, *Talking to Ourselves: Conversations with Editors of the Irish News Media* (Kenny's Bookshop: Galway, 1994).

Michael Cronin, Peadar Kirby and Luke Gibbons (eds), *Reinventing Ireland: Culture, Society and the Global Economy* (Pluto Press: London, 2002).

Gladys Engel Lang and Kurt Lang, *The Battle of Public Opinion: The President, the Press and the Polls during Watergate* (The University of Chicago Press: Chicago, 1983).

John Langer, 'Television's Personality System', in *Media, Culture and Society 3* (Sage Publications: London, 1981).

John Langer, *Tabloid Television: Popular Journalism and the Other News* (Taylor and Francis: London, 1997).

Joe Lee, *Ireland 1912–1985: Politics and Society* (Cambridge University Press: Cambridge, 1989).

June Levine, *Sisters: A Personal History of the Irish Feminist Movement* (Ward River Press: Dublin, 1985).

Lisa Lewis (ed.), *Adoring Audience: Fan Culture and Popular Media* (Routledge: London, 1992).

Robert and Linda Lichter, *The Media Elite* (Adler and Adler: Minessota, 1986).

Sonia Livingstone, *Audiences and Publics: When Cultural Engagement Matters for the Public Sphere* (Intellect: London, 2005).

Sonia Livingstone and Peter Lunt, *Talk on Television* (Routledge: London, 1994).

Myra Macdonald, *Representing Women: Myths of Femininity in the Popular Media* (St Martin's Press: New York, 1995).

Jim Maclaughlin (ed.), *Location and Dislocation in Contemporary Irish Society* (Cork University Press: Cork, 1997).

Louis MacRedmond (ed.), *Written on the Wind: Personal Memories of Irish Radio* (Raidió Teilifís Éireann: Dublin, 1976).

Gloria Jean Masciarotte, 'C'mon girl: Oprah Winfrey and the discourse of feminine talk,' *Genders*, Vol. 11 (University of Texas Press: Texas, 1991).

Christopher Morash, *A History of the Media in Ireland* (Cambridge University Press: Cambridge, 2010).

David Morley, *Family Television: Cultural Power and Domestic Leisure* (Routledge: London, 1992).

Marshall McLuhan, *Understanding Media* (MIT Press: Cambridge, 1999).

John Meyrowitz, *No Sense of Place: The Impact of Electronic Media on Social Behaviour* (Oxford University Press: Oxford, 1986).

Tim O'Sullivan, *Key Concepts in Communication and Cultural Studies* (Routledge: London, 1994).

Fintan O'Toole, *A Mass for Jesse James: A Journey through 1980's Ireland* (Raven Arts Press: Dublin, 1990).

Fintan O'Toole, *The Ex-Isle of Erin* (New Island Books: Dublin, 1997).

Michael Parkinson, *Parky: My Autobiography* (Amazon Books: London, 2008).

Senia Paseta, *Modern Ireland: A Very Short Introduction* (Oxford University Press: Oxford, 2003).

Lance Pettit, *Screening Ireland: Film and Television Representation* (Manchester University Press: Manchester, 2000).

Richard Pine, *2RN and the Origins of Irish Radio* (Four Courts Press: Dublin, 2002).

Betty Purcell, *Inside RTÉ: A Memoir* (New Island: Dublin, 2014).

Deirdre Purcell, *Days We Remember* (Hachette Books: Dublin, 2008).

Paul Ricoeur, *Hermeneutics and the Human Sciences: Essays in Language, Action and Interpretation* (Cambridge University Press: New York, 1981).

Kevin Rockett, Luke Gibbons and John Hill, *Cinema and Ireland* (Routledge: London, 1988).

Gerry Ryan, *Would the Real Gerry Ryan Please Stand Up* (Penguin Ireland: Dublin, 2008).

Robert J. Savage, *A Loss of Innocence: Television and Irish Society 1960–1972* (Manchester University Press: Manchester, 2010).

Robert J. Savage, *Irish Television: The Political and Social Origins* (Cork University Press: Cork, 1986).

Paddy Scannell, *A Social History of British Broadcasting* (Blackwell Publishers: London, 1982).

Paddy Scannell, *Radio, Television and Modern Life* (Blackwell Publishers: Oxford, 1996).

Michael Sexton, *Marconi: The Irish Connection* (Four Courts Press: Dublin, 2005).

Helena Sheehan, *Irish Television Drama: A Society and Its Stories* (RTÉ: Dublin, 1987).

Helena Sheehan, *The Continuing Story of Irish Television Drama: Tracking the Tiger* (Four Courts Press: Dublin, 2004).

Roger Silverstone, *Television and Everyday Life* (Routledge: London, 1994).

Sonia Livingstone, *Young People and New Media* (Sage Publications: London, 2002).

Colm Tóibín, *The Trial of the Generals: Selected Journalism* (Raven Arts Press: Dublin, 1990).

Andrew Tolson, *Television Talk Shows: Discourse, Performance, Spectacle* (Amazon Books: London, 2001).

Ryan Tubridy, *The Irish Are Coming* (William Collins: London, 2013).

Kenneth Tynan, *Show People: Profiles in Entertainment* (Simon and Shuster: New York, 1980).

Noram Ellen Verwey, *Radio Call-ins and Covert Politics* (Averbury: Wiltshire, 1999).

Iarfhlaith Watson, *Broadcasting in Irish-Minority Language, Radio, Television and Identity* (Four Courts Press: Dublin, 2003).

Kieran Woodman, *Media Control in Ireland, 1923–1983* (Southern Illinois University Press: Carbondale, 1985).